Pierre Toussaint
Apostle of
Old New York

by Ellen Tarry

With a new appendix
on the cause of Pierre Toussaint

BOOKS & MEDIA

Boston

Nihil Obstat: Francis X. Toner
Censor Deputatus

Imprimatur: +Terence Cardinal Cooke
Archbishop of New York

Library of Congress Cataloging-in-Publication Data

Tarry, Ellen, 1906–
    Pierre Toussaint : apostle of old New York / Ellen Tarry ; with
a new appendix on the cause of Pierre Toussaint. —2nd ed.
        p.   cm.
    Rev. ed. of : The other Toussaint. c 1981.
    Includes bibliographical references.
    ISBN 0-8198-5910-9
    1. Toussaint, Pierre, 1766-1853? 2. Afro-Americans—Biography.
3. Afro-American Catholics—Biography. 4. Slaves—Haiti—
Biography. 5. Slaves—New York (State)—New York—Biography.
6. Haiti—Biography. 7. New York (N.Y.)—Biography. I. Tarry,
Ellen, 1906– Other Toussaint. II. Title.
E185.97.T7T37   1998
305.5'67'092—dc21
    [B]   97-45108
                                                                              CIP

This book in no way judges the heroic sanctity of Pierre Toussaint.
That judgment is reserved to the Holy See.

Printed and published in the U.S.A. by Pauline Books & Media, 50
St. Paul's Avenue, Boston, MA 02130.

http://www.pauline.org

Pauline Books & Media is the publishing house of the Daughters of
St. Paul, an international congregation of women religious serving the
Church with the communications media.

1 2 3 4 5 6 7 8 9 10   07 06 05 04 03 02 01 00 99 98

Dedication

This book is dedicated to the memory of Arthur Sheehan, who spent the last twenty years of his life studying the letters and papers of Pierre Toussaint and who shared his research with this author.

Contents

Preface

I must first acknowledge that this book would not have been written or conceived if His Eminence, Terence Cardinal Cooke, had not urged me to write about Pierre Toussaint. With my pastor, Rev. Francis Philbean, C.S.Sp., I had visited the Cardinal in 1971 after a trip to Rome. I was anxious to show him a picture taken at the Vatican when I was received by His Holiness, the late Pope Paul VI, and had presented the Pope with three books written some years before.

After the Cardinal examined the photograph, he looked up at me and said: "Now Ellen, I want you to write a book on Pierre Toussaint."

Before I could answer, Cardinal Cooke handed me a letter from Rome which contained a Pontifical Blessing from Pope Paul in appreciation for the books. I was so overwhelmed that all I could say, as the Cardinal and Fr. Philbean smiled, was: "Yes, Your Eminence."

Neither the Cardinal nor Fr. Philbean had any way of knowing that Sr. Mary Timothy, S.B.S., had been writing me stories about the sanctity and heroic virtues of Pierre Toussaint (1766-1853) for years. At the turn of the century when Sister was still a little girl in Bristol, Pennsylvania, she

had read an article in *Ave Maria* magazine about Pierre
Toussaint written by Emma Carey. As a spiritual daughter of
Blessed Katherine Drexel, Sr. Timothy was a part of that
circle of Catholics who found an added outlet for their work
on behalf of social justice in the Catholic Interracial Council, headed by the Rev. John LaFarge, S.J., to whom stories
about Pierre had been passed on by his parents.

Later, Sr. Timothy began corresponding with the Pierre
Toussaint Guild, headed by Rev. Benjamin M. Horton, S.S.J.
She subsequently formed a friendship with the writer,
Arthur Sheehan, who was still researching the life of Pierre
Toussaint. Sr. Timothy started sending my letters to Arthur
Sheehan and his letters to me. I had already read the biogra-
phy of Pierre Toussaint by Arthur Sheehan and his wife
Elizabeth, but Sr. Timothy's letter exchange brought us to-
gether.

Through Arthur Sheehan I met the director of the
Catholic Negro-American Mission Board, Rev. Benjamin M.
Horton, whom the late Cardinal Spellman had asked to
promote the cause of Pierre Toussaint and organize the
Pierre Toussaint Guild. I am grateful to Fr. Horton for tell-
ing me about another Schuyler—Schuyler Warren—who
had consistently urged his cousin, Fr. John LaFarge, George
Hunton of the Catholic Interracial Council, Arthur Sheehan
and Fr. Horton to push the cause of Pierre Toussaint, whom
Mary Anne Schuyler had so long ago referred to as "Saint
Pierre."

According to Fr. Horton, Schuyler Warren's sister, Hope
Warren Wilberforce, who married a grandson of William
Wilberforce—English statesman, orator and abolitionist
(1759-1833)—lived in England. In her correspondence with
her brother, Hope consistently reminded him of the importance of bringing Pierre's charity and virtues to the attention
of the Catholic hierarchy.

I hereby acknowledge my indebtedness to Fr. Horton for

sharing his knowledge of the earliest years of Pierre's cause. I must also thank his office staff for the assistance they have given me.

Though only two years have been devoted to writing this book, I have been researching Pierre's life since my visit with Cardinal Cooke in 1971. I first wrote a Profile (of Pierre Toussaint) that left me very unhappy because I was intellectually and emotionally torn in two directions.

Soon after I told Sr. Mary Timothy about the Cardinal's suggestion, she wrote, "You do the writing. I will do the praying." A few months later Sr. Timothy died. She never knew that I was disturbed by the fact that I could not accept the version of Pierre's life that had been passed on by writers who had no blood ties to the Africa from which Pierre's and my ancestors had been torn.

Then there was Arthur Sheehan to whom this book is dedicated. I am grateful that I never had to say, "Art, you have been writing about a saintly white man with a black face. Pierre was black, and if I write about him I have to know he thought like a man with African blood who rose above racial considerations in pursuit of his own salvation."

Arthur Sheehan understood what I never said, and it was not uncommon for me to look up from my desk at the Department of Housing and Urban Development to see him standing there with a batch of Pierre's letters or a folder of the letters Euphemia, Pierre's niece and adopted daughter, had written. In addition to the book written with his wife, Elizabeth Sheehan, the letters and other papers, there were hour-long telephone conversations from my home in Harlem to Art's home on City Island about Pierre's cause, the historians the Cardinal appointed to study the Pierre Toussaint papers and how I thought Pierre reached the big decision which affected the course of his life.

Fr. Charles McTeague telephoned me in early August 1975 to tell me that Arthur Sheehan was dead. Elizabeth

Sheehan had given Fr. McTeague permission to gather
Arthur's papers on Pierre and deliver them to Fr. Horton's
office.

The Will of Pierre Toussaint, which appears at the end of
this book, was among the documents I did not get until two
years after Arthur died.

When His Holiness, Pope Paul VI, granted me an audi-
ence in 1971, I told him I would return to Rome for the Holy
Year 1975, and I did. I traveled with a group of pilgrims from
California, and as soon as I learned we would visit Florence,
I wrote my friend, Rev. Thomas McGlynn, O.P., the sculptor,
who had a studio at Pietrasanta, Italy.

It was a rainy, dreary day when I left Florence for
Pietrasanta. Traveling by train, I soon thrilled to names of
places made familiar to me in letters from my daughter,
Elizabeth Patton, when she and Angela McCord Shelby
had visited Fr. Tom. As soon as we entered Fr. Tom's living
room I saw *the* book—the Sheehan biography of Pierre
Toussaint—on his coffee table.

"I'm trying to run away from Pierre Toussaint," I blurted.
"Why is he here?"

Fr. Tom explained that his sister, Helen McGlynn
Cashin, who had left Pietrasanta soon before I arrived, had
been reading the book and left it for him. I, in turn, had to
explain my involvement.

Fr. Tom, who never placed undue emphasis on the enormous talent God had given him, told me that Cardinal
Cooke had been visiting military installations in the area
around Pietrasanta, and someone had told him about a
priest who had a studio nearby. So, he said, the Cardinal had
stopped by his place briefly.

The matter-of-fact manner in which my gifted priest-
sculptor friend mentioned the Cardinal's visit kept me from
screaming: "Now you must do a bust of Pierre!" How could I
be so emotional when Fr. Tom was so calm?

It was well past midnight when I got back to Florence.

Though I was the only female in the railroad station in a strange land, I was not really afraid. I was happy because I knew Pierre had another friend in Italy. So I have to add the name of Thomas M. McGlynn, O.P., to the list of those who offered their encouragement.

When I returned to New York, Msgr. Eugene V. Clarke, Director of Communications for the Archdiocese of New York, met with Fr. Horton and me. I lost no time in recounting the manner in which I had discovered the book on Pierre Toussaint at Fr. Tom's studio in Pietrasanta. I saw the light of inspiration in Msgr. Clarke's eyes, but before he could say it I expressed the hope that Fr. Tom would execute a bust of Pierre. The two priests agreed.

Months passed and Fr. Horton reacted to my concern about Fr. Tom's deteriorating health by commissioning him in the name of the Josephite Fathers to do the medallion of Pierre's head which is reproduced on the cover of this book. The medallion was presented to Cardinal Cooke, who then expressed the desire for Fr. Tom to execute a bust of Pierre. Fr. Tom was in the States for medical attention at the time, but he was delighted and immediately began making plans to return to Pietrasanta and begin work on the bust of Pierre Toussaint. That, however, was not God's plan, and on September 3, 1977, Fr. Thomas McGlynn died. The medallion of Pierre Toussaint's head was the last work he finished.

During Fr. McGlynn's months of confinement, he heard the results of my visit to Haiti, the trek to the Bérard habitation at St. Marc where Pierre Toussaint was born and grew up, and my appraisal of Pierre's Haitian background. Fr. Tom knew I had seen and touched the tomb of Jean Jacques Bérard, Pierre's master, and was pleased that the cardinal had paved the way for me to be a guest of the Haitian government.

Through the intercession of Ambassador Alexandre Verret and Henri C. Auguste of the Haitian Tourist Bureau, I was met at the François Duvalier Airport in Port-au-Prince by Yves Massillon, Ministre Plenipotentiaire, and Carlo Noel, Sous-Chef Du Protocole, and was extended every courtesy possible during my stay in Haiti. The wise advice of Laurore St. Juste and Jean Lanoue had prepared me for the beautiful Haiti I explored.

Yves Massillon witnessed the Rev. Joseph Saget's statement regarding Gesner Lamothe's cure, along with my Haitian sister, Lily Madiou. Though I will be ever grateful to those two, I cannot forget Gerry, the best chauffeur in Haiti, who always got me where I was to go and brought me back to the Hotel Chaucoune at Petionville. Often, as after the visit to Pierre's birthplace, it would be more truthful to say Gerry carried me into Hotel Choucoune, with Lily Madiou limping behind.

My thanks and prayers are all I have to offer my relatives, my friends and my agent, Toni Strassman, for their understanding during the years I have been living with this book. I have not found the words to adequately express my appreciation to Roderick and Laura Gittens and Lois Alexander Lane for their encouragement. Special thanks are extended to Waldemar A. Roebuck, Third Order of St. Francis, and Herbert A. Johnson, Office of Black Ministry, Archdiocese of New York, for their help during the pre-publication efforts to produce this book.

If I have succeeded in understanding and interpreting Pierre Toussaint, I must thank Pierre and the Holy Spirit, whose help I sought each day before I hit a key of my two typewriters. I am confident that those prayers were heard, and it is my hope that as a result of this small effort more of God's children will be inclined to emulate Pierre Toussaint's example and bestow love and charity on others without regard to race, color or creed.

CHAPTER 1

Clouds Over L'Artibonite

Pierre was troubled—deeply troubled. Never before had he defied his mother Ursule or his stern but wise grandmother, Zenobie. Though they were all slaves, Zenobie had taught Pierre to read and write. Now he was sitting in the library of Monsieur Jean Bérard at L'Artibonite, the parish of St. Marc on that part of the island of Hispaniola known as St. Dominique. The year was 1785, and he was wondering about the protective world in which his relatives had forced him to live.

Pierre and all of his relatives were the property of Jean Bérard. The fact that Pierre could read and write set him apart from the other slaves on the plantation. Pierre often wondered how his grandmother had learned to read. He had an idea, but he dared not ask her. Recently, there seemed to be few questions he could ask his grandmother.

Though Pierre was already nineteen and would soon be twenty years old, he felt his mother and his grandmother were reluctant to allow him to reach manhood. Now, for the first time, Pierre felt uneasy in his grandmother's presence. It was almost as if she were trying to penetrate his skull with her piercing black eyes—the better to read his thoughts. She was constantly warning him that any association with the restless slaves from nearby plantations would only bring trouble to them all. Zenobie and Ursule both made it clear to Pierre that the other slaves at L'Artibonite, the field hands, were also to be kept at a distance. These constant warnings about trouble had added to the young slave's natural curiosity.

Night after night when Pierre heard the muffled throbbing of distant drums, he felt his virile young body twitch with a rhythmic tremor. He was a black slave but he was also a man, and his heritage would not be denied.

Pierre knew, as did every other slave, that long before he was born, his ancestors had been brought in chains from far away Africa to St. Dominique, the part of the island under French rule. He knew the slaves had been brought there to work the fertile soil which yielded the lush waving cane from which sugar was extracted and refined. The black slaves nurtured the coffee bushes and the tobacco crops. They tended the trees which bore exotic fruits that sustained the colony and satisfied the appetites of the French settlers who had pledged allegiance to the French king, Louis XV and later to Louis XVI while they piled up immense riches to send back to France.

Despite the repeated warnings of his mother and grandmother, Pierre had already found ways to talk with slaves from other plantations. Though this contact was only recent, the stories Pierre had heard of the cruelty and inhuman treatment of many slaves had filled him with horror. Having never seen such cruelty at L'Artibonite, Pierre wondered how much of what he had been hearing recently was true.

As long as Pierre could remember, he had seen other slaves on Sundays when he went St. Marc to attend Mass with his family. This casual observance was enough for him to decide that few slaves were as fortunate as his family. L'Artibonite was managed according to the personal creed of Monsieur Bérard, who was a man of honor and subscribed to the belief that all men should be accorded dignity—regardless of their station in life. Because Monsieur Bérard tried to keep slave families together, insisted that all who belonged to him be baptized, allowed Christian marriages and permitted them to practice their faith, he had earned the contempt and even hatred of many of the other French planters.

Pierre knew that Zenobie was watching him. He was glad his mother was more carefree and less observant. Pierre's father, who was simply called the "older Toussaint," worked in the fields as did another son, while Pierre, his mother, sisters and grandmother worked as house slaves.

Under the supervision of Zenobie, Pierre soon learned all that was expected of any house servant. His special duty was the care and orderly arrangement of the many rows of books which lined the walls of Monsieur Bérard's high ceilinged library. Pierre had a special fondness for this beautifully decorated room in which all the furniture had come from France. Often after he finished his chores, he would sit at one of the ornate desks with its delicately curved legs and imagine himself in Paris writing a letter back to his family at L'Artibonite.

Zenobie had told Pierre many exciting stories about Paris. Whenever any of the Bérard daughters visited their homeland, Zenobie chaperoned them. So Pierre had finally decided that the Bérards taught Zenobie to read and write so that she could properly supervise the girls while traveling with them. Pierre sometimes wondered why Zenobie had not taught his mother to read, but he knew that Ursule had started bearing children at an early age.

Because Monsieur Bérard was busy with the affairs of the plantation most of the day, Pierre was accustomed to being left alone when he was in the library. He was startled when he first realized that Ursule had begun to peer in the library from time to time as if to make sure he was there. Then Pierre began to see lines of worry crease his mother's smooth, mahogany-colored forehead. Once or twice at night he awakened to see her standing over him, though each time she hurried away without speaking.

Pierre's father was Monsieur Bérard's most trusted field hand. One day when the "older Toussaint" did not come in for the noon meal, Pierre's mother asked him to carry food to the field for his father and his brother. Pierre saw that his father was uneasy about something. He also sensed an air of agitation among the field hands. When his efforts at conversation met with shrugs and grunts from the slaves, he realized that they resented him.

Pierre was too wise to mention this to his father, who had long ago decided that he was fortunate to have a wife and children who were house servants while he and his other son were assigned the easiest jobs given any field hands. Like all the other slaves at L'Artibonite, Pierre's father knew that Zenobie was responsible for much of their good fortune.

Pierre's premonition of trouble persisted and so did his grandmother's watchfulness. His mother, too, continued to find excuses for coming in and out of the library. Sometimes when Pierre was on the tall ladder to reach the shelves nearest the ceiling, he watched his mother's face as she looked around the room for him. He'd wait until he saw her start to wring her hands and then he would announce his presence with a chuckle. When his mother failed to find this amusing, Pierre knew there was some reason for the spying.

"I think they would like to keep me a captive at L'Artibonite forever," he mused.

At such times Pierre dreamed about the idea of a life away from L'Artibonite. But he had never been farther from his birthplace than Port-au-Prince, and that had been a hard journey by carriage and foot.

Then came the first of a number of moonless nights when the call of the drums had been so strong that Pierre trusted his luck and gambled that Zenobie would not wake up. He followed the throbbing sounds and climbed higher and higher, feeling his way around trees and stumps, until he almost dropped from exhaustion. But the drums led him on and on, up and up. Suddenly he came to a clearing and found himself in the midst of a gathering of slaves—angry slaves—who ignored him as he stood panting and looking around for a familiar black face. The men were showing wounds they had received at the hands of the planters and their overseers. The most vocal slaves were cautioned not to raise their voices above the dull throb of the drums. Pierre was secretly glad that none of the slaves from L'Artibonite were in the gathering. He would have been denounced as a spy for the French planters. The angry men around him might have ended his short life and consigned his body to the prowling animals whose eyes shone out from the darkness surrounding them.

Many of the slaves showed maimed limbs and bared bloody backs still raw from the whip. This was so new to Pierre as to be almost unbelievable. He was fascinated by the story a slave who sat near him told of having a brand burned into his flesh with a red hot iron. When the man finished his story, Pierre dared to run his fingers over the brand which had been burned into the fleshy part of the man's shoulder near the arm socket. It seemed to Pierre that many of the slaves were so inflamed by hatred that their eyes blazed in the dark. He listened to their patois, a combination of whatever language they had brought from their native land and the French of their masters. Pierre had often found it hard to transpose patois into the precise French spoken in the Bérard household, but the hatred of the slaves for their masters and their desire for revenge needed no interpretation. This hatred was so obvious that Pierre felt it like an entangling veil. He knew now why his mother and his grandmother had been watching him. They must have understood the message of the drums. He wondered if the slaves at L'Artibonite were meeting somewhere in the lush vegetation of the mountains overlooking St. Marc. He knew how difficult it would have been for them to escape the keen eyes of Zenobie, his mother, or even his father. Yet he, Pierre, had found this group. He thanked the fate that had prevented him from stumbling into a meeting of slaves from L'Artibonite.

"I've spent my entire life in a cocoon," Pierre mumbled to himself as he stole away from the group and sought to find his way back to L'Artibonite before the cocks started crowing and an aroused Zenobie or Ursule discovered his absence.

After following the drums into the hills, Pierre saw everything and everybody around him with different eyes. In spite of the easy lives led by the slaves on the Bérard plantation, as compared to the lives of most of the other slaves, Pierre began to understand ripples of discontent which he observed among the slaves from time to time. Their servitude alone made them inwardly resentful of the Bérards and, in a lesser measure, of Pierre and his family. He was sensitive to the attitudes some of the slaves displayed toward him, whereas they dared not disrespect his grandmother Zenobie by word, deed or even a gesture.

It did not make Pierre any happier to remember that he, too, might be working the fields from sunup to sundown had he not been the grandson of Zenobie in whom the Bérards, for many reasons, had implicit confidence. Pierre often wondered if those who had taught Zenobie to read and write ever thought that she would pass this gift on to her children. He watched the old woman labor over letters to any Bérard who happened to be away from L'Artibonite and marveled at how she found time to do so many things.

Pierre often wished that his great-grandmother Tonette, who lived on the plantation in semi-seclusion, would take him into her confidence and one day answer some of the questions he began to ask her. The wizened old woman answered him with a word or two that seldom made sense to him; sometimes they were words he had never heard before.

But Pierre kept up his visits to Tonette and never stopped asking questions.

Zenobie possessed one talent that puzzled Pierre. There were few doctors on St. Dominique and distances had to be traveled to reach them. Whenever there was an illness among the slaves or the members of the Bérard family, Zenobie was consulted. The old woman brewed teas and other medicinal potions from herbs, leaves and plant stalks. She tended humans and animals alike. Some slaves whispered that Zenobie could make people and beasts well or she could put them into a slumber from which they would never awake. Her grandson was to remember this the rest of his life.

Each day Pierre thumbed through books in the Bérard library while returning used volumes to their rightful place, inspecting them to make sure the humid climate was not crumbling the paper. While doing this, he pondered his grandmother's varied skills and wondered about their source.

A smile always brightened Pierre's face when he remembered the first day Monsieur Bérard led him into the library, stood him on a stool, put a duster in his hand and told him it was his job to take care of the books. Pierre also liked to recall the first day Zenobie put a pencil in his fist and showed him how to scrawl "Pierre." Neither the old slave woman nor the indulgent master had any idea that the boy would spend his remaining youth learning to read and write, or that many of the letters he wrote would be preserved for posterity.

Learning to read had been a slow process for Pierre, often more guesswork than anything else. But it was a challenge and Pierre's life had been devoid of any other challenge. When Zenobie saw that Pierre was determined to master the art of reading and writing, she shared her meager knowledge with him. Then Pierre began copying passages from the books that appealed to him. As he grew older

he was pressed into service whenever the Bérards entertained, and he listened intently to the book discussions
which Monsieur and Madame Bérard held with the few
friendly planters who paid regular visits to L'Artibonite.
Other times Monsieur Bérard came to the library and ordered Pierre to read passages to him, correcting obvious
mistakes as the young slave read.

Pierre had pieced together enough information to feel
fairly certain that Zenobie and her mother Tonette had
been brought to St. Dominique from West Africa. He
puzzled over the absence in the Bérard library of books on
Africa. The stories Zenobie told her grandchildren were
more often about the early Spanish settlers who came over
with Columbus, and gave Pierre few clues to what his
grandmother's life had been like in her native land. The
reverence the other slaves showed the aged and ailing
Tonette, coupled with the respect accorded Zenobie, led
him to believe they had been torn from a land in which they
had enjoyed the esteem of their people.

Nobody but the God Pierre had been taught to believe
in knew the many struggles he had with a quick temper. As
he grew older, many times he and his mother or his grandmother took measure of each other with their eyes in minor
confrontations which daily arose in the manor house. Pierre
learned to clench his fist and bite his tongue to keep back
angry words following orders from his mother, but more
often from his grandmother. This temper and the angry
words which rose to his lips was another problem Pierre took
to God in prayer. Later, people were to comment on Pierre's
deliberate manner of speech, little realizing that he had
disciplined himself to think before he spoke. But a different
world had been revealed to Pierre before he perfected this
trait.

Though Zenobie was all things to all people at
L'Artibonite and slept in the Bérard mansion as often as
with her family, Pierre's mother Ursule served as Madame

Bérard's personal maid, assisted by his older sister, Marie-Louise. There was also the older brother who worked in the fields under the supervision of Pierre's father, and Pierre's younger sister Rosalie who was Pierre's worshipful charge. During Pierre's earliest years, he looked after Rosalie during time left over from his tasks at the house and the library.

When Rosalie was little more than a toddler she had eased the pain of separation—perhaps the first—when Pierre's playmate and godmother De Pointe Bérard, along with her sisters Victoire, Felicite and the brothers Lester, Du Pithon, Des Glajeux and the oldest son Jean Jacques, had gone to France to complete their education. Pierre treasured the letters his grandmother Zenobie wrote him from France, since she had accompanied the younger members of the family.

Sometimes Pierre thought his grandmother had only returned to L'Artibonite to make sure that he did not know what was going on all around him. The truth was that the elder Bérards had brought Zenobie back to L'Artibonite to tell her that they had decided to place the management of L'Artibonite in the hands of their oldest son Jean Jacques, who accompanied Zenobie back to St. Dominique. Few of the slaves knew about the plans of the older Bérards, but Pierre had keen ears.

It was almost as if too many things were happening to Pierre at the same time, and he longed for a relative or companion in whom he could confide. The preparations for the Bérard's leavetaking were cloaked in secrecy, but Pierre had discovered a hole in the shroud. He found himself recalling the days when his little godmother had been the companion he looked up to and delighted in pleasing. He lavished his love on his sister Rosalie, who looked up to him much as he had looked up to De Pointe Bérard. Some days he sat on the banks of the winding river L'Artibonite, from whence the plantation took its name, with a book on his lap, watching over his younger sister at play as she darted in and out among the slave women who were washing clothes at the edge of the river.

Pierre relished the thought of these happier times, when he had been unaware of the turmoil which was churning the slaves and planters of St. Dominique into what would become a boiling cauldron.

As Pierre now sat on the banks of the river watching Rosalie, he liked to remember Ursule holding his hand tightly when she had led him over the hilly roads from the plantation to the center of St. Marc on Sunday mornings where they would attend solemn high Mass in the huge old church. Pierre savored memories of the music, the elaborately dressed ladies who descended from their luxurious coaches attended by red-jacketed coachmen, and the bright colored clothing of his own people. They were allowed to come into town for Mass and have the remainder of the day for rest from their labors in the field.

Pierre could remember Ursule jerking him along as he stared at the French planters in their tall hats and long coats until the two of them reached the elder Madame Bérard, who more than often gave his mother an extra coin to take Pierre to the new theater on La Grande Rue to watch the great Volange, who the planters insisted was the rage of Paris. Pierre was a born mimic, and Madame Bérard had known he would soon be delighting all who visited the Bérard household with his imitation of Volange and any other actors he heard or saw. Before long Pierre had been given a fiddle and he taught himself to coax sounds out of the instrument. His playing came near to matching the music he heard at the theater—for God had also endowed Pierre with an extraordinary memory and an ear for music. As Pierre grew older he was dressed in knee pants and was given a red jacket with a fancy shirt that had lace on the cuffs. In this outfit, with his fiddle in hand, Pierre entertained the Bérards and their guests. More than once he saw his grandmother or his mother smiling at his performance as they appeared to be busying themselves with small chores.

For a while it was as if the elder Bérard's return to France was only a matter of conversation. There came the day when Monsieur Bérard called the house servants together and revealed the plan for his and Madame Bérard's return to Paris. Later the field hands were told that young Jean Jacques would manage L'Artibonite. However, the parents deferred their date for sailing until such time as Jean Jacques thoroughly knew the requirements for running the plantation. There was also the matter of his personal life to be considered, and his parents did not want to leave their son until they were sure he was happy about the task ahead, as well as qualified for it.

There had been a flurry of entertainment at L'Artibonite upon Jean Jacques' return, because the other planters were always anxious for the latest news from Paris. The French planters had always hated and feared the sound of the drums, but now they discussed their fear of what messages the drums were sending to the slaves, and they thirsted for gossip from France.

Pierre listened as he moved back and forth among the Bérard guests, catering to their needs or entertaining with his fiddle. The younger Monsieur Bérard had already sensed the undercurrents of restlessness among the slaves, but he insisted that the source of whatever discord existed was the *gens de couleur,* men of mixed ancestry, most of whose fathers were French planters. Jean Jacques had met many of them in Paris and he knew they had every intention of fighting for their rights.

Pierre listened as his young master argued with his friends. Pierre knew the *gens de couleur,* many of whom were wealthy as a result of their French fathers' generosity, were too few to instigate a widespread revolt. The thousands of slaves who lived lives of intolerable poverty and toil in addition to being subjected to the cruelty of ruthless overseers or "factors," as some of the plantation managers were called, would have to be reckoned with.

Long before the elder Bérards planned their return to France, they had given Pierre's grandmother her freedom. Though Zenobie was no longer a slave, the Bérards knew she would never leave L'Artibonite other than in the service of their family. A mutual affection existed between the Bérards and Zenobie. Every post brought letters from the Bérard girls asking for her, and after a number of consultations it was decided that Zenobie would make her last trip to Paris with the elder Bérards, visit with the younger members of the family and return to L'Artibonite to assist Jean Jacques in any way she could.

During these years of preparation, Jean Jacques had married again, since his first wife had died of tuberculosis. The second young bride was one of the beautiful Bossard daughters from Dondon, a parish between L'Artibonite and Cap Français. Monsieur Bossard was one of the small group of French planters who were still genuinely cordial to the Bérards, with the families exchanging visits frequently. Young Marie Elizabeth Bossard Roudanes, like Jean Jacques, had lost her spouse at an early age and the two young people were attracted to each other by their mutual sorrow. Pierre's aunt, Marie Bouquement, had nursed the three Bossard sisters from infancy. So there was great rejoicing at both plantations, among the slaves as well as planters, over young Jean Jacques' marriage.

The elder Bérards often spoke to each other about the unobtrusive manner in which Pierre had assumed more and more duties during the period when Jean Jacques began managing L'Artibonite. They were also pleased at the confidence their son displayed toward the grandson of their beloved Zenobie. It was almost as if Jean Jacques thought of Pierre as an assistant, and they knew that in matters pertaining to running the household and entertaining, Jean

Jacques would have a capable advisor. Though the elder Bérards had a stubborn and persistent sense of troubles to come, they listened to their oldest son's optimism and departed for France feeling that Jean Jacques could cope with whatever happened.

Pierre was not so sure. He knew that his young master was not aware of the extent of the slaves' hatred of the French planters or the slaves' desire for revenge. It shocked Pierre to learn that his presence at the meeting the slaves had held high in the mountains was not so secret as he had thought. In the months after Jean Jacques assumed the management of L'Artibonite, the younger planter had bought three or four black slaves from nearby plantations, the better to harvest the plentiful crops of cane and coffee which his father had cultivated. Pierre seldom saw the field hands and had not come to recognize any of the new slaves by sight. But he had an experience one day which troubled him.

Monsieur Jean Jacques had sent Pierre to give a message to his father. Pierre's father was farther away from the house than had been anticipated, and Pierre found himself reflecting upon the plight of row after row of black barebacked men sweating under the rays of a blistering sun as they hacked away at the stalks of cane with swinging machetes. Pierre paused at the sight before him and was still lost in his thoughts when he was startled by the sound of his father's voice calling out to him. Just as Pierre glimpsed his father and made an effort to walk toward him, he saw something which startled him even more. The slave at the end of the row he was near had a brand mark high on the fleshy part of his left shoulder near the arm socket. Pierre peered into the man's face, which he had never seen before. The sweating slave shook the perspiration from his forehead, looked Pierre in the eye and then shook his head in an act of dissent. Pierre's father had to call him again before he covered the distance between them and delivered the message.

That evening Monsieur Bossard, the young bride's father, visited the newlyweds. As Pierre served tall, cooling drinks to the French planters and their womenfolk, he kept remembering the black men he had seen that day working in the sun. They would go home at sundown to a shack where the only cooling drink they would have would be from a bucket of water a slave woman had brought atop her head from a spring under the same broiling sun.

Pierre felt his temper flaring. He wanted to denounce the Bérards and the Bossards and accuse them of living in luxury at the expense of slave labor. His hands sweated and trembled as he strove to contain what he told himself was righteous indignation. He also had to remind himself that he, too, was a slave and the outburst with which he was struggling, if unsuppressed, could very well result in him being sent to the fields to work like the men he had pitied that day.

"Perhaps," he decided, "that might be a more honest way for a slave to live."

Young Madame Bérard, who was accustomed to a smiling, self-assured and entertaining Pierre, noticed the change which had suddenly come over the black man. She stepped away from the family circle to ask if he was ill.

"Madame, it will pass," Pierre said slowly as he drew a handkerchief from his pocket and wiped the perspiration from his brow, his entire being having identified those first few minutes with the slaves he had watched at work that day.

Pierre rushed from the drawing room, through the dining room into the kitchen to replenish the tray of sweetmeats and petit fours he was serving with the drinks. His mother, who was now personal maid to the young mistress as she had been to the elder Madame Bérard, was sitting on a stool gossiping with the cranky old cook and did not notice Pierre's entrance. He was struck by the fact that Ursule had for the moment abandoned the French she used with her mistress for the patois with which most of the slaves were more comfortable. Ursule was in the process of telling the cook that someone had told her that the new slaves the young master had bought were troublesome and that was why their former masters had agreed to part with them for a nominal price, as it was obvious that they were all young, strong and capable of a good day's work.

Pierre apologized for interrupting his mother's conversation and asked for the tray which the cook had already arranged.

Later that night Pierre lay in bed turning over in his mind all that had happened within the last few days. "No wonder *Grandmère* Zenobie and my mother tried to keep me away from the field hands and the other slaves. They must have known it would only be a matter of time before I would learn the truth."

Pierre tried to figure out why the new slave with the brand on his shoulder seemed familiar, though he was sure he had never seen that face before. Suddenly, the young slave sat up in bed. It was the brand and not the face that was familiar. He recalled the slave who had huddled near him at the meeting high up in the mountains. That slave bore what must have been the same brand. No doubt they were from the same plantation. Maybe they were brothers. Few masters hesitated to break up families, and these slaves must have been branded when they tried to run away. Pierre knew instinctively that his young master would have accepted the men if their former masters told him they were good workers. It was apparent that the men were young and healthy. Like his father, Jean Jacques would have refrained from having the men stripped down to their nakedness so that he could examine every inch and crevice of their bodies.

In spite of a latent sense of loyalty to the black men, Pierre found himself feeling sorry for Jean Jacques. If the new slaves had given trouble at the other plantation, L'Artibonite might be in for sad days.

Pierre felt a sinking sensation—as if all he had known and loved was slipping away from him. At the same time, he felt a resurgence of spirit. Despite the absence of physically cruel punishment at L'Artibonite, injustice did not exist only on other plantations; it existed at L'Artibonite, too.

Pierre had heard Jean Jacques say much trouble had broke in Paris. Pierre knew it was only a matter of time before the slaves would revolt. He saw his life changing just as he had watched the changes of the current in the winding river from which L'Artibonite took its name.

The French planters contributed astronomical sums of money to the Royal French treasury through taxes, and they were determined that the those of mixed ancestry should have no voice in St. Dominique's political life. The *mulattosan, mele, griffe, mustif* or *quateron* females were another story. The wives of the French planters considered competition with these dusky to ivory-colored females for their husbands' time, attention and money a small price to pay for the riches which were sent back to France to await their eventual return from St. Dominique.

The men of mixed blood had no such cavalier feeling about liaisons between their womenfolk and the French planters. They knew it was a game in which the cards were stacked against them. It was bad enough not to be able to compete fairly for the affections of the women you admired, but there was the matter of the *gens de couleur* being forbidden to practice medicine. The French planters were fearful of the knowledge anyone with African blood was said to possess of or about poisons. Pharmacy was closed to the men of mixed ancestry for much the same reason as medicine. Even though a biracial man might have studied for the priesthood and been ordained in France, he was not accepted as a priest in St. Dominique. "What Frenchman would confess to a man of color?" was asked. All public office was also closed to men of color and neither could they teach or engage in any occupation which might bring them modest wealth. A biracial person without a wealthy or generous French father was unfortunate, indeed. It was this group of unfortunates who raised their voices loudest in Paris and in St. Dominique.

Pierre watched his young master's surprise and chagrin when planters who had previously been friendly with the Bérard family began avoiding contact with him because he continued to treat his slaves as had his father, allowed them to practice their religion. He lost no opportunity to remind the planters that they were largely responsible for the discontent and rabblement of the *gens de couleur*.

Pierre had little time to sympathize with his young master's problems, for he was struggling with his own newborn rebellion. Even his dreams reflected his indecision. Night after night he would dream he was once more a child. His godmother, De Pointe Bérard, was still at L'Artibonite and they were spending long, lazy days in the childish play of years past. Some nights Pierre dreamt of the Sundays when his mother Ursule held his hand firmly as they walked along the hilly, rough roads leading to the center of St. Marc and the ancient church where they would attend Mass. After Mass there were the stalls in the marketplace where produce, fowls and all manner of local handicraft were displayed. In his dreams, Pierre savored the smell of the small cakes and other delicacies cooked on little braziers set up on the cobblestones.

It had not been unusual for the boy Pierre to break away from his mother after Mass as he ran to reach the stalls and taste the confections. Neither had it been unusual for him to skip through the crowd until he failed to see a familiar face among those around him. Even the dreamed sense of being lost frightened Pierre. In his sleep he cried out, "Maman! Maman!"

Pierre awoke to find Ursule standing over him.

"It was only a dream," Pierre explained, still trying to rub the sleep from his eyes and shake off the fear he had relived.

"It must have been a bad dream," his mother commented, shaking her head and grumbling as she shuffled away.

Pierre was perceptive enough to realize he was trying to return to the world he had known as a child—a world devoid of the forces now pushing him toward a decision which could change the course of his life.

It had been a long time since Pierre would admit to himself that he felt the need of advice from his grandmother Zenobie. Now he found himself longing for the old black woman who had put a pencil in his fist and guided it until he could write his name. Pierre tried to think how Zenobie must have looked as a young woman before care and responsibility had etched in tiny wrinkles. He pondered on her ancestry and station in life in whatever village of the Congo she had been stolen from. He decided she must have been a child in her mother Tonette's arms when they were captured and sold into slavery. He had often thought his grandmother's blackness was the blackness of a purple, ripe plum. He had never noticed gray hairs, but then he had never seen Zenobie without a brightly colored scarf or mouka, as the slaves called them, draped about her head. Though she was not as tall as his mother Ursule, Zenobie's was an imposing figure, due in part to her carriage and the air of authority she assumed.

Pierre's longing for the wise counsel of his grandmother was of short duration. If he dared tell her that their family had been living in an unreal world, she would have demanded justification for his statement. If he told her that he understood why the other slaves resented the preferential treatment given their family, while the rest toiled day in and day out under a sun strong enough to fry an egg on a rock and blister a man's back until the skin toughened to protect the body it covered, she would ask what slaves had expressed resentment.

Pierre knew that even the hut to which his family went each night after none of them were needed any longer in the manor house was more attractive than others in the section of the plantation where the slaves lived. Ursule and his father had marked off the space given them with stones. At one end of this enclosure stood a coconut palm from which the children sometimes took the heavy fruit before it was ripe and got a thrashing for their trouble. At the other end of the yard grew bananas and mangoes. In front of the thatched-roof hut, there were bright patches of color in the midst of green foliage. Pierre loved the orange and purple lantana and marveled at the vermillion of the coral plant. The clumps of wild scarlet canna always made him stand still for a second to inhale the fragrance.

The Bérards had allotted Zenobie and her children a small plot of land where they could cultivate foods peculiar to their background. Pierre's older brother tended the little patch of guinea peas which weighed down the bushes on which they grew. There were cocoa plants, more bananas and mangoes, and other shrubs from which Zenobie plucked leaves to brew healing potions in time of illness. Dogs seemed to thrive and multiply at L'Artibonite, and Zenobie had one shrub whose leaves she used to wash the animals in order to kill worrisome fleas.

Pierre remembered the day he had watched Zenobie, in a fury, pull up a cluster of shrubs his father had planted without her consent. He could not account for his grandmother's rage and his mother had only made a tooth-sucking sound and rolled her eyes when Pierre had asked questions. Much later Pierre learned from one of the new slaves what the plant was, and why his grandmother was so angry.

There was nobody with whom Pierre could discuss his problem. Rosalie was too young to understand. His older sister Marie-Louise was always busy assisting his mother in the house and his older brother went out to the fields each day with his father, a machete in his hand to cut the cane or inform his father when the other slaves did not.

Pierre felt himself drawn to the new slave with the brand on his shoulder. He discovered the hut where the new slaves slept and found excuses to walk in that direction. He observed that the slave with the brand on his shoulder kept to himself, while the others seemed to find comfort in each other's company after they had finished the long day's labor. Fortunately for Pierre, Tonette, his great-grandmother, lived in a hut alone that was not too far from where the new slaves lived. Tonette had long ago withdrawn from the world of L'Artibonite, and Pierre had great difficulty communicating with her. Still, a visit to Tonette was the excuse Pierre used for glimpsing the branded slave.

Then came the hot, humid night when there was no moon and no breeze to sway the trees or even stir the bushes. Pierre carried an evening meal which his mother had ordered him to deliver to Tonette. The combination of the heat and his curiosity slackened his pace as he left the old woman's hut and passed the group of new slaves who sat on the ground playing some game. Only the branded slave looked up as Pierre passed. Then he rose and fell in step beside Pierre. They walked in silence until the other slave touched Pierre's arm and pointed toward the river. Instinctively, Pierre understood that the man wanted to talk to him and would meet him later.

Then began Pierre's wait for the moment when sleep had claimed the occupants of the hut he called home. He shared a room and a bed, which was a little more that a pallet, with his older brother. But after a day in the fields, Pierre's older brother succumbed each night to sleep from which even the crowing cock had difficulty in arousing him the next morning. The older brother paid Pierre little attention, as the younger one's preoccupation with books and writing had convinced the older one that Pierre was too strange to waste time on. Still, Pierre held his breath as he slipped past the room where his parents slept with Rosalie and Marie-Louise.

Once outside, Pierre's bare feet led him toward the banks of the river. His vision improved after he became accustomed to the blackness. He felt his way through bushes and around trees until he found the slave he had promised to meet. The man sat on the river's bank, his head bowed and his body a study in dejection. Pierre walked as quietly as he could, for he had the feeling that a startling sound would make the slave jump into the waters beneath.

The story Pierre heard that night was stranger than he had imagined. Neither had Pierre read anything in the Bérard library which compared with what the branded slave told him.

CHAPTER 2

The Brand

P ierre realized that the man before him was struggling to find words to express himself. He also knew that the other slave's confidence in him was uncertain. Every slave at L'Artibonite knew that Pierre was Zenobie's grandson. They—all of the slaves—knew that Zenobie and her daughter Ursule were the Bérard's most trusted servants. Yet Pierre sensed there was some connection between this man and the branded slave whose mutilated flesh he had felt the night he had slipped away and climbed to the mountain gathering place of the rebellious slaves screaming their grievances.

"Your name?" Pierre whispered.

The man shrugged, a gesture Pierre interpreted as disdain for whatever name an owner might have given him.

"M'rice," he mumbled, and Pierre understood that he was called *Maurice*.

"He," the slave pointed toward—and then away from—Dondon, the Bossard plantation, to give Pierre some idea of direction, "he—*frère*—" and Maurice touched the brand on his shoulder, "he is Roberto."

Pierre understood that the slave he had seen high in the mountains was the brother of the man before him. He repeated the Spanish-sounding name, "Roberto?"

After a slight hesitation, the man smiled and murmured, "Berto."

When Maurice finally decided he would talk to Pierre, he told a story of a family—his family—of slaves owned by the pirates who inhabited the nearby island of Tortuga. Pierre had heard the Bérards and his grandmother talk about the pirates who came to St. Dominique to barrel salt at La Grande Saline. The French, Pierre knew, would have preferred not to have the business of the pirates. They feared that the casual ways of these colorful characters would prove a bad influence on the restless slaves. But the gold doubloons and other treasures these men had stolen from the Spanish ships they plundered and used for barter influenced the planters to continue to sell them the salt they collected from the dunes. Sometimes the pirates camped on the western shores of the island and hunted animals which they roasted over open spits to carry back to their refuge on Tortuga—the Turtle.

As Pierre listened, he learned that on one of the plundered ships the pirates had captured an African slave and his two small sons. The pirates took the African slave and the two boys to Tortuga, where they lived an easy life and waited on the pirates when they returned from their sea ventures. These slaves lived as freely as slaves could live under the circumstances, but the father always told Maurice and Roberto that they would one day swim out to a ship that would take them home.

Then came that homecoming of the pirates' ship; it returned without the men who had taken the African slave and his two sons as a prize of the sea. The Spanish caravels were avoiding waterways where they were likely to encounter the pirates, and fierce resistance followed any encounter. The Spaniards who inhabited the other part of the island, known as Santo Domingo, separated from the French by the meandering L'Artibonite, lakes and mountains, were attempting to offer safe passage to ships sent out from Spain with men and supplies not available on the Island of Hispaniola.

Though the pirates and their descendants (for the population had increased over the years) lived on lush vegetation and animals they hunted for food, they still were dependent on St. Dominique for salt and other commodities.

On one of the trips which the pirates made to St. Dominique, when the doubloons and pieces of eight were gone, the desperate pirates lured the African slave and his two sons, now approaching manhood, into making the trip with them by telling them that they were needed to barrel the salt. Instead, they were sold to a French planter, Monsieur Ducheine, who owned a plantation past Dondon and closer to the west coast. There was a high mortality rate among Ducheine's slaves, and he needed a strong African with two growing sons to work his fields. This was how Maurice and his brother, whom he called "Berto," came to know the cruelties of slavery as compared to their initial suffering of being torn from their native land and taken to a strange country where they were servants to a motley crew of pirates—some English, some French and some Spanish—but adventurers all.

Maurice's father had soon run away from the new master and hid in the mountains. The brothers had pieced bits of information together from slaves who had seen their father and others who had fed him and tried to persuade him to join the *maroons,* themselves runaway slaves. They urged him to make a home for himself in the safety of the foliage protected mountains where no Frenchman would dare to climb. They were convinced their father was determined to make his way to the Spanish side of the island and take his chances on swimming out to some anchored ship in the hope that he could work his way back to Africa.

Maurice told Pierre that they knew his father had either drowned or been killed by man or beast. Nothing short of death, he insisted, could have kept his father from getting a message to them.

"How could he get a message to you?" Pierre questioned.

"The drums," Maurice answered, as he slapped his thigh in a rhythm resembling that of the drums.

From the time the father escaped, Monsieur Ducheine had watched the two sons. Lashes on their backs were used to prod them on when the relentless sun and long hours had reduced their considerable strength. The moment they slowed their pace, as they moved amid the waving cane or squat coffee bushes, there was usually an overseer on hand to offer cups of a potion brewed from the root of the plant kingola, said to be the basis of the drink which hougans or voodoo doctors used to induce the trance in which men became as the living dead and escaped the cruel realities of their slave lives. The weaker potions gave the slaves a sense of false strength which kept them threshing the cane or picking coffee beans.

"Why did he brand you if he intended to sell you?" Pierre asked.

"We tried to find our father," Maurice explained in a combination of patois, Spanish and words from wherever Maurice had been born.

Pierre's compassionate nods made Maurice know he understood, and the slave described the abortive attempts he and Berto had made to join their father. Pierre felt nauseous as he listened to Maurice describe the pain and smell coming from the red hot branding iron when applied to their young flesh as punishment and identification for as long as they lived.

"Why did he sell you and leave Berto behind?" Pierre wanted to know.

"*Femme! Femme!*" Maurice took such a deep breath that his nostrils flared as he struggled to explain himself. "Ducheine wanted my *femme*," and he used his hands to describe the soft curves of a woman who was obviously the object of his desire and coveted by his master as well.

With some effort Maurice managed to explain how he had been subdued in the middle of the night and kept in a holding place until the master took him to St. Marc. There, for the first time, Maurice found himself on the auction block, where he was later bought by the young Monsieur Bérard. The other new slaves were from another plantation, and Maurice indicated that he had found little in common with them. He felt they had long since lost any family ties and could not understand how Maurice longed to be with his brother and his *femme*.

Pierre was trying to judge Maurice's age and how he had developed such a strong desire for and devotion to his *femme*, when there was a slight rustle in the bushes. With the motion of lightning, yet devoid of any noise, Maurice disappeared. Pierre was alone, except for some wild creature he knew was moving among the shrubbery on the bank of the river.

"He is truly a hunted animal," Pierre reminded himself as he made his way back to the Bérard plantation. "But he is also a man."

The days following Pierre's talk with Maurice were soul-searching days. Pierre had to assist his mother and his sister with the smooth operation of the Bérard household. He had to be at the service of young Monsieur Bérard, who instinctively turned to him whenever there was a problem. Pierre found himself accepting accounts of field happenings from his own father in order to explain a situation in language Jean Jacques could readily comprehend.

Each time the young master said: "What would I do without you, Pierre? At least I can trust you," Pierre wanted to scream out the doubts and fears which were plaguing him. There was nobody he could talk with. During this period Pierre's almost total reliance on prayer was born. God was the only one he could turn to.

Only the young mistress seemed to understand that Pierre was experiencing emotional changes. He had no appetite for the food the cook or his mother set before him. Yet with Ursule watching him, he had to attempt to eat in order to avoid questions and suspicions.

Pierre's nights were hours of tossing and turning sleeplessness. His face was soon drawn and his clothes hung loosely. When company came and the Bérards asked for a song from Pierre, the tunes he drew from his fiddle were plaintive as he cradled the old instrument in the crook of his neck, shutting his eyes while he drew the bow across the strings.

"*Mon cher ami,*" the young mistress spoke softly as she asked Pierre to sing a French favorite his grandmother Zenobie had taught him. "What is troubling you? Are you grieving for the *grandmère?*"

Pierre forced a smile and nodded slightly as he made himself sing the French ditty he had learned as a little boy. The planters applauded, but Pierre was ever to remember the quizzical look on young Madame Bérard's face. Her sincere concern had not been unappreciated. Pierre was relieved when his mother appeared and signaled to him to serve refreshments. As he moved among the Bérard's guests, Pierre prayed silently that he would not throw caution aside and denounce those he served as parasites and human scavengers before he made a final decision as to what he would do with the remaining years of his life.

Pierre avoided Maurice for a few days. He went to the Bérard library and read the sermons of the French preacher Jean-Baptiste Massillon, who had been a powerful figure at the court of Louis XV. Pierre had often read these sermons to the elder Monsieur Bérard as the Frenchman nodded in approval. Now the slave Pierre found no comfort in reading the works of the French writer. He could in turning the pages remember his first clumsy efforts when Monsieur Bérard had insisted that he continue. The memory of those early years was the only solace Pierre got from the writings of Massillon; the lessons were lost in his inner disturbance.

In his personal misery Pierre was even irritable with little Rosalie, who had been accustomed to bringing all of her problems, real or imaginary, to him. One day the little girl came to her brother holding up a mashed thumb.

"You're such an *enfant*," he snapped. "Why bother me? Go soak the thumb in hot water."

Rosalie, who had never known anything but loving and protective care from her brother, cried so loud that her mother dropped her chores and with her mistress close behind her, followed the sound of Rosalie's cries.

Long after Ursule took Rosalie to the kitchen where her older sister Marie-Louise soaked the injured thumb and cajoled her younger sister into stopping the tears, Madame Bérard sat in the library staring at Pierre. She sensed that he would have liked to snarl at her as he had at his sister.

The French woman, only a few years younger than Pierre, recognized an inner conflict in the slave. But Marie Elizabeth Bossard Bérard, like Pierre, had led a sheltered life. Pierre's aunt Marie Bouquement, who was Zenobie's oldest daughter, had nursed and cared for all of the Bossard girls. The young mistress' parents, being wealthy, had lavished the trappings of their wealth on their children. There had always been smiling slaves to gratify their every desire. Though young Madame Bérard had indeed heard her husband arguing the case for and against the *gens de couleur,* she could never imagine that this situation would affect Pierre. The young Frenchwoman had never seen the slaves at work on her father's plantation or at L'Artibonite. She would have sworn all the house slaves at Dondon and in the Bérard household were happy and contented. Then she remembered the French saying *cherchez la femme*—look for the woman.

"Pierre," she asked hesitantly, "is it *amour?*"

Pierre thought of Maurice and his *femme*. The young

woman's obvious concern only tightened the invisible trap he felt closing in on him. Pierre still refused to talk. He did not trust his ability to express all he felt without referring to the slaves' meeting and the story Maurice had told him.

"Only God knows the source of my turmoil. And only God can help me," Pierre finally said. He spoke slowly and with such intense feeling the young woman felt herself dismissed and left the library.

Pierre paced the room and looked at row after row of books. He examined the titles, still hopeful even though he knew he had never seen one book which would give him a clue to his true identity and origin.

Pierre had heard old Tonette speak of "Guinee" as home. Still he had no idea of Guinee other than as some place on the continent of Africa. He had heard that other slaves had been brought from Dahomey and still others were from the tribe of Nigerians known as Ibos. Pierre wondered if Maurice's father had been an Ibo, as they had the reputation for killing themselves rather than remaining enslaved.

Unmindful of the time, Pierre began pulling down books from the shelves. He searched until he found a thin, worn and faded volume, not much more than a pamphlet. He noted a fading, almost tattered royal seal—the seal of King Louis XIV. He soon discovered this was the *Code Noir*. When Pierre had finished reading as much of the old document as was legible, his chest was heaving with mixed emotions. The pamphlet was dated 1685. The decree purported to have been drawn up for the purpose of saving the slaves from the superstitions they were alleged to have brought with them from Africa and to convert them to the Christian religion. Pierre remembered Zenobie telling him about Columbus who sailed three ships from Spain. According to Zenobie, Columbus had sailed across the ocean until he came to the island where they lived, which he had called Hispaniola. Zenobie said Columbus had to land on the island because his sailors had been on the ocean so long they were afraid they were going to sail on and on until they sailed off the earth. The old woman told her children that Columbus had settled in a little town not too far from L'Artibonite which he called Navidad. Then, Zenobie always said, Columbus went back to Spain to tell Queen Isabella and King Ferdinand what a beautiful island he had discovered.

When Pierre had asked his grandmother if she was living at the time Columbus came to the island, she laughed and said there was nobody on the island then but the natives—the Arawaks, she called them. When Pierre asked what had happened to the Arawaks as he had only seen slaves, Frenchmen, pirates and *gens de couleur,* she looked sad and said all of the Arawaks died a long time ago.

It came back to Pierre that his grandmother had usually found a way to change the subject when he asked more questions about the natives who lived on the island before Zenobie or her mother Tonette came to St. Dominique. Many years later when Pierre read the writings of Moreau de St. Mery he learned how the Arawaks were exterminated by the Spaniards. The Spaniards later supplied the French planters with slaves to work the fertile meadows and hillsides which they expected to take from the French and unite with the other half of Hispaniola which remained under Spanish control.

Pierre understood how a man of principle like the elder Monsieur Bérard would have a problem with his conscience over being a slave holder. He also understood how the Frenchman might have salved his conscience with the knowledge that he made sure all of his slaves were baptized and allowed the privilege of practicing the Christian faith. And yet Pierre asked himself how Monsieur Bérard could actually reconcile his religious beliefs with buying human beings much as he might have bought a horse, a hoe or a pickax to help till the soil of the property he owned.

Then Pierre's thoughts turned to his grandmother Zenobie. Somehow he excluded Tonette, for he had decided she must have been the one to undergo the agony of being captured and stolen from her African home and relatives, then made to adjust to the life of a slave as opposed to Pierre's previously surmised position of her being held in esteem by her peers. Tonette's acceptance of life as a slave, Pierre reasoned, had been half expediency and half expectation of deliverance. Her daughter Zenobie had followed the mother's example. The lack of male ancestors bothered Pierre, but he had heard vague reference to an uncle whose death was ever to remain shrouded in mystery. As best as Pierre could discern, Marie Bouquement, who nursed all of the Bossard girls, had been born to Zenobie while she was little more than a child.

Pierre first had feelings of resentment about Zenobie. Why, he asked himself, had she entered into a life of accommodation? Then he wondered about who had fathered his aunt and his mother. For his own father, Pierre felt only toleration. It was the sort of tolerance one felt for any human being locked into a position from which he could not free himself.

Pierre felt more trapped than ever. His mother was part and parcel of Zenobie. She knew the difference between the lives of house servants and slaves who worked in the fields. Her husband and children were favored as the descendants of Tonette and Zenobie. Ursule never let her husband forget the life they might have been compelled to live but for the generosity of the Bérards.

That night, after the day Pierre spent in the library trying to arrive at some decision about his identity, he vomited the food he was served for an evening meal. As in a trance, he found himself making his way to the hut where Tonette sat rocking without rockers on her chair and chewing without food to chew, in the way of the very old. His many questions about Africa and her life before she came to St. Dominique fell on ears that refused to hear that which might be painful. The only word he could distinguish was "Guinee-Guinee."

On his way back home, Pierre observed Maurice sitting apart from the other slaves as usual. Pierre was so absorbed he showed no sign of recognition. Neither did he slacken his pace. He had walked some distance before he felt Maurice's presence beside him; the slave's bare feet had made no sound as he approached.

Pierre felt a gentle nudge, then Maurice pointed toward a moon shrouded in clouds. Maurice nodded his head and pointed toward the bank of the river where they had met before. Pierre secretly wished he had never seen Maurice's brother or looked in the face of Maurice after he saw the brand on his bare shoulder that day in the field. In the distance there was a faint sound which Pierre recognized as drums in the hills. Pierre decided that Maurice's insistence that they meet later was connected with whatever message the drums were sending.

Just as Maurice had intimated, dark clouds still covered the moon. Once the candles in the Bérard house had been snuffed, Pierre went out into the blackness of the moonless night.

Pierre had reached the stage where he had wearied of accounting to his mother for his every movement. This night he would meet Maurice without going through the pretense of feigning sleep until he knew the rest of the family was deep in slumber. Instead he walked slowly in the direction of the hut where the new slaves lived. A few paces from the slave hut, Pierre recognized the outline of a figure emerging and walking in the direction of the river. That, he surmised, would be Maurice, who was going before him. In a few moments, the other figure had disappeared among the thickets leading to the bank of the river. Pierre continued to walk, but he could hardly see his hand in front of him. He leaned against a tree and decided to wait until Maurice found him. Soon Pierre felt a touch on his arm. It was Maurice and he pointed toward the river but shook his head violently. Then he pointed in the direction of the distant mountain which the slaves called *Morne du Diable*. The drums were now beating louder and louder. Pierre surmised they were calling the slaves to a rendezvous in the highest ridges of this grim and foreboding mountain fastness bearing Satan's name.

Maurice went ahead but waited for Pierre each time he dropped behind. This went on and on until Pierre was almost out of breath, but their climb did not end until they pushed aside the thick foliage in a dense thicket and found themselves on a natural plateau ringed with more slaves than Pierre had ever seen at one time. Then Pierre saw a thatched arbor or *tonnelle,* inside which was a crude altar bearing a cross beneath which was carved a serpent. In front of the altar was a coconut shell. Inside the shell burned a tiny flame which seemed to float from one end of the shell to the other. Slave drummers were on either side of the altar, and the throbbing song of the drums along with the flame dancing in the coconut shell induced in Pierre a feeling of being more asleep than awake. He saw calabash bowls of food and a bleeding cock whose blood was draining into a larger bowl.

Pierre looked around for Maurice who had disappeared. As before, Pierre did not see a familiar face, until Maurice reappeared bringing his brother Berto with him. After Berto had greeted Pierre with a nod, the three slaves sat on the ground among the others. By now Pierre had realized he was to see a voodoo ritual. Slaves at L'Artibonite whispered about voodoo, and though Pierre had been curious, he had never thought he, as a Christian, would ever see the ritual. Pierre looked about him and wondered why there were no females in the gathering. He remembered the pride with which Maurice had spoken of his *femme* and thought other slaves might have brought women with them.

Then the tempo of the drums abruptly changed. The music slowed, then became softer before it picked up a feverish beat. Pierre blinked his eyes when a young, barefoot female appeared and began a wild dance. She went through a series of gyrations and sensuous contortions until she fell exhausted at the foot of the altar. As if by magic, another young slave woman appeared. She stepped over the first dancer and repeated much the same performance as the first until she likewise sank to the ground in exhaustion.

The drummers produced a roll of the drums which made Pierre think of the thunder and lightning accompanying storms which had so frightened him as a child.

With a wild leap, a third dancer jumped over the prone bodies of the other two and stood in front of the altar, both hands on her hips while she looked around as if counting the black slaves sitting on the ground.

The drums fell silent as the dancer prowled with her eyes. Then the drums started again, this time like a continuing roll of thunder, and the woman began her contorted body movements which seemed to torment the seated slaves, though not one of them moved.

Pierre thought the dancer was the most beautiful woman he had ever seen. From her aquiline nose and thin lips, he deduced that her African blood had been diluted by that of some French planter. She did not wear the mouka most slave women wore on their heads, and her hair was not as tightly curled. As the drums mounted a tormented beat, she writhed as if in agony and pulled at the strands of her hair until it stood about her head like a halo. Then she gave a string of whimpers which made Pierre think of a wounded dog. Finally there was her wild piercing scream of "Damballa! Damballa!" and she collapsed at the foot of the altar with the wooden snake, then rolled over and over until she lay still, as if dead.

Pierre remembered having heard slaves whisper about Damballa, the god to whom the snake was sacred. Now Pierre began to understand Maurice's longing for his *femme.* He—Pierre—experienced a sensation he had never known before. He wanted to go and pick up the beautiful dancer, take her in his arms and tell her she could forget Damballa. Our Lord and his Blessed Mother would see that no harm came to her. But suddenly the first two dancers came to life and picked up the beautiful one, whose body appeared to be as rigid as a board, and bore her out of his sight.

Pierre had hardly recovered from this shock when there was another roll of the drums and a tall black man wearing a red ceremonial robe stood before the altar. There was movement and knowing whispers among the slaves.

"I must be the only one here who does not know who he is," Pierre decided, but he refrained from asking the man's identity.

A young black boy, naked except for a cloth about his loins, appeared with a knife in his hand and slit the throat of the bleeding cock, tasted the blood in the bowl and then handed it to the tall man who threw back his head in a defiant gesture and drank until the bowl was emptied of the cock's blood.

Pierre actually felt the ripple of movement in the crowd. He marveled that this pagan rite could still sway men, now generations from Guinea or wherever they came from, to such an extent.

Then the man began to speak. Pierre had heard enough brilliant conversation in the Bérard drawing room and parlors to recognize eloquence; this man was an eloquent speaker. Sometimes he used the familiar patois. Again he spoke French, then resorted to words which had no meaning for Pierre but evidently conveyed a meaning to some of the slaves.

"If only Tonette had given me a smattering of her native tongue," Pierre wished.

Maurice and Berto sat on either side of Pierre, almost as if they were guarding him. He noticed that the two brothers were leaning forward as if straining to understand the speaker. Pierre wondered why they had taken him into their confidence. They sat so close to him he became uneasy. He began to wonder if he was destined to suffer the same fate as the cock whose throat had been slit.

Pierre's concern for his own safety gave way to a state of confusion in which he began to wonder if what he had seen and was still seeing was real or the result of an overactive imagination. Yet, he reasoned, the beautiful dancer had to be real because he had never seen a woman like her. Her piercing eyes and her beautiful face was a joy to remember. Pierre's own manhood had been controlled by a mixture of religion, dedication to his duties and the strong, ever-watchful influence of his mother and his iron-willed grandmother. Tonight Pierre's religion seemed a remote influence. Neither his mother nor his grandmother were present, and he felt no sense of duty to the Bérards. All he felt was the puzzlement over the spectacle before him and a yearning to protect the beautiful dancer from Damballa. This shed a new light on Maurice's yearning for his *femme.*

The speaker intruded on Pierre's yearning, and he decided he would have to find out the identity of this man who had conducted a pagan rite of voodoo and was now calling on the god of light and goodness to deliver the black men on St. Dominique from the cruel French planters who had stolen them away from their homes across the sea and forced them to work and live as beasts of burden.

"Who?" Pierre asked Maurice softly, pointing to the speaker.

"Boukman," Maurice replied.

"Who is his master—what plantation?"

These questions amused Maurice and his brother. "He has no master! He lives as he wills. He will lead us!" Berto said with conviction.

For the next hour Pierre heard Boukman harangue God, Damballa, Erzilie—goddess of the sea—and every angel or saint he had ever heard of, imploring them collectively to rain fire and brimstone on the planters and grant freedom with revenge to the slaves.

Then Pierre heard names he had never heard before as the speaker permitted the squatting slaves to join in planning the destruction of the planters. This was obviously not the first time the uprising had been discussed, and the men who squatted nearest the altar were evidently familiar with the plans.

For the first time Pierre heard a name similar to his—the name of Toussaint Louverture—who he later learned was a coachman at Breda, a beautiful estate just three miles from the capital city of Cap Français Breda. He had heard the Bérards say that Breda was owned by Comte de Noe and under the supervision of one Monsieur Libertat.

Like Pierre Toussaint, the other Toussaint had somehow learned to read and write. Some said there had been a godfather who had taught Louverture the rudiments of reading, writing and numbers. Monsieur Libertat was so impressed with the young coachman's judgment of men, weather conditions and situations concerning the productivity of the estate that he made Louverture the steward at Breda, a position heretofore unknown to be held by a slave. It was not unusual for the French planters to give their male offspring by slave concubines such authority, but no other slave was known to have been made a steward.

As the steward at Breda, Louverture had access to the library of the Comte de Noe, and there is no doubt that this young slave studied the military strategy of the great soldiers of the world just as Pierre read French sermons and classics in Monsieur Bérard's library.

That night on *Morne du Diable,* Pierre heard other names which were to make him shudder whenever he heard them.

What bothered Pierre as he listened to the slaves call names like Dessalines, Christophe and Pétion was that only the name of Christophe was at all familiar. He vaguely remembered Zenobie talking about the struggle of the colonists to the North who were fighting to win their freedom from England and how slaves from St. Dominique had gone to some place in the colonies called Savannah, where a fierce battle was fought, the slaves fighting side by side with the colonists. The only slave whose name Pierre remembered Zenobie calling when she told them about the slaves fighting at Savannah was that of Christophe. And now Pierre was hearing about Christophe again, but this time the slave would be fighting the French planters for the freedom of slaves.

Pierre looked around him—past Maurice and Berto. He had no doubt that the men who were talking harbored such intense feelings of rage and hatred for the white planters that they would not hesitate to kill every white man, woman or child they saw. It was obvious they were only waiting for the coachman at Breda to tell them when to strike. Pierre marveled that the slaves had so far succeeded in keeping secret their plans to drive the French planters away from St. Dominique by force and violence. He felt pity for men like Jean Jacques Bérard who insisted it was the *gens de couleur* who were stirring up strife and discontent.

Without any word of indication, the drums were silenced and the slaves began disappearing. Pierre felt ill as he and Maurice made their way back to L'Artibonite. Berto had left them halfway down the mountain, and Pierre was glad that only Maurice saw him when he stopped to empty his stomach. Maurice seemed to understand and tore a handful of berries from a nearby bush that caught their clothes and ordered Pierre to eat them to settle his stomach.

The two slaves parted before they emerged from the trees and thickets into the clearing around the slaves' quarters. Just before they parted, Maurice gripped Pierre's hand and held it so firmly Pierre winced, yet he strove to prevent the other slave from noticing his discomfort. Maurice said nothing, but his labored breathing indicated deep emotional concern. After a few minutes, he dropped Pierre's hand and smiled. Pierre understood that Maurice felt that he was with him and not against him in this battle for freedom. Pierre knew that Maurice would inform him when the leader who bore part of his name gave the signal for the slaves to strike the first blow in their effort to drive the French from St. Dominique.

CHAPTER 3

Reprieve or Postponement?

Pierre knew few waking moments when he was not formulating one plan after another for the course of action he would take when Toussaint Louverture gave the signal for the slaves to launch their revolt. His first reaction was that he would protect the Bérards with his own life. Then Pierre tried to picture himself warding off the blows of Maurice, who was determined to avenge his own suffering. Though Maurice's life at L'Artibonite had been less arduous than the cruelty he suffered at the hands of Monsieur Ducheine, memories of his father and his *femme* kept the slave from developing any feelings but hatred for any planter. It was not hard for Pierre to imagine Maurice with a machete in his hand attempting to behead Monsieur and Madame Bérard. Pierre knew that Maurice had not made many friends since he came to the Bérard plantation, but the temptation for him to dispose of the Bérards and take over the plantation was a possibility Pierre had to consider.

Again Pierre was assailed by the feeling of being alone—without any confidant but God. He knew that his older brother and sister had decided that anybody who spent as much time with his head in a book as Pierre was different from anybody they knew. They only exchanged the conversations one has to exchange with a member of the family with whom one lives. Rosalie, still little more than a child, spent most of her time playing with the other slave boys and girls and, Pierre thought, giggling over anything and everything.

One night after Pierre had made sure all of the candles had been snuffed, he decided it would be a good idea to start bolting the doors to the great house. Pierre had only bolted the door to the main entrance when he heard a light noise and turned to see his young master descending the stairway.

Jean Jacques demanded to know why Pierre was bolting a door that he could never remember having been bolted. Pierre, who was not adept at lying, attempted to remain silent but his young master was insistent.

"One never knows," Pierre began without knowing how he would finish, "one just never knows when men or animals decide to prowl."

Jean Jacques was perplexed. He had never known Pierre to be evasive. Yet his wife had told him that Pierre did not appear to be his usual self. Perhaps, his master reasoned, he is reacting to Zenobie's absence and the added responsibility I have given him.

Pierre secured the other doors and went home. He had developed the habit of walking softly and his parents did not hear him enter.

"Something is wrong with Pierre," Ursule was telling Pierre's father. "I think he spends too much time with his head stuck in a book. What good is all of that reading going to do a slave?"

"Zenobie taught him to read," the other Toussaint reminded his wife.

"As if I did not know that," Pierre detected a note of irritation in his mother's voice. "I just wonder...."

"You just wonder if he wants a wife," the father spoke haltingly.

"How could you think of such a thing?" Pierre heard his mother demand.

"You and your mother have forgotten that our sons are flesh and blood—as well as Monsieur Bérard's slaves."

Pierre waited for an explosion. He had never heard his father speak with so much feeling.

"You must have had too much tafia,"[1] Ursule began, "or else you must have grown more of that *kingola* since Zenobie went to Paris."

"I don't have to be drunk or drugged, *chérie*, to know that my sons are men and will soon be taking wives," Pierre heard his father insist. To Pierre's surprise his mother remained silent, and Pierre tiptoed to the bed where he slept.

Pierre's father's remarks pushed aside his fears of the slaves' revolt. That night he thought only of what his father had said. Then his thoughts turned to the beautiful dancer at the voodoo meeting. Surely one so delicate in appearance could not be a *mambo* or voodoo priestess. If only he could find her again, Pierre reasoned, he was sure he could persuade her to forsake *Damballa* for Jesus Christ and his Mother, the Virgin Mary.

"How do I know what might have driven her to voodoo?" Pierre asked himself, then trembled when he thought of the many possibilities. Again his thoughts darted back to the conversation he had overheard. "The *kingola* my mother mentioned," he decided, "must be the plant I saw Zenobie pull up. It must be a drug."

Another day was breaking and Pierre was no closer to solving the riddle of what he would do when the slaves rose up to kill the planters or how he would find the dancer who had aroused his dormant male passions.

After the evening meal, Pierre walked outside into the softness of the night and looked around. He watched birds flying from tree to tree and decided that even the birds were

---

1. A raw rum made from sugar cane.

freer than he was. He heard the sound of chatter coming from the direction of the slave quarters and started in that direction, but remembered that his mother and Zenobie had kept him so isolated he only knew a few of the slaves well enough to converse with them. Any attempt at friendliness now would arouse their suspicion. Perhaps he could find Maurice and ask him about the voodoo dancing girl. Before Pierre decided what he would do, he heard the sound of galloping horses.

Pierre stood wondering. It would be most unusual for Monsieur to have guests without having made any preparation for their entertainment. Yet he found himself accepting the reigns from two horsemen who had stopped at the main entrance and ordered him in a loud voice to tie up their horses as they ran up the steps and presented themselves at the door.

Pierre saw the frightened look on his sister's face as she opened the door and called to her mother, while the two Frenchmen stamped their feet and used words Pierre had never heard in the Bérard household. Pierre quickly tied the horses to a hitching post and reached the door of the house just as his mother appeared and the impatient men made as if to push her aside, demanding to see Monsieur Bérard immediately.

Pierre took a deep breath as he threw himself between the Frenchmen and his mother. "Pardon," he forced a fixed smile on his face, "what is it the messieurs wish?"

"We want the master, and hurry and get him!" the taller of the two men bellowed as Pierre's frightened mother ran through the house calling for Monsieur Bérard, who was pulling on his jacket and straightening his ascot as he came out of the drawing room.

It was apparent to Pierre that Monsieur Bérard did not know the men when they gave their names, and he sensed that their presence meant trouble. The taller of the two said he was Monsieur Ducheine and the shorter, heavy-set man was the Monsieur Caradeux, the merciless slave master Pierre had heard the slaves describe at the first clandestine meeting he had attended. Monsieur Caradeux, the slaves said, was the most inhuman of all the planters in the area.

"We're looking for two runaway slaves!" Monsieur Ducheine bellowed.

"Why come to L'Artibonite?" Monsieur Bérard asked.

"The one I'm looking for is a brother to a slave I sold you. I branded both of them for trying to run away once before. I should have crippled them then," Ducheine swore.

"And you, Monsieur?" Pierre's master addressed Monsieur Caradeux. "What brings you here?"

Pierre heard the second planter explain that he had sold young Monsieur Bérard three slaves at the time he had bought the brother of the slave who had run away from the Ducheine plantation.

Pierre said a silent prayer that Maurice was not hiding his brother Berto as the three planters walked in the direction of the hut where Maurice slept. Though Pierre assured his mother and Madame Bérard that the young master was in no danger, he reinforced this assurance by immediately following the planters.

Pierre was alarmed inwardly when he heard the slave hunters cursing. They came out of the hut where Pierre knew the new slaves slept, and he decided their curses meant they did not find the slaves they sought. He heard grunts and laughter, then he saw the planters walk to a clearing at the edge of the wooded thicket leading to the banks of the river. Pierre saw the slaves enjoying a wrestling match, and Maurice threw another one of the slaves to the ground as the Frenchmen approached them.

Ducheine made a springlike movement toward Maurice, who was surprised to see his former master. In a flash young Jean Jacques intercepted the movement and with determined civility informed Ducheine that he, Monsieur Bérard, would question Maurice about his brother. Pierre knew that

Maurice would never give any indication of understanding the questions asked him. He listened to Maurice's muddled denials and hoped they were sincere. He also hoped that Berto was high in the mountains with the *maroons* and free of Ducheine forever.

Monsieur Caradeux was more diplomatic than Ducheine, though Pierre never doubted that he could be the more vicious of the two men. Caradeux gave Monsieur Bérard the names of his runaways and told him to tell the other slaves he would give them a reward for any information they might supply if the runaways dared to seek them out.

Pierre walked quickly back toward the house and untied the horses. After he stood beside his master and watched the two planters disappear, the young master turned to him and spoke.

"Buying slaves from those two was the first mistake I made after my father turned L'Artibonite over to me. Were I a slave, I am sure I, too, would have run away from them."

Madame Bérard was in the high-ceilinged parlor with Pierre's mother and his sister. All three of the women had been frightened by the coarseness of the two visitors' appearance and language, and they awaited the young master's assurance that there would be no further trouble.

After the women had been calmed, Pierre walked his mother and Marie-Louise home. Ursule continued to dramatize the manner in which Pierre had stepped in front of her when Monsieur Ducheine had attempted to push her aside.

Pierre felt sorry for his mother. She had so few opportunities to be proud of her menfolk, he thought. Then Pierre decided it was the other way around; his mother's menfolk had so few opportunities to assert their manhood.

Pierre knew there was no way he could sleep that night without talking to Maurice. For the first time, Pierre found

Maurice in a group with the other slaves who shared the hut. The sight of Ducheine and Caradeux, he discovered, had reminded them anew of the cruelties they had suffered at the hands of these two planters. Though Pierre attempted to converse with all of the new slaves, only Maurice would answer any of his questions. Pierre soon decided that the men knew nothing about the whereabouts of the runaways. He thought that Maurice appeared more distracted than the others even though he answered the questions Pierre asked. Yet Pierre knew Maurice well enough to decide he had not heard from Berto yet; otherwise he would have been on his way to join him as soon as the slave owners disappeared.

The story of the runaway slaves spread from plantation to plantation. The following Sunday morning when planters and slaves alike went to the old church in St. Marc for Mass, Pierre knew by the conversations around him that the planters were disturbed and the slaves were fearful that their masters would curb small privileges they might have been granted.

After Mass Pierre walked through the crowd hoping against hope that he might have the good fortune to see the beautiful dancer. If longing could make her appear, he knew she would be there. Instead he heard his mother's voice call out to him.

"Pierre," Ursule whispered once she had overtaken her son, "Madame is disturbed by the gentlemen talking with Monsieur. André, the coachman, is holding the door open. I think the young master would appreciate it if you offered to escort Madame to the coach."

For half a second, Pierre was inclined to tell his mother that Madame Bérard could walk to her own coach while he looked for a woman of his own. Then he took another look at his mother and wondered how she had ever taken time away from the Bérards to have a family of her own. Before he could voice any of his sentiments, he felt the gentle touch of

Ursule's hand on his arm as she steered him in the direction of the group of planters and one or two of the ladies who were engaging in an animated conversation.

Pierre looked at the men in the shiny-buttoned long coats and high hats, with their hair in perukes which they fastened with black ribbons. The women were dressed in elaborately fashioned muslins with lacy frills and large sleeves. The ladies' skirts covered full petticoats also edged in lace, which showed as they entered or descended from their coaches. Pierre walked toward the planters with his mother but looked back from time to time as a gaily dressed slave girl or groups of the more somberly clad *gens de couleur* passed.

Snatches of heated conversation drifted toward them as Ursule continued to steer Pierre to the Bérards and their friends. Pierre could tell it was the same old argument; who should be feared, the slaves or the *gens de couleur?* Pierre knew his master was still insistent that it was the *gens de couleur,* with the higher degree of intelligence gained from education and special privileges, who posed the greatest threat. The other planters saw the flight of the two runaway slaves as a sign of things to come.

Pierre felt his mother's grip on his arm tighten. She knew he was more intent on overhearing the conversation than rescuing Madame Bérard.

"*Bonjour,* Madame," Ursule called softly to her mistress. "Pierre will assist you to the carriage."

The young Frenchwoman warmly thanked the two slaves for helping to get her away from the agitated Frenchmen and followed Pierre to the carriage, which as long as Pierre could remember was always left near the rectory. André, the coachman, was still holding the door and Pierre helped his young mistress as she gathered her skirt and petticoats to step up and into the waiting vehicle. Ursule was arranging the cushions for her mistress as the horses shifted from foot to foot when Jean Jacques Bérard appeared, his face red and perspiring. For a moment the young Frenchman stood and looked at Pierre. Then he shook his head and joined his wife.

Pierre looked after them as the horses' hooves and the carriage wheels raised a cloud of white dust on the unpaved street. He knew his young master was wrong in advising the planters that they should not fear the slaves. But the knowledge Pierre had gained was his secret—his and thousands of angry slaves. He could not betray the slaves who had trusted him. But neither could Pierre kill a Bérard. The answer to his secret problem was as illusive as his longing for his secret love—the beautiful voodoo dancer.

"Maybe—maybe," the thought came to Pierre with such force he felt his lips forming words silently, "maybe I will have to take to the hills like Berto."

The impact of this thought surprised Pierre. He realized that subconsciously he had decided that Berto had taken to the hills and cast his lot with the *maroons* in the hope of finding liberty or at least some trace of his father.

"Have you been drinking tafia, too?" Ursule demanded.

When Pierre's older brother and his two sisters joined them, she insisted that their smart brother was acting like he was drunk. Pierre's brother and older sister laughed as if they thought their brother was usually drunk. Rosalie took Pierre by the hand and half-skipping, half-pulling, led him over to the cobblestone marketplace where she cajoled him into buying her a chocolate confection before they started the long walk back to L'Artibonite.

Pierre avoided Maurice after he decided Berto had fled to the mountains where he had first seen him. He felt guilty harboring the thought, but he could not risk actual knowledge of Berto's whereabouts. His young master had been extremely restless since the encounter with Ducheine and Caradeux. Each night when Pierre heard the echo of the drums in the hills, he wished he had learned to understand the messages they were sending. He wondered if the drums where telling Maurice about Berto.

Then the sickness came. First the chickens and later the dogs crawled around and then collapsed. After that the male slaves fell between the rows of cane and the coffee bushes.

"If only I had kept Zenobie here," Jean Jacques lamented as Ursule and Marie-Louise went from hut to hut trying to help the women nurse the sick. Pierre remembered hearing his grandmother and his aunt, Marie Bouquement, mention a doctor who had a plantation near Dondon, the home of the young Madame's parents, and so informed the young master.

"I will ride over for the doctor," Jean Jacques told Pierre. "I'll take Madame Bérard with me for company on the drive. Then I will encourage her mother to urge her to stay until we know what the sickness is. Tell your mother to pack a valise for Madame—but make sure André puts it out of sight so she will not become suspicious. I have no idea what this sickness is. Do you, Pierre?"

"It must be something they drank—something in the water from one of the streams. Nobody in the house has been felled and few of the women are sick," Pierre commented. "I'm trying to remember what my grandmother did in cases where the slaves appeared to have been..." and Pierre shied away from the word *poisoned*.

"I will leave as soon as Madame is ready. Make sure the coach is at the door when I bring her down. She will be full of questions about so sudden a trip."

Monsieur Bérard had barely reached the top of the stairway when Pierre called out.

"I've just remembered," he almost shouted. "*Grandmère* Zenobie always said 'purge them' in cases where symptoms such as we are seeing were shown."

"Purge them with what?" the Frenchman had run back down the stairs.

"I—I'm not sure," Pierre admitted. "But my mother might know what *grandmère* used. You go for the doctor, and I'll see what we can do while you are away."

As the coach drove off in the direction of Dondon, Jean Jacques saw Pierre walking with his mother toward the garden. Pierre was annoyed when his mother couldn't remember what her mother had used to brew the purging potion. Pierre watched her as she went from tree to shrubs to bushes. She sniffed the scent of the leaves on one thick bush, tore off a leaf and chewed it. She made a face and spat out the vile tasting juice.

"Go to the house and help the cook fill as many pots as you can find. Then start boiling the water. Make sure there is enough firewood and hurry," Ursule ordered as she started stripping the bush of its leaves.

As Pierre started toward the Bérard house, he was surprised to see his father and brother coming in from the fields so early.

"Out of over a hundred men I only have twenty-five who can work today, and this boy of mine acts like he is sick, too," Pierre's father said. "I think they are all lazy—or planning something. I've been hearing some strange things ever since those two slaves ran away."

Pierre felt his brother's forehead, then whispered "fever" to his mother before he ran in the direction of the manor house to boil the water.

Pierre closed his ears to the cook's complaint about him using all of her pots and throwing so much of the cut wood on the fire. Then Pierre searched his memory for every single thing he had seen Zenobie do when she was treating the sick. High fever was one of the symptoms of this illness. He recalled seeing his grandmother make a poultice out of the leaves from a certain tree outside their hut. The poultice was used to lower the fever, but first they would have to use the tea from the leaves his mother was gathering to purge the patients.

The water was boiling by the time Ursule came into the kitchen with an apron full of leaves. As soon as she added the contents of her apron to the pot, a stench hit their nostrils.

"What is that you're making?" the cook wrinkled her nose.

"Bring me a bottle of the juice from the cane that you use for sweetened," Ursule ordered. "This tea is to purge the sick ones. But they'd die before they drank enough of it to do them any good unless we sweeten it."

As soon as the brew was sweetened, Ursule stuck her tongue in a few drops she put in a spoon. Then she filled a cup and handed it to Pierre. "Run to your brother and make him drink this. Pour it down his throat if he refuses. By now he is probably too weak to fight you. I wouldn't be surprised if your father came down with it, too. They've both been drinking from one of the streams. My mother has told them over and over only to drink from the springs or the well that supplies this house with water."

Pierre was already on his way as his mother talked. His brother lay on the pallet-bed they shared, sweating profusely and glassy eyed. Pierre put the cup to his brother's lips. The older boy took one sip and looked at Pierre as if he were an executioner. Sensing his brother's helplessness, Pierre tilted the cup until it was drained of its contents. The older youth gagged, but Pierre held his lips with his fingers until he saw his brother take a deep swallow.

There had been little affection between these two brothers. Zenobie had made no secret of which one she favored and neither had the Bérards. But the sick boy knew his brother was trying to help him. When Pierre found a cloth and wiped the perspiration from his brother's brow, he smiled up at him.

Just as Zenobie and the Bérards had shown their favoritism toward Pierre, the father had shown his preference for his firstborn son. Pierre's father had seen the other slaves fall out and he said they were lazy. Now his favorite son was felled and he was dazed by the turn of events.

Pierre knew his mother would need all of them to help administer the brew she was concocting. He also knew the fever would have to be controlled until they were completely purged. He led his father to the tree where he had seen Zenobie gather leaves for poultices.

He urged his father to strip the tree and any other like it he could find, then explained why they needed the leaves. He warned his father to save enough of the strippings to make a poultice for his son after the tea had rid his body of whatever had caused the ailment.

When Pierre ran back to the house, he chuckled when he found Rosalie ladeling the tea while his mother and Marie-Louise trotted from hut to hut until they succeeded in getting the women and children who were not afflicted to come to the kitchen door and get the tea for those most in need.

The old cook, who was disdainful of the whole process, criticized everything Ursule and Pierre did.

"Wait until Zenobie gets back. You'll change your tune then," Ursule reminded her.

The old woman covered her chagrin with a cackle. When Ursule asked her what was funny, she said she was thinking about what a busy night this would be at L'Artibonite because so many of the slaves would be going out into the bushes.

"That means you knew this tea would purge them. Why didn't you mention it before?" Ursule demanded. "You must have seen Zenobie use it."

"Nobody around here knows anything but you and that smart son of yours," the old woman stood akimbo as she said what she must have wanted to say ever since Zenobie went to Paris with the elder Bérards.

"Just for that," Ursule picked up a small pot of the unsweetened tea and walked toward the defiant older woman, "I should make Pierre hold you while I pour this down your throat."

The cook let out a loud squeal and ran through the house screaming for Madame Bérard—who was on her way to Dondon.

It had been a long, long time since Pierre had laughed, and it felt good to have something to laugh about. His father came in with a basket of leaves to be used for poultices. There would be time for the women to soak the leaves, then mix them with enough of the clay from the rich soil to make a pack which would be put between wet cloth and placed on the foreheads of the feverish ones—after the tea had done its work. Pierre heard his father tell Ursule that he had already made a poultice for his brother and would make another if the fever did not break.

Darkness settled over L'Artibonite and a pale moon shone. Pierre might have admired it at another time but now he was bone weary. Some of the slaves still hung around the kitchen door, one of whom was Maurice. Pierre had been touched by the way Maurice had helped to carry the medicinal tea to the sick slaves in the huts farthest from the Bérard mansion. He had made Pierre understand that some of the slaves did not have clean cloths to use for the poultices and Pierre invited him into the house where they went to the linen closet and tore old sheets into strips. Pierre saw out of the corner of his eyes that Maurice was awed by the rich furnishings as they passed through the dining, drawing rooms and spacious parlor. But Maurice gave no indication of his thoughts as they tore the strips, and Pierre's only slave friend hurried to get the cloths to the sick ones who needed them.

There were over a hundred field hands, seventy-five to eighty slave women and at least a hundred black children on the Bérard plantation. Pierre tried to remember a crisis such as the one they were going through. The only calamity he could remember happened when Pierre was no more than four years old. One night a loud rumbling awakened him. It was like the earth was moving up and down. His mother and

Zenobie had gathered the children together and tried to quiet them until the earth stopped trembling. Later Pierre had been told that what he felt was an earthquake. When they went into St. Marc for Mass, he had seen piles of debris where buildings had stood and was told the buildings had been destroyed by the trembling earth. Pierre could remember the elder Madame Bérard crying because the one theater in St. Marc had been among the buildings destroyed.

An exhausted Pierre sat in the kitchen alone, while his mother and sisters lay on the rugs in the parlor napping. The old cook dared not show her face. Pierre was wondering why it was taking Monsieur Bérard so long to drive to Dondon, get the doctor and come back, when he noticed the moanful sound of distant drums.

"If only I could decipher their message," Pierre wished again.

The kitchen door was opened abruptly. Pierre sat up and stared at Maurice. Only today he had entered the Bérard house for the first time, and here he stood in the kitchen again.

"The drums!" Maurice pointed toward the hills.

"I hear them," Pierre answered as he noted the frightened look on Maurice's face.

"Bad!" Maurice whispered, "bad! bad!"

"What are they saying?" Pierre asked slowly, hoping to calm the slave.

"Dead! Dead!"

"Who is dead? Who?"

Maurice beat his breast and whispered, "They tell me—me. Maybe it's Berto."

Before Pierre could question Maurice further, they heard the sound of approaching horses. "That must be the master returning," Pierre told Maurice. "We must go outside. He will want me to take the doctor to the huts. Come—you can help me."

André the coachman had taken another slave with him

on the trip, and Pierre saw a lighted lantern held outside the coach. Pierre instructed Maurice to help with the horses as the men would be tired from the return trip, but Pierre was aware that Maurice was in a trancelike state.

Soon the carriage was at the door, and the young master jumped out. Then instead of the doctor, Pierre's aunt, Marie Bouquement, stepped from the coach followed by a slave woman Pierre had never seen.

Jean Jacques Bérard saw the questioning expression on Pierre's face. "The doctor had an accident," he explained hurriedly. "His horse stumbled and fell on him. Both legs are broken and they had to shoot the horse. I had to get this woman," he motioned. "They say she is almost as good a nurse as your *grandmère*. But I had to ride over to Ducheine's place. He had her helping with some slave woman who was giving birth. When he heard that the slave woman had died, Ducheine acted like a human being for the first time," Jean Jacques added.

Pierre greeted his Aunt Marie as his mother and the girls emerged from the house. Monsieur Bérard explained again why the doctor could not come and asked about the condition of the sick slaves. Pierre was saved the necessity of an answer as his mother and Marie-Louise began telling their relative and the slave nurse what they had done with the tea and poultices.

Pierre felt Maurice's hand on his shoulder. "Ask who the slave girl was at Ducheine's," Maurice begged.

"Pardon," Pierre addressed the old nurse, "but would you remember the name of the slave girl at Ducheine's who died after giving birth?"

The woman, who carried in a bag she had fashioned out of a scarf whatever remedies she intended to use, noticed Maurice for the first time. She ignored Pierre and walked over to Maurice, then looked at him carefully before she spoke. "Her name was Collette," she said without taking her eyes off Maurice's face.

"The baby? The baby?" Maurice insisted.

The old woman sighed. "The baby died, too. But the baby wasn't yours—for sure!" she cackled.

A groan—a low, rumbling groan—escaped from Maurice's lips. He started running and before Pierre could catch him he had disappeared among the trees and thickets which led to the banks of the river.

"Collette must have been his *femme*—the one Ducheine wanted," Pierre reasoned. "That's what the drums were telling him. I'll be surprised if I ever see him again."

Pierre's Aunt Marie and the old nurse were amazed that not one slave had died from the illness which had befallen L'Artibonite. But many of the slaves were still running high fevers and few of them were strong enough to go to the fields. Ursule was with her sister and the nurse as they went from hut to hut.

Pierre was physically and emotionally spent. He went home and made sure his brother's fever had abated. Then he spread a sheet on the floor beside the sick one and stretched out, hoping that sleep would wipe out the happenings of the day for a few hours. Yet he found himself more wide awake than ever. Pierre was certain that Collette was Maurice's *femme,* and that she had died giving birth to a baby Ducheine had fathered. Pierre thought about the beautiful voodoo dancer, as that was the only woman he had ever wanted to take in his arms. He wondered how he would have reacted if he had been in Maurice's position.

He decided that Berto must have been in the hills and had tried to warn Maurice with the drums. Then Pierre sat up on the floor. Maurice had always met him on the banks of the river. Pierre had heard that some Africans thought of death as a passage to a better life in another world. What if Maurice had plunged into the river in an effort to end a life he felt no longer had any meaning?

Pierre tiptoed outside and looked up for the moon which had bathed the plantation in a soft glow earlier. Now clouds had erased any trace of that beneficent moon. In the distance, thunder joined the moan of the sad drums. Pierre shivered. He could hardly see, but he knew he had to look for Maurice. Pierre searched the banks of the familiar river until slivers of light were slipping between the trees and the dense foliage. In spite of his determination, Pierre was not sure he would find Maurice—alive. He walked cautiously when he retraced his steps and again approached the spot at the river's edge where he had first met Maurice. There was no sign of his friend.

Pierre was about to give up his search and go back to the plantation when he stopped to admire the spectacle of the sun rising like a glowing orange ball from the waters of the L'Artibonite. Then he saw what looked like the figure of a man made small by distance—silhouetted against the back-drop of the rising sun. Pierre wasted no time. He ran until he was close enough to see it was Maurice. He was sitting on the jagged stump of a tree that had lost the rest of its body in a wind storm.

Pierre's happiness vanished when he saw Maurice's face and heard his first words.

"I will kill Ducheine," the tortured man said quietly. "He killed her. I will kill him," and Maurice held up his huge black hands, the fingers spread wide apart. "I will kill him!"

Pierre, who had seldom been at a loss to find words, was speechless before the other slave's passionate desire to kill.

"Berto not dead," Maurice continued. "He told me on the drums. First I find Berto. Then I kill Ducheine. Many slaves would like to kill him. They will make it easy. But I— Maurice—I will kill!"

"Please," Pierre finally spoke, "I must not know your plans. If you run away the master will hunt you down. He saw us together last night, and I will be the first one he will question."

The other slave rose from his tree-stump seat and took Pierre's hand.

"I—I will pray for you," were the only words Pierre could manage before he broke away and started back toward the plantation.

"Your God blind!" Maurice laughed mockingly, and Pierre felt little consolation in the prayers he tried to mumble as he stumbled toward the Bérard mansion with Maurice's laughter echoing in his ears.

Pierre had barely opened the door to the kitchen when he heard a carriage coming up the driveway. He ran outside in time to assist Madame Bérard. He learned that she had insisted that her father, Monsieur Bossard, drive her back to L'Artibonite to be with her husband because she suspected he was in danger of contracting the illness which had felled so many of the slaves. Jean Jacques, who had also heard the carriage, was still pulling on his jacket when his wife rushed into the house and met her husband at the foot of the staircase. Pierre could not help but think of Maurice when he saw the young Frenchman and his wife locked in a warm embrace, murmuring soft terms of endearment. Pierre's sister, Marie-Louise, ran to take the young mistress' bonnet and help her to her quarters since Pierre's mother, his aunt and the old nurse were still tending the slaves who could not throw off the fever.

Day was breaking.

As was her way, the cook was still grumbling. In spite of the weariness from a sleepless night and sympathy for his tortured friend, Pierre set about preparing the table for breakfast. Jean Jacques had already instructed André to prepare the coach for a drive to Cap Français, where a friend from Paris was to arrive by boat that day.

Monsieur Bossard lingered over coffee with his daughter after her husband drove off for the Cap. Monsieur Bossard asked Pierre to send Rosalie in search of Marie Bouquement so he could find out how much longer she would be needed at L'Artibonite. The young mistress, relieved that her husband was in no danger, chatted with her father and Pierre alternately. She told Pierre what she knew of the friend who was arriving by boat. "You know," she added, "Monsieur Bérard misses the gaiety of his student days in Paris."

"My *grandmère* has told me many wonderful things about Paris. Perhaps we will all go there one day soon," Pierre wished aloud.

"Hadn't you heard?" the young Frenchwoman asked. "There is all kinds of trouble there, too. That is why Jean Jacques is so anxious to get the latest news. As tired as he is, he had to meet his friend."

Pierre was about to ask about Zenobie and the elder Bérards when he heard voices in the kitchen. One was a man's voice, and he excused himself to find out who the cranky old cook was arguing with. Pierre opened the door to the kitchen and saw his father.

"She wouldn't go for you," his father looked at the cook, "and neither would she let me go inside. Come, I must talk with you—it's trouble—bad trouble!"

Pierre followed his father, who did not slacken his pace until they were some distance from the Bérard house. "Zenobie and Ursule always told you not to get too friendly with the field hands," he said.

Pierre agreed that his mother and grandmother had always warned him about being friendly with the other slaves, but he was not quite sure why his father was so upset.

"They—all of the slaves—know you have been friendly with that one the young master bought from Ducheine."

Pierre felt an inner alarm he did not intend to show his father.

"Maurice is my friend," Pierre said.

"Then you had better find him before the master returns."

Pierre heard himself asking if Maurice had run away, but his father had already turned away from him and was walking toward the fields. A handful of black slaves were well enough to cut the cane under the brilliant sun he had seen rise that morning before he had found Maurice. Pierre wondered why he had been at all surprised to learn that Maurice had run away. He should have known that the slave was too distraught to even attempt to cut cane or pick coffee beans.

Pierre had to admit that his father was right; the master had seen Maurice with him the night before. Pierre almost wished for the courage to follow Maurice's example and run away. Then he remembered Maurice's vow to kill Ducheine. Pierre knew that this was one time when his family could not help him. He could only pray that Maurice was wrong—that his God was not blind—and that Jean Jacques Bérard would accept his explanation.

It had been painful to Pierre, when he was serving dinner, for him to have to be polite and listen to Madame Bérard's nervous chatter. He knew she was trying to gloss over her concern for affairs at L'Artibonite. Aside from the humane aspects of an epidemic among the slaves, this could also cause a financial disaster. Her husband was anxious to prove himself capable of managing the plantation. Yet every day the slaves were ill was a day the master lost their labor, which in turn meant a decrease in the crop they would harvest and then sell.

Marie Elizabeth Bérard had lived with slaves all of her life. Yet this night there was a quietness at the plantation that worried her. She could hear no distant sounds of laughter, no tirade of an angry wife nor any songs of love or hate coming from the slave quarters. The more she tried to draw Pierre out so he would give her some clue to her uneasiness, the more he had seemed to retreat. She was glad when the dessert was served and Pierre bowed courteously and left the dining room.

The young Frenchwoman was overcome by her feeling of desolation. Her father had gone back to Dondon. Her husband was somewhere between Cap Français and their plantation. Her maid Ursule and Marie, her nurse from infancy, were still nursing the sick slaves. Separated from her parents and her sisters by many rocky miles, Marie Elizabeth felt afraid for the first time since she had married Jean Jacques. She had no idea that Pierre was even more afraid.

Pierre looked away when his mother and his aunt came to the house, and the young Frenchwoman fell into the arms of her nurse and sobbed out her fears.

When the candles had all been snuffed and the doors bolted, Pierre went to the hut where Maurice had lived. But the other slaves were all asleep or, he decided, pretended to be when he tried to question them about Maurice's last known movement. Pierre found himself drawn once again to the river. He could hear the drums in the distance spelling out a message he could not understand. He felt another rush of resentment toward his mother and Zenobie. They had schemed to rob him of his identity and make of him a court jester for the Bérards.

"If only I could hate," Pierre muttered, "then I could fight. I hate the evil that men do, but can I, as a child of God, hate another man? Can I dare to hate Monsieur Ducheine for all he did to Berto and poor Maurice?"

Recalling all the two slaves had suffered brought tears that Pierre had been taught were not manly. The more he thought of the event which caused Maurice to run away, the more he cried. An animal stirring in the bushes reminded Pierre of where he was, and that Maurice would remember that he had begged not to know of his plans. It was not likely that he would see Maurice tonight—or ever again. With a shrug of resignation, Pierre went home and spread a covering on the floor beside his brother who was still weak and sleeping off his fever.

The next morning Pierre had already had one argument with the cook and set the table when he heard the Bérard carriage pull up to the door. Pierre ran out to assist his master, who looked the worse for his journey. Pierre was puzzled when Jean Jacques barely greeted him and ran into the house and up the main stairs to his wife's quarters without any of his usual pleasantries. André the coachman looked as glum as his master, and Pierre wondered what had happened in Cap Français.

The cook complained about having to keep the breakfast warm. She insisted that the coffee would not be fit for the dogs to drink if the Bérards did not come to the dining room soon. For the first time, Pierre was glad to listen to the woman's complaints; they took his mind off the problem of his relationship with Maurice. His family seemed to be avoiding him. He suspected that they expected the young master to accuse him of having aided Maurice in his plan to run away.

When the Bérards entered the dining room, Pierre thought his master still looked troubled. Jean Jacques shared information with his wife about Cap Français and the friend from Paris. But several times Pierre heard him refer to *the letter*. And Pierre wondered why *the letter* was so important and what had been the contents.

Pierre dreaded to see the meal end, because he had decided to tell Jean Jacques about Maurice before anyone else had the opportunity. Almost as if on cue, the young mistress begged to be excused and went to her quarters as soon as the meal was finished.

Once again Pierre found himself groping for words he did not want to utter. Jean Jacques rose from the table.

"Pierre, I've never seen you like this. You—you are trembling. What is it? Did one of the field hands die?"

Pierre took heart from the fact that the young master did not use the word slave. "Monsieur Bérard," he began, "Maurice is gone. He has run away."

"Who is Maurice?" Jean Jacques asked.

"The slave you bought from Monsieur Ducheine—who was here with me the night you brought the nurse and Aunt Marie back from Dondon."

"What happened? Had he been fighting with the others?"

Pierre omitted the manner in which he had first become

friendly with Maurice, but he told his master all Maurice had told him of his life and ended by explaining that Maurice had been in love with the slave girl who had died at the Ducheine plantation after giving birth to a white baby.

Jean Jacques closed his eyes for a second then motioned for Pierre to sit down. "I told you before," he began, "buying those slaves was my first mistake after my father turned his estate over to me. Pierre, things here and in Paris are much worse than either of us has imagined. I am going to have to make a decision very soon which may change the course of our lives.

"My friend who returned to the Cap from Paris brought me a letter from another friend who warned of impending trouble."

Again Pierre had the feeling of being trapped. "What kind of trouble, Monsieur?" he heard himself ask.

"It's the *gens de couleur*. They have organized in Paris. Their society has been founded by Brisson de Warville, who has visited in the colonies to the North. A society has been founded for the purpose of promoting the cause of men of mixed blood and is known as *Les Amis Des Noirs*. They will come to St. Dominique to press their cause and there will be bloodshed. I want no part of it. There is great unrest in Paris. Angry debates over political issues are being held which lead me to conclude there will be uprisings in France, too."

"What of your family and my *grandmère*?" Pierre asked.

"They are safe, for the time being. Zenobie will soon be sailing for home. But I am not sure we are safe here, Pierre. The *gens de couleur* will strike. As soon as Zenobie returns, I intend to take Madame for an extended visit. Monsieur Bossard has asked me to take her two sisters with us."

"But if there are rumors of trouble in Paris, where will you go?"

"We have just decided today and I must get a letter out by the next boat. We will go to New York. I know several

Frenchmen there who are well connected. With a modest investment, we should have an income which will provide gracious living. Nothing as lavish as L'Artibonite, but then this will only be a vacation until the unrest has passed. We will plan accordingly. The decision has been made."

"But what about Maurice?" Pierre asked. "Will you warn Monsieur Ducheine and report Maurice to the authorities?"

Jean Jacques pushed back his chair and began pacing the length of the room. After what seemed to Pierre to be an interminable time, he spoke. "If what you tell me is true—and you have never lied to me—that slave—that man—has suffered enough. Pierre, I trust your judgment and my parents have stressed your honesty. I will not report Maurice as a runaway slave. I will not conduct any hunt for him, and if Ducheine dares to come here, I will remind him that he sold Maurice to me and has no further claim on him. As for you, Pierre, I place no blame on you."

Jean Jacques walked out of the room, then wheeled around and came back to where the dumbfounded Pierre was still standing. The young planter placed a hand on both of Pierre's shoulders. "When we go to New York, it would be a great consolation to have you go with us," the young Frenchman said with feeling. "Perhaps you and Rosalie can go, along with Marie Bouquement and a couple of the other servants to take care of the house we propose to rent. I have already discussed this with Madame Bérard. Will you consider it, Pierre?" the young planter asked.

"I will speak with my parents," Pierre answered with a calmness which was forced.

This time when the Frenchman left the room, he did not stop until he had reached the steps to the upper floor, and he took them two at a time. He was anxious to carry out his plan.

Pierre felt drained. The last three days had been like no other three days in his life. "He asked me—a slave—to *consider* going to New York with him. And I was worried about

whether I would have to kill him or be killed trying to
protect him and his family. God, have mercy on your doubt-
ing child!" Pierre prayed.

Pierre was inclined to fall on his knees and pray for more
guidance, but he heard the cook rattling pots in the kitchen.
He knew she would ridicule him if she found him on his
knees.

"If I consent to go to New York," Pierre recovered his
composure, "I shall make sure that Monsieur does not take
that one," he pointed toward the kitchen and then went out
to face the grouchy cook.

CHAPTER 4

St. Dominique and New York—1787

Pierre did not discuss the details of Jean Jacques Bérard's proposal to take him to New York with his family for some time. The young slave was not sure why he delayed informing his parents of the young master's proposal, but he finally admitted to himself that he had misgivings about the journey to New York.

There was a constant round of visits between L'Artibonite and Dondon as Jean Jacques was making arrangements for Monsieur Bossard, his father-in-law, to manage the estate during the time the Bérards expected to be in New York. The two Frenchmen made no effort to conceal their plans or change the conversation whenever Pierre happened to be serving them in one capacity or another. Years later Pierre was glad he had listened.

In the midst of Jean Jacques' feverish preparations to take his wife and her two sisters to New York until the trouble he anticipated had been resolved, the young Frenchman had to make many trips to St. Marc and to Cap Français to conclude certain business affairs. The young planter was on such a trip to St. Marc when one of the dock hands told him that the captain of a ship anchored in the harbor had a letter for him from France. Fortunately, the captain was on the wharf checking supplies he had ordered when Jean

Jacques found him. The seaman handed the young planter the letter after apologizing for being so late getting to St. Marc, because his vessel had run into rough weather soon after leaving France.

Jean Jacques later told Pierre how he had read the letter from his father immediately, but it was only after he noted the date that he realized Zenobie, Pierre's grandmother, was on a ship that would be arriving at the Cap within a few days.

Jean Jacques rode back to L'Artibonite in a thoughtful mood. He was happy that he had told André the coachman not to prepare the carriage and had elected to ride a sure-footed mare who knew her way home over the rocky, rutted roads regardless of how he held the reins. He was delighted at the thought of seeing the old slave woman whom he knew would bring greetings from his parents as well as his brothers and sisters. The young planter chuckled and his horse broke into a lively trot when he thought of how Zenobie and his parents had probably shopped for weeks before the old woman set sail. He was willing to wager that one trunk would hold the latest Paris creations for his wife, with fetching bonnets to match. He knew Zenobie's trunk would be partly packed with suits and shirts for him that his father considered to be in good taste for a young man of his means.

What Jean Jacques Bérard did not know was how Zenobie would react to his proposal to take Pierre, Rosalie and Marie Bouquement to New York. He could not remember ever having done anything that displeased Zenobie or caused her to scold him. Now, more than ever, he needed her approval. Though Monsieur Bossard had promised to manage L'Artibonite, Jean Jacques knew Zenobie would control the slaves and care for the house. Pierre's father, who had a fear mixed with respect for Zenobie, would know that she expected him to make sure the slaves worked the fertile fields. Eventually Zenobie would make the final decisions.

As Jean Jacques and his horse came into view, Pierre wondered about the gait of the animal. Thinking something was wrong, the slave ran to meet his master. When the Frenchman threw the reins to Pierre he also tossed him the letter from the elder Monsieur Bérard and told him to read it.

Pierre's first reaction was one of joy at the thought of seeing his grandmother. Then he looked up at his master's face as Jean Jacques hesitated before dismounting, and he realized they both felt accountable to Zenobie for whatever they did. Neither of them could be sure what her reaction to the New York sojourn would be.

Pierre forced a reassuring smile. "After you have informed Madame Bérard and my mother," he said, "we must make haste to be certain that the *grandmère* can find no fault with the way L'Artibonite has fared in her absence."

The young planter nodded. Pierre had given him the key to winning Zenobie's approval of his plan. He would talk to Ursule who had a tendency to imitate her mother without being conscious of the trait. She would make sure the house looked as if Zenobie had not been away a day. Pierre's father would be instructed to goad the field hands into the greatest productivity possible.

Pierre smiled morning, noon and night as he observed the quickened pace at L'Artibonite in anticipation of Zenobie's return. Jean Jacques suggested that Pierre take the long ride with André to the Cap, though the master would also go along to check and sign for the baggage. The women would stay home and welcome Zenobie on her return to L'Artibonite.

This would not be the first time Pierre had joined in a welcome to his grandmother after a voyage overseas. He knew from experience that the Bérards and his family would all receive gifts. The other slaves would sing and dance after the special meal they would be served following Zenobie's return. They would sing and dance whether they were glad she was back or not. Then the old woman would go from hut to hut. By the time she retired, Zenobie would know everything that had happened at L'Artibonite while she was in France.

Zenobie's homecoming was just as Pierre had anticipated. He watched her as she inspected the kitchen, the dining room and the parlor of the Bérard manor on the pretext of getting a good look at the scenes she had longed to glimpse during her stay in France. He detected a glimmer of pride when Monsieur Bérard and several of the slaves told Zenobie how Pierre and his mother had nursed them during the sickness at L'Artibonite.

Pierre knew he could no longer delay consulting with his family about Jean Jacques' offer to take him to New York, but he wanted to give his master time to first tell Zenobie. The young slave was also troubled by reports that the planters, Ducheine and Caradeux, had been seen riding around the fields farthest from the house.

The morning after Zenobie's return, the old woman was later than usual making her appearance. As Pierre poured his young master's coffee he said softly, "I have waited to tell my family about New York. I thought you would wish to be the first to tell the *grandmère*."

Jean Jacques wrinkled his forehead in a make-believe frown. "I will speak to her as soon as she presents herself," he answered, and the two young men, one the slave and the other his master, laughed at their mutual understanding of the other's dilemma.

Zenobie had been refreshed by a good night's sleep and the happiness of being reunited with her relatives when she went in to talk with her young master. Though she was taken by surprise to learn of the proposed journey to New York, she had heard enough talk in Paris and aboard ship to know that there was trouble brewing on the island.

Like Jean Jacques, Zenobie considered the *gens de couleur*

to be the instigators of the unrest, and she was not fooled by the explanation that the trip to New York was merely to be an extended vacation. She knew that Jean Jacques had been friendly with many of the young students of mixed blood while in Paris, and she understood how the young planter would wish to avoid this conflict if possible. However, when Jean Jacques told Zenobie he wanted to take Pierre, Rosalie and Marie Bouquement with him, the old woman winced before she regained her composure.

"I cannot question your decision, but I will hold you responsible for their safety," Zenobie said. "I will expect Pierre to look after Rosalie and Marie—and any others you feel you will need. You had an English tutor when you were a student in Paris, and you will have to coach Pierre in English so he will know how to shop for you and Madame and look after the slaves as well. L'Artibonite will await your return."

Jean Jacques watched the old woman as she excused herself by explaining that his wife had promised to furnish her with paper and a quill so she could write the elder Bérards and inform them that she had arrived safely.

"I trust you have already informed your parents of your plan to go to New York for an extended vacation," Zenobie said before she went in search of Madame Bérard.

Jean Jacques was relieved that this conversation had ended. He knew how important it had been to Zenobie through the years for her family to be kept together. His only consolation was that this separation would only be temporary.

That night Pierre told his parents that Monsieur Bérard wanted to take him and Rosalie as well as his Aunt Marie to New York. Pierre's father found it hard to believe that young Monsieur Bérard had asked Pierre to go rather than to tell him, but Zenobie joined the family group and corroborated Pierre's version of the conversation with the master. Rosalie, Pierre's older brother and his sister were then called in to be told of the trip to New York. For a brief second Rosalie looked frightened at the prospect, but she saw Pierre's reassuring smile as he held his arms open, and she ran to his embrace. Pierre's parents and Zenobie told him the decision was up to him.

"As long as I can take my little sister with me, I won't be lonesome," Pierre said as Rosalie snuggled even closer to her brother.

"And Marie will be there to keep an eye on the two of you," Zenobie reminded them. "The young master knows some English, Pierre. He will begin coaching you so you will be familiar with the money and foods you will have to buy for the house. I will find an old ledger for you so you can write out a few of the words and phrases you will need."

Pierre, too, knew how slaves hated to see a family separated. He knew it would not be easy for his parents to part with two of their children. His grandmother, who previously had only to visit Dondon to see her daughter Marie, would feel the separation even more keenly. Still, Pierre marveled at the way the old woman faced the situation and set about making sure that he was prepared for whatever responsibility was given him.

"The Bérards knew what they were doing when they taught her to read and write," he mused. "She will run L'Artibonite as long as there is breath in her body." He had no way of knowing he had made a prophecy.

Pierre was surprised and pleased when Jean Jacques suggested that he pick out the books he thought they might like to take with them to New York and see that they were properly crated. The library soon became the repository of all kinds of articles to be packed, with Pierre and sometimes Jean Jacques overseeing the operation. Rosalie was so happy to be with Pierre she did whatever he told her, and most of the time he kept her busy outside the library.

Jean Jacques started Pierre's English lessons with the days of the week. He knew how Pierre had trudged the distance from L'Artibonite to the old church at St. Marc from the time he could walk, so he explained that what he called *église* would be "church" in New York and *Dimanche* would be "Sunday." Pierre jotted down the English words opposite the French in the midst of packing.

Pierre and Jean Jacques had gone through a drill on the days of the week and started on numbers the day Zenobie found an excuse to come to the library and observe the process. After a few seconds she left. Pierre had only gotten as far as the English for the numeral ten when Zenobie reappeared. She stood at the door holding an old book behind her back.

Jean Jacques, who had secretly decided he was not equal to instructing a pupil as apt as Pierre, was puzzled by the expression on the old woman's face. "I'm trying to help Pierre with his English so he will be prepared for New York," he explained. "Is there something you would like to say?"

The slave woman walked over to the young planter and handed him an old copybook.

"Zenobie! Where did you get this?" the astonished Jean Jacques asked, as he examined the tattered book. "I haven't seen this copybook since you and my mother decided I did not need any more English and shipped the tutor back to England."

Zenobie refused to comment on the part she had played in getting rid of the English tutor who had made the grave mistake of attempting to be overly familiar with the slave woman. "Just before I left Paris we found this copybook in an old trunk you left in the attic. I decided that since the colonies to the north had their freedom it might be a good idea for you to refresh your memory. Now you can share this with Pierre. Though I did not like that old Englishman, I suspect he might have been a better teacher than young Monsieur Bérard."

Pierre and Jean Jacques looked at each other in amazement. They could hear Zenobie chuckling over her coup as she closed the door.

Soon the two young men were turning the pages of the old copybook. Pierre was delighted to discover similarities between French and English, but Jean Jacques had to drill him on pronunciations. They both knew this old book would save each of them valuable time.

Though Pierre had soon memorized the contents of Jean Jacques' old copybook, he had a hard time trying to share his newly acquired knowledge with Rosalie. Zenobie told him that Rosalie would be forced to learn the new language once they were in the States.

Pierre was not surprised to discover that Zenobie soon appeared to know everything that had happened at L'Artibonite while she was in France. She let Pierre know that she was aware of his friendship with Maurice, the runaway slave, and she also knew about the trouble which the planters Ducheine and Caradeux had caused.

A few days after Zenobie mentioned Maurice to Pierre, she told him that Ducheine and Caradeux had been seen near L'Artibonite. Had Pierre not been so busy with the copybook and getting his young master to help him with the pronunciation of the English words, he would have been alarmed over the thought of Ducheine and Caradeux riding around the outskirts of the Bérard property.

Pierre did not realize that Jean Jacques welcomed this opportunity to refresh his memory of the English he conversed in during his student days. The Frenchman was interested to note that Pierre had written English words opposite the French equivalent just as he had done years before. In drilling Pierre, he often laughingly reminded him that his own English was accented by his French, and some tradespeople might have difficulty understanding him.

Early one morning, a few days before the date scheduled for leave-taking, Pierre paused outside the hut which was his home. He decided the trees and flowers were all a part of a huge bouquet being prepared to wave one last farewell.

Later as Pierre poured strong, steaming coffee for his

young master, he was still under the spell of the mood induced by the beauty and fragrance of profuse bougainvillea, acacia, the inverted lilies called *trumpets of the angels* and the gracefully swaying palms.

Still moving as in a trance, Pierre had just removed a napkin from a tray of warm croissants he was about to serve when he heard screams coming from the direction of the slaves' huts. He dropped the tray as Jean Jacques pushed him aside and ran outside to investigate. Pierre's thoughts immediately darted to what Zenobie had told him about Ducheine and Caradeux. At the doorway he could see his master running toward the huts. Before Pierre could decide what he should do, he saw Madame Bérard running down the stairs with his mother following.

"Who is screaming? Where is Monsieur Bérard?" the frightened woman asked.

Pierre was almost sure he knew what was happening. Though he realized his young master needed him, he did not want the young Frenchwoman or his mother to witness a scene with Ducheine and Caradeux. He was in the process of giving them a delayed excuse so he might go to Jean Jacques, when the dining room doors opened and Zenobie marched out and blocked the main doorway. Pierre knew Madame Bérard and his mother would never get past Zenobie, whom he also knew would want him to go to Jean Jacques.

The screams continued and slave women ran beside Pierre telling him that the planters were trying to kill the slaves they were accusing of harboring their runaways. When Pierre reached his master, Jean Jacques was demanding that Ducheine, Caradeux and another henchman explain what right they had to invade his property and brutalize his slaves. Ducheine was insisting that the slave who lay at his feet unconscious was Berto. Several other slaves were beaten and mourning their pain.

Pierre examined the unconscious slave. He knew the

brand was one way to identify Berto and explained this to
Jean Jacques in a hurried whisper. From the position in
which the slave was lying, an old blue shirt torn from the top
of his body, they could see there was no brand on his arm
near the shoulder.

"You will leave my habitation immediately!" Jean Jacques
ordered.

"If he is not Berto, he knows where Berto is because one
of the other slaves told me," Ducheine screamed. "And I'm
not leaving here until I beat the truth out of him!"

Pierre saw Jean Jacques turn and sprint toward the
house. He saw Zenobie, who was standing on the steps, one
arm behind her and the other akimbo, move to let the
young master in. Now the planters were questioning the
slave women. There was so much going on Pierre had no
idea what would happen next. He was almost afraid to
breathe for fear the noise of exhaling would stimulate
Ducheine's desire to beat the truth out of the prone slave.

Then Pierre saw his young master running toward the
planters. Jean Jacques was carrying the long pistol which the
elder Monsieur Bérard had kept in a box lined with velvet,
which hung over a mantle in the library.

"My poor young master," Pierre thought as he looked at
the guns the other planters were wearing in holsters,
"doesn't know that pistol has never been fired."

"You will leave my property immediately or I will open
fire on you!" Jean Jacques announced.

As Jean Jacques and the other planters argued among
themselves, Pierre saw his father running in from the field
followed by a crowd of slaves with their machetes raised.
Then he heard his grandmother's voice and saw her advanc-
ing toward Ducheine and Caradeux with a long kitchen
knife, which he realized she had been holding behind her
back until reinforcements arrived. Then Pierre saw his
mother, whom he realized had carried the message to his
father, standing beside Zenobie. For a second Pierre saw the

humor enacted by the little group of loyal slaves. Then he realized that neither Ducheine nor Caradeux would consider the horde of machete-waving slaves a laughing matter.

"Thank God Monsieur will not have to try to fire that pistol." Pierre watched the planters disappear into a thicket where he surmised they had hidden their horses. He knew his father would not order the slaves back to the field, and he watched Zenobie and his mother bend over the unconscious slave. Then he saw his father and several other men improvise a litter to lift the injured man to the hut where Maurice had once slept. The slave women were tending the wounds of the others who had been mistreated by Ducheine and Caradeux.

"This is life in St. Dominique," Pierre muttered, "and I've been a long time discovering it."

Pierre followed Jean Jacques, who went directly up the stairs to his living quarters, his arm about the weeping wife, assuring her that he was unharmed.

When Pierre's mother and grandmother joined him in the kitchen, where the old cook was still hiding in a corner, he decided they obviously were determined to act as if the recent confrontation was of little importance. Pierre was not fooled by their nonchalance and laughed when Zenobie pulled the cook out of her corner and ordered her to prepare a menu which included most of Jean Jacques' favorite dishes.

After a late midday meal had been served, Pierre and his grandmother talked over their coffee. Pierre's mother was still with Madame Bérard, who insisted on believing that Ducheine and Caradeux might return.

"I did not know what to think when I saw Monsieur Bérard with that pistol," Pierre admitted.

"I've known him all his life, but I've never known him to be like that before. It takes a lot to make one so even-tempered turn into a madman. I've never even seen Jean Jacques swat a fly."

"He never had to swat a fly," Pierre mused, "because he always had a slave to swat the flies for him."

Later that night, after Pierre had bolted all the doors and made sure the candles were snuffed, he stood outside the Bérard house and looked up at the cloudless sky. He wondered how many of those machete-bearing slaves would have rallied to Jean Jacques' defense if they had not known that Zenobie had ordered his father to bring them in from the field. He wondered about the slaves' fear of Zenobie. And yet they turned to her whenever illness or misfortune befell them. The slaves were also in awe of old Tonette, his great-grandmother. Pierre wondered if the parents of the field hands had told them something his parents had never told him. As he approached the slaves' huts he saw a group outside the one where Maurice had slept. He heard moans and realized the badly beaten slave had regained consciousness.

Outside the Toussaint hut, Pierre saw his father and older brother in close conversation. He decided the day had provided one of the few instances he could remember when his father had the opportunity to act like the head of his family.

Though Monsieur Bérard had booked passage for Pierre to accompany the family to New York, Pierre was still asking himself if he really intended to cast his lot with this French slave-owning family. After Jean Jacques faced Ducheine and Caradeux with the pistol, Pierre felt closer to his young master than ever. Each day after the English lessons, he also felt kindlier toward his grandmother, whose devotion to the Bérards he had begun to resent. When members of his family had previously asked him questions about the proposed trip to New York, he had been evasive. Now he began to speak positively about the "visit," and when he wasn't practicing his English he was packing and marking crates destined for the colony to the north. Along with André the coachman, he made many trips to St. Marc, where the huge cartons were left on the wharf for shipping.

Once Pierre had accepted the idea of actually making the trip, he determined to push everything unpleasant out of his mind. Still, he could not help but sense that the slaves around St. Marc were involved in some plot to overthrow the French planters. Whenever Pierre or André, who made the last-minute trips to St. Marc without Jean Jacques, came within hearing distance of the groups of slaves who gathered around the wharf, it was obvious that the subject of the conversation was immediately changed. Pierre knew that the slaves would await a signal, or maybe an incident would incite them. Even then he knew any action they took would be preceded by much whispering and secret meetings. He began to pray that the Bérards would be far away when the revolt came—as come it would.

Pierre did not worry too much about his own family. With the Bérards away he was confident that revolting slaves would hesitate to harm Zenobie or her family. He still chuckled when he thought about the day Ducheine and Caradeux had invaded L'Artibonite, and he looked up to see his grandmother walking as erect as if there had been a tray of fruit on her head, with one hand on her hip and the other hand behind her back holding a butcher's knife. Even if the field hands left L'Artibonite, Pierre knew his family could grow enough food to feed themselves.

The night before the Bérards were to sail for New York, Pierre lingered in the library where he had spent so many of his young years. The shelves were not all empty, as Jean Jacques insisted they were only going on a visit. But there were big gaps between the books where he had selected volumes and packed them for shipping. He snuffed out the candle, locked the door and looked fondly at the key he would give to his grandmother to add to those she already carried on a string around her waist covered by a huge apron.

There was much activity in the house, with Monsieur Bossard and his two daughters already on hand for the drive to St. Marc the next morning. Pierre hurried outside to escape being pressed into service. He knew his own hut would be crowded with well-wishers watching his mother pack for Rosalie. His aunt, Marie Bouquement, would be in the Bérard manor with the Bossard sisters, but there was "Old Cabress" and the girl Célie, who would also be sailing with the Bérards. He knew there would hardly be a quiet spot in the slave quarters, and Pierre wanted to be quiet this night.

The young slave stood far enough away from the house so he would not be seen, and he sniffed the fragrance of the flowering bushes all around him. Pierre went from palm tree to palm tree rubbing his hands across the rough ridges of the bark. He found himself walking toward the spot on the bank of the meandering river where he had first met Maurice. Suddenly he heard a noise. Pierre froze, then smiled at his own wishful thinking when he saw his only company was a bird—a pale, long-necked tourterelle—who took flight as soon as Pierre moved. Then Pierre realized the drums were silent. He hoped Maurice and Berto, wherever they were, had been sent a message about his leave taking.

"It is better for all of us that we not meet again. But I will never forget that they taught me the price of freedom," and Pierre turned his steps toward the hut where he would rest until dawn.

Pierre saw the flickering flames from fires in front of a number of the huts. He had smiled secretly when Monsieur Bérard told the slaves that absolutely no food was to be carried aboard ship. He knew very well that each of the slaves in the Bérard party would have a small package of food prepared by a friend or relative. Pierre would not be surprised if he found a packet of his favorite sweet cakes between his shirts and underwear when he unpacked.

As the procession of Bérard and Bossard carriages drove away from the Bérard habitation, Pierre turned for a last look. He saw Zenobie standing as erect as an ebony statue at the foot of the steps leading to the house. His father was consoling his mother, weeping at the sight of two of her children leaving L'Artibonite. His older brother and sister were waving as they had both begged Pierre to send for them one day. Marie Bouquement's daughter Adéle appeared dazed. The other slaves were also waving vigorously, and their loud chorus of adieus rang in Pierre's ears for days afterward.

Pierre rode in a carriage with the other slaves. Old Cabress was dry of eye, but Rosalie and the girl Célie cried all the way to St. Marc. The more Pierre tried to comfort them, the more they cried. He finally put a strong arm about each of their frail young bodies, and when the entourage reached St. Marc he had to awaken them.

The old wharf at St. Marc was crowded with slaves and planters who had come to see the Bérards before they sailed. Pierre had to leave the girls to assist Monsieur Bérard, who had the awesome task of making sure that all the personal belongings of his wife and her two sisters were aboard ship.

"They must think there will be a ball every night and a promenade each afternoon," Jean Jacques muttered to Pierre as he entrusted the bulging trunks, valises and bonnet boxes to the sailors to carry aboard.

Pierre was grateful that his mother had packed his belongings and Rosalie's clothes in one bag. Old Cabress and Célie had packed together, and Pierre knew that his Aunt Marie had put most of her clothes in the boxes the Bossard sisters had already shipped.

The excitement of boarding the ship and the demands which Madame Bérard and her sisters made of Old Cabress and the two girls reduced the young ones to an occasional sniffle. As the ship pulled away from the wharf, Pierre ran to the deck outside his master's stateroom where he had been unpacking the suits Zenobie had brought Jean Jacques from Paris.

Pierre turned his head from side to side to get a view of

all he could see. Sprawling mountains rose on one side. Downstream he saw a group of naked slave boys who had climbed out of the water to stand on the shore under the palms and watch the ship pull out to sea.

In passing the open doors of the other staterooms, Pierre had noted that Madame Bérard and her sisters were also resorting to tears, though they had appeared to be almost vivacious when their father took leave of them and walked down the gangplank. Pierre supposed that Monsieur Bérard was trying to console the ladies.

As Pierre continued to watch the fading landscape, he took a deep breath of the exhilarating sea air. Suddenly he sensed that he was not alone. Then he heard his master's voice.

"We will have a pleasant vacation; the trouble will be over before too long and we can all come back to L'Artibonite," Jean Jacques declared.

Pierre closed his eyes before he replied: "We must take it as God sends it!" and hurried away to finish unpacking.

Pierre observed that it did not take young Madame Bérard and her sisters long to make friends with other passengers. His young master was more reserved. Several times while performing some chore for him, Pierre looked up to see Jean Jacques gazing at him as if to fathom his thoughts. Old Cabress and Marie Bouquement were good sailors, but it was soon apparent that Rosalie and Célie would stand the roll of the ship with ill grace.

When the vessel docked at Cap Français, Pierre thought of Toussaint Louverture at nearby Breda and wondered when he would give the signal for the slaves to take up arms against their oppressors, the French planters. Pierre attempted to avoid the Bérards while the ship was in port at the Cap, but a number of their friends had come aboard to bid them adieu and he had to assist with the service of their entertainment. Even then Pierre was conscious of the puzzled look on Jean Jacques' face when he moved among the guests.

By the time the last of their guests from the Cap had departed and the ship nosed its way out of the Windward Passage into the Gulf Stream which would carry them to New York, Pierre knew that Rosalie and Célie would require service instead of rendering it; they were two little seasick girls.

Pierre had watched the Cap and the rocky land surrounding it until there was nothing to see but water. He had thought of Ursule, Zenobie, his father, his brother and sister and wondered if and when he would see them again.

"I'll have to take a dose of my own medicine," Pierre mused, "and take it as God sends it."

The trip to New York was a joyous voyage for Madame Bérard and her two sisters, because most of the other passengers spoke French. Pierre's Aunt Marie catered to the whims of Mademoiselle Adeline Bossard and Madame Marie Anne Dessource, while Old Cabress looked after young Madame Bérard and Pierre took care of the master and the two seasick slave girls. Once the sea calmed and Marie Bouquement produced a packet of carefully wrapped soda crackers for Rosalie and Célie to munch on, the girls emerged from their cabin and showed signs of regaining their strength. They made the trip as passengers—not servants.

Pierre suspected that Rosalie and Célie might have recovered much quicker if Madame Bérard had not been so sympathetic. Both Pierre and his Aunt Marie had silently hoped their young mistress would run out of her long list of remedies for sea sickness much sooner. The concoctions she suggested only gave them more work as they aggravated the girls' nausea. Lazy and napful days on the ship steadied by the calmer waters restored the girls' health and their spirits. By the time land was sighted and they glimpsed the harbor of New York with ships flying flags from nations all over the world, Rosalie and Célie were on deck squealing with excitement and jumping up and down like much younger children, to the delight of the other passengers.

Pierre, his Aunt Marie and Old Cabress were too busy packing and relabeling the baggage to be amused by the girls' antics. Pierre and the older slave women wondered how the three sisters would ever wear all of the gowns and bonnets they had brought.

By the time the ship nosed its way to the pier at the foot of Wall Street, Pierre was standing beside his master and a small mountain of trunks and boxes. Madame Bérard was busy giving letters and instructions to the captain, who had promised to deliver them the next time he stopped at St. Marc or the Cap. Marie and Old Cabress were always within calling distance of the womenfolk.

"I wish I could say I was as happy as the girls," Jean Jacques told Pierre as Rosalie and Célie ran around the deck.

"Are you troubled?" Pierre asked cautiously.

"I'm not sure, Pierre," Jean Jacques was frowning, "but I have a strange feeling—a very strange feeling. I've even begun to think you are holding something back from me. And Pierre, please don't tell me I will have to take it as God sends it."

Pierre laughed. "Monsieur Bérard, I, too, feel a sense of change—great change. But I still tell myself I will have to take it as God sends it."

Both men were laughing when the women and the two excited girls joined them.

As early as 1787, New York harbor was crowded with sailing ships and cargoes from every corner of the world. Though barely recovered from the destruction of the War of Independence, New York City already showed signs of becoming one of the most powerful ports of the world. The Bérards and their slaves, with the exception of Monsieur

Bérard, who had lived in Paris, were only accustomed to the bustling harbors of St. Marc and the Cap, where ships took on cargo of coffee, sugar cane, cotton, indigo and some rice. Here in New York harbor they saw cargo they could not identify and many flags they had never seen before. Even the trees they saw in the distance looked nothing like the palms at St. Marc or L'Artibonite.

Pierre noted how protectively Jean Jacques Bérard held his wife's arm as he scanned the crowd for a familiar face. Pierre knew his master had a friend in New York who had found a house for him and had also advised him on investments. Though Pierre did not know this man by name, he decided he must have been the portly gentleman he saw push his way through the crowd and, after a word with the officials guarding the gangplank, run up to greet Monsieur Bérard before the other passengers were allowed to debark.

"Jean, we're so glad to see you!" Pierre heard the man say as Jean Jacques stepped forward to greet his friend. "We were afraid you would not get out in time."

Pierre was glad the women were adjusting their hats and making small talk when he saw his master frown and place a finger at his lips before he embraced his friend. Pierre knew then that trouble had begun in St. Dominique during the weeks they had been aboard ship. Yet he could not be sure whether it was the revolt of the slaves or an uprising among the people of mixed ancestry. He did not miss the look his master gave him before he presented his wife and her sisters to his friend, who spoke halting French. Neither did Pierre miss the "I knew you were holding something back from me" look his master gave him, but he was more concerned with trying to hear the conversation between Jean Jacques and his American friend.

The man explained that he had a carriage and a dray waiting to take them to 105 Reade Street, the house he had rented for the Bérards. The women followed the lead of the men to the conveyances while Pierre and Jean Jacques followed their mountain of luggage through the official red tape.

Madame Bérard and her sisters were still bidding other passengers adieu and inviting them to visit their new home when Monsieur Bérard and Pierre joined them with the luggage and crates. Pierre had been given the address and told to put the slave women on the dray with most of the bags and to have the porter who had attended them trundle the remaining trunks and boxes to their new home. Some of the boxes they sent had already been delivered, they were told.

An awareness of a strange land, strange houses and a strange tongue had sobered Rosalie and Célie as Pierre helped them on the dray and assisted the porter with loading the baggage. Marie Bouquement and Old Cabress counted the trunks and compared the numbers with the list Pierre held before they found a place to sit on the dray beside the driver. Every inch of space was occupied, and Pierre knew this meant he would have to walk to his new home with the porter who was to deliver the excess baggage—mostly the hats and dresses Madame Bérard and her sisters had insisted on bringing, along with the meager belongings of the slaves.

Pierre did not mind walking. It felt good to be on firm ground after almost three weeks at sea. He smiled as the porter pushed and shoved to get away from the crowd and reach the cobblestones of what he called "Broadway." Each time a hat box fell off the pile, the porter cursed. Pierre found himself straining to catch English words his master had drilled him on, then wisely decided he would never need to know the meaning of what the perspiring porter was saying.

Pierre was happy that the people became fewer and fewer as the pier was farther and farther behind. He was also glad that the weather was balmy and the skies blue. Otherwise, he might have found the straight lines of the houses and lack of tropical color depressing. Some of the buildings still showed signs of the recent war and, according to the porter, a more recent fire.

When the cobblestones ended, Pierre was glad to be walking on dirt roads again. But for the scowls of the porter whose patience dwindled each time another hat box fell victim to the ruts in the dirt road, Pierre would have rid himself of the shoes his master had provided him for the trip. He was proud that he had mastered enough English to point as they passed a familiar-looking building and say, "Church?"

"St. Paul's," the porter answered and wiped his forehead with the back of his hand in a gesture familiar to Pierre.

Then came the green trees and grassy lanes. In the distance Pierre could see neat farms and houses he recognized from books as being of Dutch architecture. Pierre's spirits rose as he realized they would be living a distance away from the crowded pier which had been his first glimpse of New York. When the porter turned off Broadway to enter Reade Street, Pierre felt a sense of relief as the single houses seemed to him to be more inviting than the straight, box-like buildings closer to the busy harbor.

When Pierre and the porter finally reached 105 Reade Street, his Aunt Marie and Old Cabress were still directing the driver of the dray as he struggled to unload the last of the trunks. Madame Bérard's sisters pounced on Pierre as he began to gather their hat boxes. The carriage in which they rode had passed Pierre and the porter just as two of their hat boxes had fallen off the cart, and the porter gave out with language that even the proper Mademoiselle Adeline Bossard recognized as curses.

"I hope you did not let that vulgar man ruin our best bonnets," the young French woman admonished the slave.

"Mademoiselle Adeline," Pierre sighed, as he secretly

wished he would never again have to see another hat with a trailing veil or a pointed feather, "I can assure you that you will find everything as you wish."

In the weeks following their arrival in New York, Monsieur Bérard and Pierre marveled at the speed with which Madame Bérard and her sisters made contact with other French refugees and began planning parties.

Pierre and his master had come to terms over the situation in St. Dominique. Pierre soon found his way back to the wharf and learned from sailors that the leaders of the group known as *Les Amis Des Noirs,* The Friends of the Blacks, were stirring up sentiment against the planters at home and abroad. Pierre informed his master, who insisted that the *gens de couleur* were causing all the trouble. The young slave was equally sure that the real conflict in his home would erupt when Toussaint Louverture gave the signal for the enslaved black men to revolt. This was a part of Pierre's secret.

Pierre did not have as much time to mull over the situation in St. Dominique as his master. Finding shops and markets where he could make his French-accented English understood so he could shop for the household was a difficult task. Then trying to overcome the malady of homesickness which the slave women who had accompanied them displayed at different times, in different ways and in varying degrees, kept Pierre drawing on his considerable reservoir of ingenuity.

Pierre's Aunt Marie and Old Cabress were the first to show any signs of adapting to their new home. Rosalie and Célie kept to the house, refusing under one pretext or another to even accompany Pierre to the market he had discovered. It was owned by an old seaman who had stopped shipping at an early age because of an injury which had cost him a leg. The storekeeper had sailed in and out of St. Marc, the Cap and other French ports long enough to learn a French jargon which allowed him to help Pierre with his

shopping English, as well as the currency of the young republic. The merchant was surprised when Pierre began to
correct him after carefully scrutinizing the bills the man
prepared for Monsieur Bérard. He had not expected a slave
to learn so quickly.

Pierre was beginning to feel small stirrings of pride over
the way he had adjusted when his master unfolded a plan
that was to change the course of the young slave's life.

CHAPTER 5

A New Way of Life

P ierre was in a joyful mood. His aunt, Marie Bouquement, had gone with him to another market he had discovered not too far from the wharf. Here Pierre had found avocados, guava, papaya and stalks of sugar cane. It was so early when they set out from Reade Street that the dew was still on the grass around the farm houses they passed. Others might have complained of the heat on such a sun-drenched morning, but to Pierre and Marie Bouquement the day was beautiful.

Pierre's delight at finding fruits that would please the Bérards was infectious; even his Aunt Marie, whose dignified bearing bordered on being austere, was smiling broadly when they mounted the steps to 105 Reade Street.

Rosalie opened the door. "Monsieur Bérard is waiting for you in the parlor," she whispered to Pierre as she relieved him of all but one of the packages he was carrying.

Pierre found his master pacing the floor. "Monsieur Bérard," the young slave said, "look at these," and he pulled three huge green avocados from the bag he was carrying.

Jean Jacques paused before he spoke. "You are indeed clever, Pierre. In New York I have not seen the likes of this fruit you have just shown me."

"But that is not all." Pierre was anxious to tell about the other finds of his shopping trip.

"Pierre," his master interrupted, "I appreciate all you are trying to do to keep Madame, her sisters and—the others— happy. But the time has come for us to talk as two men."

"Have I offended anyone?" Pierre was puzzled.

"Far from offending, you have extended yourself in every way possible. We had barely unpacked when you found a nearby church for them—St. Peter's. You shop for the household, arrange this endless round of parties Madame and her sisters insist on giving and then entertain their guests.

"But your grandmother is holding me responsible for your welfare," the Frenchman reminded, "and I think it is time you are given a trade. Every man should have one trade or profession at which he excels." Jean Jacques smiled in an attempt to put the bewildered Pierre at ease. "I have made arrangements for you to be apprenticed to Mr. Merchant, the coiffeur."

"The coiffeur?" Pierre repeated in amazement.

"Yes, Mr. Merchant has a shop. He has been impressed with your manners and the intelligence you have displayed when he came here to wait on Madame Bérard and her sisters. He has agreed to teach you the fine art of dressing and styling ladies' hair. I have already made a payment to him for your apprenticeship," Jean Jacques added in the hope that Pierre would not think this was a ruse to abandon him.

"But, Monsieur, do you really think I can learn this trade?" Pierre asked, as he tried to imagine himself with curling tongs and scissors, cutting and curling women's hair.

"Pierre," Jean Jacques sat in the nearest chair and pulled out another for his servant, "you are no ordinary man. The women in this house go to you with their problems—whatever they are—before they come to me. I only hear about the problems after you have solved them.

"And I will be the first to admit that arranging for you to be apprenticed to Mr. Merchant was not completely an unselfish act. Madame Bérard, as well as Mademoiselle Adeline and Madame Dessource, will be delighted to have their own coiffeur here in the house."

"I will do as you say," Pierre replied after some time. "When do I start?"

Though stunned by his master's proposal, Pierre was not sure of what else he could do. He was a slave in a strange land.

"Tomorrow. And here is Mr. Merchant's address."

"I know his address," Pierre spoke politely. "I have delivered requests for his services for Madame Bérard and her sisters."

The next day Pierre began his apprenticeship with Mr. Merchant. Marie Bouquement, Old Cabress and the slave girls were as puzzled by this new job for Pierre, as he had been when the subject was first mentioned. This also meant that Marie and Old Cabress would have to shop in the stores and markets they had visited with Pierre. Rosalie and Célie would have to assume more duties with Madame Bérard and her sisters.

Pierre, who had been thoughtful of others all his life, anticipated the reaction to the change. After his first day with Mr. Merchant, he rose earlier than usual, went down to St. Peter's to Mass, returned to 105 Reade Street for coffee and took one of the older slave women shopping before he went to the coiffeur's.

Though Pierre had watched Mr. Merchant dress Madame Bérard's hair and was familiar with the styles of the day, the old coiffeur insisted that he start out by learning to cut hair, and the children of Mr. Merchant's customers became Pierre's responsibility. The stately black apprentice with the little gold earrings in his ears who sang French songs while he cut their hair soon became a favorite of the children he served. Though Pierre enjoyed singing for the children, he listened to their English chatter and struggled to master the new language. By the time he could introduce himself in English on arrival and exchange polite conversation on departure, many of the parents of the children were requesting that Pierre serve as their barber also.

Pierre was a born imitator and noted every detail when he accompanied Mr. Merchant to the homes of the society leaders, who required the services of a coiffeur to style their massive and ornate hairdos before the social activities of the evening. As the months passed, some of Mr. Merchant's most prominent customers were requesting Pierre to style their hair before an evening's festivities.

Madame Bérard and her sisters continued to give their parties. The New Yorkers remembered the help that King Louis XVI had given the colonies, and the French were well received in the society of the young country. Though working each day with Mr. Merchant, Pierre was always on hand when the Bérards entertained. At a second's notice he would set down his serving tray and comply with a request to play a tune on his old fiddle or sing some familiar song that evoked a mood of nostalgia among the French refugees.

Pierre was not unaware of young Jean Jacques' brooding. Pierre, too, longed for L'Artibonite, especially after the cold weather stripped the trees along Broadway of their leaves and the winter snows began to fall. It was difficult to keep the house at 105 Reade Street warm with wood-burning fires, and Rosalie and Célie went about their duties shivering with chattering teeth until Pierre used the gratuities he received from Mr. Merchant's customers to buy woolen skirts and petticoats along with sweaters to keep them warm. Old Cabress and Marie Bouquement had learned through the years to fend for themselves, and when Madame Bérard and her sisters went shopping, the older women always managed to get a few items of warm clothing for themselves included in the shopping list. Though they all managed to survive the first winter in New York, Pierre whistled a French ditty all the way to work the day he saw the first buds on the trees lining Broadway.

That summer there was much excitement in New York City, the capitol of the thirteen colonies. On July 26, 1788, the Constitution as drafted had been accepted and was being ratified state by state. This was marked by a spirit of jubilation. There was much speculation and debate over who would head the country. Many claimed that George Washington, who had been first in war and first in peace, would be first in the hearts of his countrymen. Others claimed that John Hancock had played the more important role in wording the Constitution. Then there were those who pointed out the eloquence of Patrick Henry, and many an argument erupted when an admirer held forth on Thomas Jefferson's skill in turning a meaningful phrase with ink and quill. Nobody dared deny the influence John Adams of Massachusetts had wielded over the Continental Congress which finally, on July 7, 1776, had proclaimed that "these colonies are and of a right ought to be free and independent states."

Pierre was glad when it was finally decided to hold an election and friends of George Washington insisted he would be the first to head this young country. Though months were to pass before the event actually took place, elaborate plans were already being made for the inauguration of the first head of state. Pierre knew that meant he would be called on to fashion the massively fancy hairstyles for the society ladies who now made no secret of their preference for Pierre over Mr. Merchant.

As Pierre had thought, the social pace quickened when committees were organized even before the election to plan the inauguration. The young slave hairdresser used his heated tongs so much that each night he dreamt of the mountains of tiered curls he had fashioned during the course of a day.

Still, Pierre never neglected his young mistress and kept

a record of her social calendar. He thought of new styles for her and her sisters and would rush home from an appointment to make sure they were beautifully coifed before they entertained or went out to a soirée or a ball.

Like his master, Pierre never lost his yearning for news of L'Artibonite. He would depend on sailors with whom he had cultivated friendships to give him reports of happenings on St. Dominique. Only once did a letter come from his grandmother Zenobie to Monsieur Bérard. The slaves were all told that Zenobie sent her love to all of them, but Pierre decided that his young master's moods grew even more somber after the letter came.

From the sailors, most of whom had secondhand information, Pierre learned that those of mixed ancestry were still demanding that they be accorded the rights due every French citizen. The French planters were determined not to give them those rights or allow them any voice in the government of St. Dominique. Some had met mysterious deaths and others had been imprisoned. Pierre wondered when the slaves would join them. He worried about his own family and remembered them each morning in his prayers at St. Peter's on Barclay Street.

The winter of 1789 was rugged. Rosalie and Célie were layered in sweaters. Pierre often smiled at the difference between the girls and the two older slave women who protected themselves from the cold by adding more petticoats and skirts. Madame Bérard and her sisters remained in bed until the house was warm. If they were out for the evening there was a carriage to transport them, and when they returned they found their beds had been warmed by the hot water bottles placed between the sheets by Marie Bouquement.

Pierre rushed from one place to the other at such a pace that he became acclimatized much sooner than the other Bérard slaves. But even New Yorkers complained about the weather during that historic winter.

The heavy snows left the roads in such a condition that it was difficult for the members of the newly-elected Congress to gather. March 4, 1789, had been set as the date on which they were to convene, but there were not enough members present to form a quorum to count the votes cast by the electors. It was not until weeks later that enough members could reach New York and count the votes. As had been forecast, they promptly declared George Washington, Esq., the winner and John Adams, Esq., to be second in command.

Pierre, who made it a matter of principle never to repeat the conversations he overheard in the homes he frequented to style the ladies' hair, heard much talk of the debate between members of the Congress as to what title the chief magistrate should hold. It was said that John Adams insisted the title should be "His Highness, the President of the United States and Protector of their Liberties." The congressional committee set up to confer titles and make final plans for the inaugural ceremony decided the title should simply be "The President of the United States."

In discussions of this debate at the Bérard home, the Frenchmen all thought the title should include "His Highness." In the homes of the New Yorkers he served, Pierre heard them argue that "The President of the United States" was ample.

It took some time for General Washington, who had awaited the news of his election at Mount Vernon in Virginia, to reach New York. By the time he arrived, many of those who had fought under him had joined his party, and New York gave the cavalcade a rousing reception. The roads had been too bad for Mrs. Washington to make the trip.

Pierre had worked so hard he found it difficult to spring from his bed and light the fires when the guns began to boom at sunrise on the morning of April 30, 1789. He was still weary when he made his way to St. Peter's for Mass, but he found the streets already crowded.

Pierre did not see the inauguration ceremony. He sat in
Mr. Merchant's shop and wrote out the many requests for
service which servants continued to bring. But he did hear
the roar of the crowd, and as soon as he could push his way
to the first appointments, he heard the gentlemen of the
houses describing how George Washington had rode in a
coach to the Federal Hall escorted by carriages, troops on
horseback and loyal followers on foot. It was said that the
crowd went wild when their hero general came out on the
balcony and gave a courtly bow.

The women Pierre attended all seemed disappointed
when they were told the new President wore a simple brown
suit. Many of them said they had expected him to wear his
military dress uniform. New York's Chancellor, Robert
Livingston, had read the oath prescribed by the Constitution. It was whispered that the committee in charge of the
ceremony forgot to provide the Bible, and members from
the nearby St. John's Masonic Lodge produced one at the
last minute. Washington repeated the words of the oath after
Chancellor Livingston with his right hand on the hastily
borrowed Bible. At the conclusion, they said George Washington kissed the Bible and the crowd cheered all the louder.

That night the taverns were crowded and the sky lighted
up intermittently with fireworks. A number of the ladies
whose hair Pierre styled that day were preparing to attend a
party to be given by the Spanish minister Don Diego de
Gardoqui at No. 1 Broadway. The day after, all of the ladies
were talking about the spectacular colored lights which had
decorated the minister's residence and added an air of en-
chantment to the lavish affair. The other story that went the
rounds of polite society was that the streets were so crowded
that the carriage President Washington was in on his way
home from the festivities could not move one way or the
other, and the weary man got out and walked from Chancellor Livingston's house back to the Presidential mansion,
unrecognized by his enthusiastic admirers.

Pierre heard so many versions of how George Washington had kissed the Bible and how he had to walk home the night after his inauguration that he began to feel sorry for a man on whom all eyes were focused and whose every movement was discussed. Later when Pierre was to observe the President leaving his home at No. 3 Cherry Street, he still thought the chief executive showed signs of being burdened. Pierre noted that the somber brown suit had been replaced by one of black velvet, and the President carried his dress sword at his side.

Though it was some time after the inauguration that Mrs. Washington arrived in New York, Abigail Adams, the wife of Vice-President John Adams, who lived in the distant section known as Greenwich Village, held a number of small receptions until the First Lady could assume her duties as the official hostess. Other famous hostesses of the day followed suit, and Pierre and Mr. Merchant were busier than ever. These "at homes" were the chief form of entertainment for the ladies and gentlemen that Pierre attended, because there was only one recognized theater—the John's Street Theater—in New York at that time.

The news Pierre gleaned from sailors continued to give him cause to worry. From a distance, he had observed his master at the pier talking with one of the captains they knew best. Madame Bérard and her sisters continued to entertain, as the Bérards appeared to have no financial worries. Pierre, who had begun to wonder if he would ever see L'Artibonite or his family again, would rush home from work, don a red jacket and serve the guests so often assembled at 105 Reade Street. When he took out his fiddle and entertained with some lively French song, he often wondered what would have happened if instead he had played a lament expressing his fears and longings.

Jean Jacques Bérard was not as good an actor as Pierre. When he rushed home from some merchant's office—where he had heard news that a revolt in St. Dominique seemed inevitable or that trouble was brewing in Paris and the monarchy was in danger—to find the drawing room crowded with guests, the young Frenchman could not conceal his annoyance. Pierre would try to distract his master with favorite tunes, but he shared the same fears.

Madame Bérard pouted over her husband's moodiness, but she had no idea of the state of affairs in St. Dominique. Her father had managed to write two or three letters to his daughters but he, too, refrained from telling them of the threatening clouds hanging over St. Dominique.

When months passed without any word from Zenobie or Monsieur Bossard, Jean Jacques Bérard decided to go back to St. Dominique—alone. Pierre was the first and only one to know of his master's decision for some time.

Pierre had suspected that his young master had always entertained the hope that in the event of a revolt, the French government would resolve the matter in a manner acceptable to both sides. When Pierre heard that the States-General, which was the French Parliament, had been summoned for the first time in 150 years to debate the authority of the monarchy, he knew St. Dominique would have to solve its own problems. So did Jean Jacques Bérard.

For a while the two men kept Monsieur Bérard's plans a secret. Pierre knew his master was hoping for a miracle that was not likely to come.

The ladies of the new republic were still having "at homes" and "levees" when word was received of the fall of the Bastille and the end of the *ancien régime.* The National Assembly in Paris had decided to support the claims of the men of color from St. Dominique. Their leaders, Vincent Oge and Jean Baptiste Chavannes, were rumored to be on their way to St. Dominique to demand their political rights from the island government.

Jean Jacques Bérard knew there was small hope that his family could ever return to L'Artibonite, but he hastened to book passage on the first ship leaving New York for his home. He confided to Pierre that he would determine what could be salvaged, but more importantly he would get the remainder of Zenobie's family and the other Bossards out before their departure would be impossible.

Pierre prayed for his master all day. Not only was the fate of L'Artibonite in doubt, but there were the elder Bérards and their children in Paris to worry about. Young Madame Bérard and her sisters persisted in their belief that all would soon be well in France, and the French would deal with the problem so that they could all go back to L'Artibonite.

Pierre heard his young master make feeble attempts to warn his cheerful wife of the gravity of conditions on their island home, and he knew the warnings fell on ears that did not wish to hear the truth.

Marie Bouquement and Old Cabress had talked with slaves of refugee families newly arrived from St. Dominique, and they now knew that the seven hundred thousand slaves throughout the island were ready to apply the torch to the fields and the homes of the French planters whenever their leader Louverture gave the signal. Pierre listened as the older women approached him with the stories they had heard. He cautioned them against sharing this information with the young madame or the two slave girls. He assured them that their master knew the danger he would risk, for once Jean Jacques began packing for his return trip, it was no longer a secret.

The first thing Pierre did each morning was to make his way to Barclay Street where he attended Mass at St. Peter's. That was also his last stop on the way home. He prayed that his master would be protected from harm. He also prayed for the wisdom to discuss the situation with Jean Jacques in such a manner as to convey the need for the utmost caution while not betraying the trust Maurice and Berto had placed in him when they took him to the meetings where the slaves were making plans for their revolt. He knew Jean Jacques still labored under the impression that it was only the *gens de couleur* who would be causing trouble.

After several attempts to caution his young master, Pierre was intrigued by the similarity between Madame and Monsieur Bérard; they both insisted on believing what they wanted to believe regardless of facts. Pierre finally decided that the only thing he could do for the Bérards was to continue to pray as much as he could and work as hard as he could to keep the women—slaves included—reasonably happy.

Jean Jacques Bérard sailed for St. Dominique in 1789. Unlike the Bérard's arrival in New York in 1787, this leave-taking was tearful. Once Jean Jacques boarded the ship alone, his young wife began to realize that affairs in St. Dominique must have been grave for her husband to make the trip without her. Pierre and Marie Bouquement attempted to be as consoling as they could but the young Frenchwoman's awakening to the state of affairs was painful.

Pierre had assured his master that he would supervise the housekeeping at 105 Reade Street and keep him informed on all important matters.

Neither of the men were aware of the magnitude of this promise.

CHAPTER 6

The Long Wait

Pierre was saddened by the drastic change in young Madame Bérard after her husband's departure for St. Dominique. He never forgot that Marie Elizabeth Bossard Bérard was the first person to be aware of his own turmoil after Maurice had taken him to that fateful meeting in the mountains, where he had heard the slaves making plans to drive the French planters out of St. Dominique. Her sensitive awareness of the personal torment he was undergoing without having any idea of the nature of his conflict had been a comfort he could not forget.

Unlike Madame Bérard, Pierre knew the cause of her worries. With Jean Jacques in the home, the young Frenchwoman had felt secure and protected. With her husband back in St. Dominique, she felt inadequate and frightened of what the future might hold for her.

Pierre continued to be in demand as a hairdresser. Still he hurried home from St. Peter's each morning, oversaw details of the housekeeping, and between appointments found time to visit the wharves around New York's waterways to beg sailors and dockhands for news of happenings on St. Dominique. Though Pierre was fortunate enough to get bits of information from time to time, he was reluctant to share what he heard with his mistress. Their island home was in

117

turmoil, and he refused to further alarm Madame Bérard or the other slaves. Jean Jacques, Pierre decided, could not have chosen a worse time to return to St. Dominique.

Oge and Chavannes, the leaders, had returned to St. Dominique in triumph after the National Assembly in Paris debated their claims and voted to support them. They argued that the recently promulgated Rights of Man assured equality for all—including people of color—born in the French colonies.

Pierre dreaded going home the day he met a group of refugees who had just escaped from St. Dominique. He learned that the planters had refused to honor the claims of the *gens de couleur*. During the ensuing violence, Oge and his little band of followers had been put to death in the public square at Cap Français. While the *gens de couleur* had not been numerically strong enough to force the French planters to accede to their demands, their effort had served as a spark to ignite the pent-up anger of thousands of slaves all over the island. There were sporadic outbreaks of violence, with slaves killing their masters and driving their families from the vast estates. This was the incident Pierre had feared. He wondered when Louverture would give his signal.

Madame Bérard, who somehow knew Pierre was haunting the wharves, became obsessed with the idea that he was withholding news about Jean Jacques from her. She mentioned this to Pierre's Aunt Marie, who playfully chided her for lack of confidence in Pierre.

Then the frightened young Frenchwoman began to question Old Cabress secretly about what she might have heard from the other slaves who had come to New York with the steadily increasing number of French refugees from St. Dominique. When Old Cabress divulged what she had heard and told Madame Bérard that everybody she had questioned who had escaped from the island told her the slaves had decided to revolt rather than wait and be killed like the others, the young Frenchwoman put her hands over her ears.

Pierre was aware of all that was happening in the Bérard household, but he avoided any discussions there of events in St. Dominique. He would manage a daily visit to the wharves and then rush to some society lady's house to fashion an elegant style of mountainous curls and poufs in an effort to block out his fears for his young master. The concern for his own family made Pierre's suffering all the greater.

The dock hands and sailors spoke of Pierre as the stately black man with the tiny gold earrings who came every day to ask if there were any letters or messages for the French family Bérard.

As the weather grew colder, Pierre bought himself a heavy, capelike coat, wore thicker stockings with his knee breeches, and added an ascot, which also served as a windbreaker and showed through the winged collar on his jacket. The warmer attire and a tri-cornered hat helped protect him against the cold gusts which rippled over the water and forced the dock hands to build open fires to warm themselves. As Pierre shivered from the damp coldness of New York's waterfront, memories of the wharf at St. Marc were bittersweet.

Pierre developed the habit of appearing to be a disinterested bystander on the wharves as he strained to catch bits of conversations among passengers leaving ships, hoping to catch a chance account of happenings in his island home. One such day a dock hand met Pierre as he made his way toward the gangplank where a number of passengers were debarking.

"From St. Dominique!" the man shouted to make himself heard above the din and pointed in the direction Pierre was already headed. Pierre immediately positioned himself so it looked as if he was waiting for a passenger. He recognized one or two of the people at the foot of the gangplank as refugees from St. Dominique. As the passengers left the shop, they began describing to their welcoming friends the conditions which had forced them to flee from their homes

and possessions. Though it was good to hear his native
tongue spoken, Pierre's depression was deepened by what
he was hearing. As he already knew, the reports of sporadic
violence were confirmed. The refugees kept saying they
were lucky to have escaped with their lives.

Pierre suddenly felt the same sort of nausea he experienced that night in the mountains when he heard the slaves
plotting to kill the French planters. He had turned to leave
the wharf when he saw a ship's captain he knew standing at
the stern of the vessel. Pierre whirled around. It was true—
the man was waving a letter at him. Pierre steadied himself
as he saw the captain hand the letter to a sailor who ran
down the gangplank to Pierre and handed him an envelope
addressed to Madame Jean Jacques Bérard in his master's
handwriting.

Pierre was mindful that there was only a short time before he was due at the home of one of the ladies he had
begun to call his "patrons." But he could not force himself
to go about his work without first delivering this long-
awaited letter to Madame Bérard. He stopped by a flower
shop and bought a bouquet for the parlor. As he hurried
toward 105 Reade Street, Pierre prayed silently that Jean
Jacques Bérard would return to New York before the full-
fledged revolt of the slaves was underway. He also prayed
that this letter would contain messages from his family and
from Marie Bouquement's daughter Adéle, whom they surmised was still at Dondon with the Bossards.

Afterward Pierre smiled all the way to his appointment,
remembering how eagerly his young mistress had accepted
the letter. He saw the glow of happiness in her eyes that he
had not seen since soon after her husband went back to St.
Dominique. Pierre had not had a moment to spare and was
forced to leave before his young mistress had read the letter.

Once Pierre arrived at the appointed address and started
working, the lady patron commented on his high spirits as
he hummed all the while he was styling her hair. Pierre even

surprised himself by the speed with which he executed a difficult and elaborate style and was soon on his way back to 105 Reade Street.

Pierre let himself in with the key he seldom used. The parlor and sitting rooms on the first floor were deserted, so was the dining room. In the kitchen he found Old Cabress kneading dough. His Aunt Marie was sewing but neither of the women looked up when Pierre called out a cheerful greeting. He sensed that something was wrong. Quickly he climbed the stairs to Madame Bérard's bedroom. He hesitated, then knocked softly on the closed door. At the sound of a faint, "Come in," Pierre entered the room where he found Madame Bérard and her sisters seated on a sofa. It was obvious that they had all been crying, and his appearance shattered whatever calm they had affected.

Once more Pierre had to listen to what he already knew. Madame Bérard, in a trembling voice, told him about the murder of the leaders of the *gens de couleur* and the baleful affect it had on the slaves. She told him that her husband said the planters feared for their lives.

As the Frenchwoman talked, Pierre could not help but realize that this was the first time Jean Jacques Bérard had ever conceded the possibility of a revolt by the slaves.

"Your family is still at L'Artibonite," Madame Bérard explained, "but many of the slaves have disappeared. My husband fears it will be some time before we can return to St. Dominique—if—if ever. It has not been possible for him to visit my father at Dondon because of the fighting between rebellious slaves and their masters. I wish—oh, how I wish—he had never gone back!" Madame Bérard and her sisters again gave in to a tearful sadness that Jean Jacques' letter had aroused.

Pierre had to think quickly. "We must all be grateful that Monsieur Bérard is in no immediate danger," he told the sobbing women. "I am delighted to know that my family is well. The slaves at L'Artibonite have never been mistreated, and I doubt that any of them would harm Monsieur. Let us pray that the fighting around Dondon has stopped. In a few moments it will be time for the evening meal, and I am sure you will all wish to attend to your toilette."

Pierre closed the door softly and rushed up the steps to the floor where the slaves slept. He heard a familiar sniffling sound coming from the room Célie and Rosalie shared. He opened the door without knocking, determined to shame them for the tears he knew they were shedding. His resolve to be stern gave way to pity when he saw the two girls lying on their beds like little rag dolls, sobbing.

"Ma mère? Ma mère?" Rosalie, who had made little effort to learn English, cried as soon as she saw her brother, while Célie continued to whimper.

"Your mother is all right," Pierre spoke from necessity rather than conviction. "And so is your mother, Célie. Can either of you imagine any slave at L'Artibonite daring to disobey your grandmother Zenobie?"

Pierre's question stopped the girls' tears as they both giggled at the thought of what might happen to any slave who dared defy a fierce and protective Zenobie. Pierre stayed with the girls until he felt it appropriate to remind them that Madame Bérard and her sisters would soon be requiring their services.

When Pierre returned to the kitchen where Old Cabress and Marie Bouquement were busy preparing the evening meal—in silence—he braved their wrath and opened pots until he knew what would be served. As he descended the steps to the wine cellar in search of two bottles of Madeira, he called out, *"Tante Marie,* I hope your meat is as good as Madame Cabress' bread smells. I will furnish the wine and the music!"

There was no answer from the old women. Pierre knew it would be harder to allay their fears than it had been to induce giggling in the girls. He found the wine he sought but still dreaded ascending the steps and facing the two slaves he knew were masking their fears with the pretense of being totally engrossed in their work. Pierre rushed through the dining room into the parlor trying to perfect his plan of action. Looking around he realized that both of these rooms could have been set inside the spacious dining room back at L'Artibonite with space to spare. This, however, would make it easier for him to try to create an air of coziness to compete with the mood of sadness he had to dispel in order to retain his own sanity.

Pierre took the bouquet he had bought earlier from the parlor and placed it on a small serving table. Marie Bouquement had already placed a damask tablecloth and set out gleaming crystal in the dining room. It was customary for the women in Pierre's family to work hardest during times of stress, and he was happy that his aunt was running true to form.

By the time Pierre had lighted candles on the table, he could detect the sound of the girls' footsteps upstairs as they ran from one room to another helping Madame Bérard and her sisters to dress.

Pierre drew scowls from the older slave women when he insisted that a cloth be placed on the kitchen table, then proceeded to adorn that table with flowers.

When Rosalie and Célie came into the kitchen, their eyes were full of questions. But Marie and Old Cabress looked so forbidding, the girls were afraid to ask about the tablecloth and flowers. They just sat and looked puzzled even when Pierre rushed to the kitchen, announced that Madame Bérard and her sisters were in the dining room and placed a bottle of Madeira in the middle of the table.

When sounds of music drifted into the kitchen, the slave women knew Pierre had taken out his fiddle. Old Cabress and Marie Bouquement had to remind the girls that they were servants, not guests, and the evening meal had to be served—by them.

Once the Frenchwomen saw the delicious food placed

before them, Pierre watched their expressions change. Quickly he put aside his fiddle, opened the wine and filled the crystal glasses for his mistress and her sisters. He went to the kitchen and filled glasses of wine for the slave women, then ordered them to follow him to the dining room, where he filled a glass for himself.

"Madames and Mademoiselles," he lifted his glass to the amazement of the women, "I shall propose a toast: Here's to the safe return of Monsieur Jean Jacques Bérard. May God protect him and also all of those we love!"

Madame Bérard and her sisters rose and drank to the toast Pierre had proposed. "Pierre," the Frenchwoman smiled, "your concern and thoughtfulness at a time like this, when I know you are sorely troubled about the safety of your own family, warms my heart. It also makes me ashamed of having despaired of God's mercy. As long as I have you, I should know I am not without protection. My sisters join me in giving thanks to God for all of you," and she included the other slaves with a wave of her hand as her sisters nodded and wiped away stray tears.

Pierre took up his fiddle as the slaves finished serving the three Frenchwomen. He knew he had stopped the tears for the night, but as he played he wondered how he would deal with all of these women the next day and the days which would follow. He was wracked by fears for his own family but dared not show it. It was to cope with this situation that he stopped to pray each time his footsteps took him past St. Peter's.

As soon as one of Pierre's patrons gave him a picture of a new hairstyle she wanted him to copy, he would sketch it so as not to lose sight of how each curl, pouf or roll should look and then try the style on Madame Bérard and her sisters, making allowances for differences in heights, shapes of faces and complexions.

When Pierre had exhausted his supply of new hairstyles, he hit upon the idea of entertaining the Frenchwomen with plans for the *fête* they would give when Monsieur Bérard returned.

It continued to go easier for Pierre to calm the fears of the Frenchwomen than it was for him to do the same for the slaves. He knew Marie Bouquement had begun to seek out newly arrived slaves from St. Dominique to ask about her daughter Adéle and the Bossards. Old Cabress kept her own counsel, but she had a knack of locating refugee families who lived as far away as Greenwich Village, then making friends with their slaves. Rosalie and Célie alternated between preening when they chanced to meet young black males and indulging in hysterical weeping as the months passed and there was no word from Jean Jacques or their parents.

Pierre had great confidence in Fr. William O'Brien, the pastor at St. Peter's. He unburdened his fears to the priest and begged for prayers and Masses for his young master and the members of his own family. He was also friendly with Fr. Matthew O'Brien, a curate at St. Peter's, whom many people, especially the refugees, found more approachable than the stern, matter-of-fact pastor.

Through these two priest-friends, Pierre was alerted to the arrival of many Frenchmen who fled the anger of the slaves on St. Dominique or the terrors of the approaching French Revolution after the king had been removed from power.

Though the French planters from St. Dominique brought slaves with them, Pierre heard the same stories over and over and he knew the worst was still to come. It was heartbreaking, day after day, not to find among the new arrivals a single slave or planter who had any information about L'Artibonite. Sometimes Pierre felt that he had dreamed of those meetings in the mountains with Maurice and Berto. Memories of his family began to seem unreal also. Then he began to hear about fighting in and around Dondon, and he gave up hope for the Bossards. Yet he could not bring himself to share this disturbing news with the other slaves.

It was around this time that the French nobility and wealthy members of the French merchant class were beginning to seek sanctuary in New York and other cities of the young republic in ever-increasing numbers. Some of those who arrived from France, like the refugees from St. Dominique, claimed to have escaped from the rebelling masses with only their lives and the clothes on their backs. As Fr. Matthew O'Brien described the plight of some of these proud but impoverished people, Pierre envisioned a plan whereby he could entertain his mistress and her sisters, keep the slave women too busy to question him each and every night, and feed some of the refugees at the same time.

Though Pierre's patrons were generous with him, he was trying to save money to buy Rosalie's freedom and eventually send funds back to his family. He had to weigh his newest plan against this desire to purchase his sister's freedom and help his family in St. Dominique as soon as he could establish contact. After much prayer and many long conversations with Fr. O'Brien, Pierre decided it was a matter of the moment for him to undertake to encourage Madame Bérard to give a series of parties for the French refugees, though he knew he would have to defray part of the expenses, for he was beginning to understand that his mistress' insecurity extended to paying bills.

Pierre paved the way by feeding Madame Bérard information concerning the most recent families to arrive from Paris, avoiding mention of St. Dominique. Then he would begin to regale her with social chatter about how the American ladies were entertaining. He told her that Mrs. George Washington had special days for her parties. New York society, he said, was vying for invitations to the "at homes" held by Mrs. Abigail Adams, the wife of the vice-president, in Greenwich Village. Mrs. John Jay, wife of the statesman, jurist and diplomat, and the wife of General Henry Knox were almost as famous as Abigail Adams for their afternoon entertainments where, Pierre told his mistress, gentlemen and their ladies would present themselves to their hostess, make the customary bow and curtsey, then sip coffee or tea and indulge in polite conversation before summoning their coaches to drive away from Greenwich Village and back downtown.

In addition to all the other planning for this series of parties, Madame Bérard asked Pierre to assist in addressing the invitations to their friends and the list of refugees he had drawn up with the cooperation of Fr. O'Brien. Then, still between appointments, he might have to accompany Marie Bouquement to the Fly Market down near Wall and Water Streets, for the freshest vegetables and fruits. Or they might have to go to Catherine Market, which was said to have the sweetest fish to be found in New York. When Pierre ran short of time he often found it easier to shop at the Oswego on Broadway near Maiden Lane.

Pierre began to combine his trips to the wharf, where he doggedly continued to seek information about St. Dominique, with a hunt for bananas and oranges that might have been brought in by some ship from the West Indies, as it was difficult to find these fruits in the markets at that time.

After a long day of going from house to house dressing the hair of rich ladies, Pierre would hurry home, slip on his red jacket, make sure all was in readiness for the evening's entertainment and then get out his fiddle so that guests arrived amid an air of merriment.

When there was no festivity planned for an evening, Pierre tried to store up bits of pleasant conversation to please his young mistress when he returned to 105 Reade Street at the end of a long day.

St. Peter's, the church on Barclay Street attended by the Bérards and their slaves, was the only Catholic parish in the city at that time. Twenty-three Catholics, under the leadership of the French Consul to New York, Hector St. Jean de Crevecoeur, built the church in 1785.

Besides the consolation Pierre derived from his daily Mass and frequent visits with the pastor and the curate, he often observed events which he delighted to relay to Madame Bérard. She had taken to her bed with a headache that day in 1790 when Pierre rushed in to tell her about seeing Thomas Jefferson, a witness of the ceremony at the wedding of De Crevecouer's daughter America who was married to Louis Guillaume Otto, Count of Mosloy, later to become Napoleon's minister to Vienna. Pierre was an able raconteur, and as he described the many notables attending the wedding at St. Peter's, Madame Bérard forgot about her headache and called her sisters in to hear Pierre's account of this memorable affair.

The pace Pierre had set for himself was wearying, and fatigue was depleting his supply of ideas to ward off despondency among the women at 105 Reade Street. But neither weather nor weariness kept him away from the waterfront. Jean Jacques had said in his one letter that there was nothing to do but wait and pray. Pierre was beginning to find the waiting a heavy cross. Wherever he went Pierre heard open conversation about the Revolution in France, but as he approached there were only whispers about what was happening in St. Dominique.

On one of his trips to the waterfront, a ship's captain greeted Pierre warmly and handed him a letter addressed to Madame Jean Jacques Bérard. Pierre's joy gave way to apprehension when he saw the penmanship was not that of his young master. Slowly the young man made his way back to 105 Reade Street. He turned the letter over and over, trying to remember if he had ever seen the handwriting before. By the time he reached the house, Pierre knew the script was totally unfamiliar and he suspected that the contents of the letter would confirm his fears that ill-fortune had befallen his master.

Pierre stood and looked at his young mistress as she greeted him cheerfully and continued to concentrate on the embroidery design she was working. He had been holding the letter behind him and he took a deep breath before he spoke. "Madame, you have a letter from St. Dominique. It was given me by a certain ship's captain to deliver to you."

Elizabeth Bérard reached for the letter but drew back when she saw the strange handwriting. "Pierre, will you read it for me?" she asked, dropping her embroidery as one hand clutched at her chest and she closed her eyes.

The letter was a short note from a business associate of Jean Jacques. It only took Pierre a moment to scan the two or three sentences. Jean Jacques Bérard had died suddenly of pleurisy in St. Dominique. The writer gave no further details. There was no mention of L'Artibonite or anyone else.

"What is it? What has happened? Did they kill him?" the young woman demanded.

"Monsieur Bérard died of pleurisy," Pierre heard himself saying as he struggled to control his own emotions before the pale young woman who slumped in her chair.

Pierre ran from the room to find Madame Bérard's sisters and to inform the slaves that the young master was dead.

CHAPTER 7

Pierre's Inheritance

There were days when Madame Bérard did not leave her bed. Neither her sisters nor her beloved "Memin," as she called Marie Bouquement, could console her. The lack of information about the where, when or how her husband met his death caused her great anguish, and she would ask endless questions of whoever was with her. Pierre would rush home at night to relieve Madame Bérard's sisters and his aunt, as he knew they had spent most of the day trying to console the tormented woman.

Over and over Pierre told his young mistress that her husband had not been killed; he had died of pleurisy. He tried to assure her that Zenobie and his parents would have seen to it that Jean Jacques Bérard was properly buried in the family cemetery at L'Artibonite. Pierre spoke softly and with Marie Bouquement applying compresses to the young woman's forehead, they usually managed to induce sleep.

This state of affairs might have gone on much longer had it not been for the mysterious visitor who called on Madame Bérard one day. None of the slaves had seen the man before, but when Marie Bouquement showed the young Frenchwoman his card, she sent word that she would receive him.

Madame Bérard instructed Marie to close the parlor door after she greeted the visitor. Nobody knew when the man left, but the woman closeted herself in her room and spoke to no one until she came downstairs for the evening meal.

From that day on, Madame Bérard appeared less grieved than preoccupied. Pierre often had to ask her a question a second time before she gave any sign of having heard him. Pierre saw telltale circles under his mistress' eyes, and he became more curious about the mysterious visitor.

In August 1791, not too long after Jean Jacques' death, Pierre heard that Louverture had finally given the signal. From a few blacks who escaped with their masters, he heard that a small number of desperate slaves met on a stormy night deep in the vastness of a forest no white man would dare penetrate. Pierre was told later that it was Boukman, the runaway slave he had heard swear vengeance against the planters, who stood before these impatient slaves and harangued them with his half-voodoo, half-Christian prayers and rituals until they had all taken the oath to kill every Frenchman on St. Dominique.

The northern plains of St. Dominique were to become the battlefield. Dessaline and Christophe, the latter having been trained in military tactics at the Battle of Savannah, under the direction of Toussaint Louverture, marshalled the forces of the slaves and led the fight for freedom on St. Dominique.

Sailors who had been on ships anchored in the harbor at Cap Français later told how men, women and children threw themselves in the water to escape death at the hands of the slaves who murdered, burned and looted until there were few if any white families left in the vicinity. Properties of great value were put to the torch and the air reeked with the combined smell of burning sugar cane and charred flesh.

Under the command of Toussaint Louverture, Dessaline and Christophe led the marauding slaves down from the mountains and across St. Dominique. Pierre knew the day he had dreaded was at hand.

There was great sadness in the Bérard house on Reade Street. Even Pierre found it hard to rise above grief over his young master's death and stories of the destruction of all he had known from youth to manhood. He knew the planters were reaping a harvest of bad seeds they had planted, but he shuddered at the thought of so much violence.

Day after day Pierre had to listen to Madame Bérard and her sisters talk constantly of going back to St. Dominique as soon as the French soldiers arrived on the island to put down the rebellion. Pierre wondered how they could be so confident of help from the French when France was currently embroiled in her own revolution. Pierre had been reminded of the chaos in that country when he talked with Fr. O'Brien about writing the elder Bérards concerning Jean Jacques' death. The priest suggested that the Bérards might have fled Paris to avoid the conflict. Pierre could only hope that the man who wrote his young mistress would also have written Jean Jacques' parents.

Though neither Pierre nor any of his relatives had any knowledge of what had happened at L'Artibonite, they all had enough confidence in Zenobie's ingenuity to believe she would find ways to protect the family. But Marie Bouquement was fearful of what had happened at Dondon. Like Madame Bérard and her sisters, she worried about the Bossards and her own daughter Adéle, who also had a family.

In the meantime Pierre continued to assume responsibility for the supervision of the Bérard household. Both Pierre and Marie Bouquement shared their concern over the sudden change they were observing in Madame Bérard. Neither Pierre nor the old nurse could cajole her into accepting invitations for entertaining anymore. Her sisters continued to talk about going back to St. Dominique, but this youngest of the three had reached the stage where she paid little attention to their prattle other than to stare at them vacantly.

One day Pierre came home earlier than usual as one of his patrons had been taken ill and the appointment was cancelled. After greeting the other servants, he ran up the stairs to ask Madame Bérard if she or her sisters wished him to style their hair.

"You are home early," Madame Bérard said quietly. "I was just thinking of a favor I must ask of you."

"Madame, I am at your service," Pierre smiled as he bowed before the solemn woman.

"Here," she said as she handed him a velvet bag which had been resting on a nearby table.

Pierre was puzzled. He knew the young Frenchwoman kept her most prized pieces of jewelry in that bag. "I do not understand what you want me to do," he said.

"Open it," the woman ordered. "You will see it is jewelry. There is a brooch from my father, a necklace you saw Monsieur Bérard present to me on the first anniversary of our marriage, the engagement rings and one or two other pieces. I want you to sell everything in the bag—at once!"

"But why would you part with jewelry that has so much meaning for you?" Pierre asked.

"Because I am penniless!" Madame Bérard spoke between clenched teeth.

"How can that be?" Pierre demanded. "Monsieur Bérard told me he had invested wisely."

"Pierre, the firm in which my husband invested has failed. The man who called on me a few days ago informed me of this misfortune and demanded that I pay him a small sum of money he had advanced Jean Jacques. Now will you do as I have asked?"

Pierre bowed his head and had his hand on the doorknob when Madame Bérard called him back.

"Please," she struggled with the request, "please do not tell the others."

"It will be our secret," Pierre promised, and he rushed

from the presence of this sad but proud woman. It was a secret he lived with for many years.

In the little room he occupied on the top floor of 105 Reade Street, Pierre sat and looked at the bag. He remembered hearing about the mysterious visitor who had called on Madame Bérard. He knew how hard it had been for her to part with jewelry from her father and her husband. He knew Jean Jacques was dead and it was almost certain that Monsieur Bossard was also dead. And to have to ask him—a slave—to sell these precious keepsakes was added gall.

"I have wronged that sad young girl," Pierre mused. "She has never treated me like a slave but always like a friend. I will be as loyal to her as she has been to me. Monsieur Bérard would expect that of me."

In the days following, Pierre was conscious of the expectant look in Madame Bérard's eyes whenever he was in her presence, but he smiled away her unspoken questions.

Less than a week after receiving the jewelry, Pierre knocked at the door of Madame Bérard's bedroom and entered with two packages which he handed his mistress.

Pierre remained standing as the young woman opened the first package containing the amount of money she had said she needed. Then she opened the second package. It was the velvet bag containing the jewelry she had given him to sell.

"Where did you get this money?" Marie Bérard demanded.

"It represents a part of my savings. Monsieur was always most generous, besides being kind. Our Lord must have known we had a need, for I have received several unexpected gifts since the day you confided in me."

"But, Pierre, how can I accept this money from—from—you?"

"Monsieur Bérard would not want you to part with that jewelry! Neither would my grandmother Zenobie. They would urge me to prevent it. When—when your claims to the property are settled," Pierre attempted to be glib, "you will be in a position to repay me for any sum I might have loaned you."

"But of course," the woman agreed eagerly. "Napoleon will take care of the slaves and we can all go home again."

As Pierre closed the door, he saw Marie Bérard pressing the bag to her bosom. He knew he had led the young Frenchwoman into further self-deception, but that was the only way he could help her to retain her dignity.

Pierre said nothing to his Aunt Marie or his sister Rosalie, but he instructed all of the merchants to give him any bills for the Bérards. Then he would wait a few days until he accumulated the necessary funds and pay the bill. When he handed the slip to Madame Bérard the bill had been stamped "paid." At first she kept up the pretense of not wanting to accept this arrangement. Always she reminded Pierre that he would be repaid as soon as they could return to St. Dominique and reclaim L'Artibonite and Dondon.

Marie Bouquement and Rosalie overheard conversations between Madame Bérard and her sisters which indicated that their mistress was without funds. When the merchants continued to accept their orders of food and supplies and Pierre continued to produce bills marked "paid," they knew there was only one answer.

Marie Bouquement was torn by her loyalty to the three young women she had nursed from infancy. Rosalie was outraged that her brother, still a slave, was supporting the Bérard household—family and slaves. Old Cabress only shook her head in amazement when Marie Bouquement and Rosalie told her of their discovery.

Rosalie had another concern. From time to time Pierre had made remarks which made his little sister know that he looked forward to the day when he could buy her freedom.

Though what Pierre said in this respect was usually more a hint than an outright statement, Rosalie knew her brother never indulged in idle talk.

Though Rosalie shared a room with Célie, her best friend at that time was a girl of fifteen, Juliette-Noel, also from St. Dominique. Juliette was more robust than Rosalie, and because she also had a serious air about her it was easy for people to think she was older than she really was.

Events had moved so swiftly since the Bérards and their slaves had come to New York, there had been little chance for Pierre to socialize. But the admiring glances Pierre bestowed on Juliette-Noel had not escaped Rosalie's attention. Since one of Juliette's distant relatives was also the object of Rosalie's romantic yearnings, Pierre's sister was happy to note that her brother admired her best friend.

Everybody at 105 Reade Street knew that Pierre was kept busy by the constant demands which many of New York's wealthy ladies made for his services as a coiffeur. Servants bypassed Mr. Merchant's shop and came directly to the Bérard's house to ask for Pierre. And Rosalie and Célie had spied on Pierre one evening when he was counting his money. Rosalie had to put her hand over Célie's mouth to smother the other girl's giggle. For fear of being detected, they had to run back to their room before they could observe Pierre's hiding place for his money.

Rosalie was sure Juliette would agree with her that Pierre had no obligation to support Madame Bérard. She knew her Aunt Marie would be reluctant to side with her though she, too, knew Pierre had no obligation to assume the responsibility it was apparent he had accepted. Rosalie was confident that her friend would share her views. The next time Juliette came to visit, in the presence of Marie Bouquement and Old Cabress, Rosalie proceeded to air her grievance as she looked toward her friend for support.

"Are you sure of what you are saying?" Juliette asked. "How do you know Madame Bérard is penniless and Pierre is supporting the household?"

Marie Bouquement, who knew that Juliette trusted her, though everybody was aware that Pierre had always pampered his youngest sister, felt she had to speak up.

"It is as Rosalie says," and tears filled the older woman's eyes. "A gentleman we had never seen came here one day and when he left, Marie Elizabeth was like a different person. Several days later she broke the news to her sisters. Both Adeline and Marie Anne have a small sum between them, but they want to go back to St. Dominique to look for their parents. They all still think the French will put down the revolt and they will reclaim Dondon and L'Artibonite."

"How do you know Pierre is supporting Madame Bérard?" Juliette insisted.

"He brings Madame Bérard all of the bills marked paid," Rosalie said.

"I heard Marie Elizabeth tell her sisters that she is accepting loans from Pierre until their claims are settled," Marie Bouquement said sadly. "And Adeline and Marie Anne want me to go back to St. Dominique with them."

"As a slave?" Rosalie asked bitterly. "They are always asking us to do this or that, but I don't see them giving anybody their freedom—not even Pierre, who is putting bread in their mouths. I think he has taken leave of his senses."

"Rosalie, I think you are too harsh on your brother. Pierre is respected by all who know him," Juliette declared. "I've heard you all speak of the tie between the Bérards and your grandmother."

"Aunt Marie," said the girl as she put an arm about the older woman who had begun to weep quietly, "you were the one who told me how young Monsieur Bérard trusted Pierre and relied on his judgment. He must also have been concerned about Pierre's future when he arranged for him to be apprenticed to Mr. Merchant. Otherwise it would have been to his advantage for him to keep Pierre here as a servant. Pierre accepted the responsibility of the household when Monsieur went back to St. Dominique. He had no way of knowing death would prolong that responsibility. Pierre gave his word and he is keeping it. We must wait and see what Madame Bérard does."

None of the women had any idea that Pierre had stopped by the house to leave a bouquet and some bananas he had bought for Madame Bérard, whose appetite reflected her gloomy outlook on her present mode of living. He was about to ascend the stairs when he heard Rosalie say he had taken leave of his senses. He was surprised and delighted at Juliette's passionate defense. He had always admired the girl, but Pierre knew then that his admiration was more; he was in love with Juliette-Noel.

"If only she was a little older and I a little younger," he sighed as he tiptoed up the stairs. He placed the bouquet and bananas outside Madame Bérard's room and put his finger to his lips when she opened the door as he concentrated on leaving the house as quietly as he had entered.

A few days after Pierre overheard himself being discussed, two things happened which gave him much concern. First, Madame Bérard informed him that her sisters were making plans to book passage back to St. Dominique.

Though Pierre made every effort to keep secret the misfortune which had befallen the Bérards, news of the present state of Madame Bérard's financial affairs leaked and was discussed. Mr. Merchant lost no time in demanding that the remaining sum due on Pierre's apprenticeship be paid. Pierre was with Madame Bérard when the elderly coiffeur presented his bill. The young apprentice listened to his teacher and was surprised when his young mistress asked what further instruction Pierre needed. Mr. Merchant admitted that there was little, if anything, he could teach Pierre. All three were aware that most of the prominent society ladies had begun to request Pierre's services exclusively.

They also knew that walking from house to house to service his clients was hard on the older man.

"Mr. Merchant, I regret that you have seen fit to trouble Madame Bérard with this matter," Pierre spoke gravely, but in the usual manner reserved for his elders. "The debt will be settled, but I will respectfully request that Madame be spared the details—which we can determine at the shop—if that meets with your approval."

The old coiffeur agreed to Pierre's proposal and when they returned to the shop Pierre made a bargain with his old teacher and paid him a sum greatly reduced from the amount Mr. Merchant had demanded of Madame Bérard.

Pierre chuckled as he left Mr. Merchant's shop for the last time. He had long since wanted to open a shop of his own but had felt such a move would be disloyal to the man who had taught him the fundamentals of his trade. Now all he had to do was locate a small store where he could open a business and notify his many patrons.

Madame Bérard offered her usual assurance that all debts would one day be repaid as Pierre finally presented her with the receipt from Mr. Merchant, which indicated that the sum for Pierre's apprenticeship had been paid in full.

When Pierre found a shop nearby, he approached Madame Bérard for a favor. "I would be most appreciative if you would permit the girl Célie to come to my shop each day and accept messages for me," he requested.

"I will tell Célie at once," Madame Bérard promised.

Pierre then told the other Bérard slaves of his plan to open a shop of his own. He asked Old Cabress to help him find a boy who could serve as a messenger apprentice. Rosalie and Pierre's Aunt Marie were pleased.

Old Cabress lost no time in producing Jerome, a young slave boy whose impoverished refugee owners had abandoned him. The boy had no home so Pierre made room for him in his own cramped quarters at 105 Reade Street and informed Madame Bérard of the arrangement.

Pierre's new venture was an immediate success. As the demands for his services increased, so did the bills at 105 Reade Street. Madame Bérard no longer made any pretense of settling these financial matters, but in several instances Pierre suspected that merchants were attempting to take advantage of his young mistress. Though his services as a coiffeur were sought and he was accepted in the homes of New York's most prestigious ladies, Pierre was mindful that in his dealings with merchants he was just another slave. He found ways to pit his wits against those of the suspect merchants and more than once uncovered a loophole in their billing system, which enabled him to reduce the monies to be paid.

Célie enjoyed working for Pierre, and Madame Bérard was pleased at the arrangement as she felt this was small reward for all Pierre was doing. The young slave girl continued to help with the evening meals and entertained the other slaves with news of the happenings at the shop. Jerome, the messenger-apprentice, was still struggling with his English and trying to master the fundamentals of hairdressing by observing Pierre at work and assisting him when permitted.

Pierre noted that while Jerome lacked the aptitude which had enabled him to assimilate so quickly all Mr. Merchant taught him, the young slave boy had shown a determination to learn the trade. Pierre was happy that his venture had worked out so well and for a brief period he had a sense of well-being.

Young Madame Bérard's lack of interest in everything but the hopeful wishing which led many of the refugees from St. Dominique to believe the French would soon put down the revolt of the slaves and make it possible for them to regain their holdings, continued to trouble Pierre. By June 1792, Cap Français had been burned and ten thousand Frenchmen, their families and slaves were reported to have escaped. They were pouring into New Orleans, Charleston,

Philadelphia, Boston and New York. It was estimated that approximately five thousand of these refugees from St. Dominique eventually made their way to New York City, bringing tales of the burning, looting and killing which caused Pierre many a sleepless night.

A house of hospitality was set up for the refugees on Vesey Street, not far from St. Peter's. This influx of refugees was augmented by the arrival of hundreds of Frenchmen fleeing the French Revolution. The Bérard household became a gathering place, and with the help of a Monsieur Gabriel Nicolas, formerly of St. Dominique, Pierre was able to detect a faint flicker of interest in Madame Bérard's eyes when Frenchmen and their wives she had known at L'Artibonite visited her.

Gabriel Nicolas, who also had been wealthy in St. Dominique, was a gifted musician. As a refugee he was reduced to making his living playing his violin wherever his services were required. Monsieur Nicolas was one of the few who could flatter Madame Bérard and receive a smile as a reward. Pierre encouraged this relationship and Marie Bouquement was also pleased. Though Madame Bérard's sisters enjoyed seeing old friends and meeting others who had come over from Paris, once they were alone they impressed upon their old nurse how important it was for them all to go back to St. Dominique and Dondon as soon as possible.

Pierre's work carried him into homes where he met many of the most distinguished French refugees. His services were constantly required at the home of the beautiful Angelica Schuyler Church, wife of the wealthy Englishman John Barker Church, now a resident of New York. Mrs. Church was the daughter of General Philip Schuyler, who distinguished himself and won fame at the Battle of Saratoga. Angelica Church was also the sister-in-law of Alexander Hamilton. Her daughter, who later became Mrs. Peter Cruger, was to become one of Pierre's most beautiful patrons and a dear friend.

It was said that Angelica Church had been instrumental in helping many of the better-known French refugees to reach America. She was a woman of uncommon beauty.

Madame Bérard's sisters, Marie Anne Dessource and Adeline Bossard, were secretly annoyed that Pierre, though always the epitome of graciousness, never shared any of the gossip they knew he must have heard. Whatever the account he gave them of news gleanings, it was always in good taste and never cast any adverse reflections on his patrons.

Among the most distinguished Frenchmen that Angelica Church was said to have helped reach America and freedom were such notables as Talleyrand and Beaumetz. Charles Maurice de Talleyrand-Perigord was far from an affable person. This unfrocked bishop with the club foot was later to become Napoleon's Minister of Foreign Affairs and wield uncontrolled power throughout Europe. The more affable Beaumetz had been a deputy in the French National Assembly. St. Memin, who had achieved recognition for his Amercian engravings, and the author Voney, as well as Colombe, one time aide-de-camp to Lafayette, were also among those who frequented Angelica Church's home.

Though Pierre refrained from mentioning it at 105 Reade Street, he had heard that when Lafayette was a prisoner in Austria at the height of the period in French history referred to as the Terror, Madame Lafayette feared for the life of her son, George Washington Lafayette, and begged President Washington to grant him asylum. Later, young Lafayette did come to the United States and was a guest of the Alexander Hamiltons until it was deemed safe for him to return to France.

Of all the French refugees of this period, Pierre found Moreau de St. Mery to be the most colorful. St. Mery had been born in Martinique, educated in France and later practiced law at Cap Français in St. Dominique. During the early stages of the French Revolution he had served as president of the Paris electors. For a short time after the fall of the

Bastille he governed Paris. But he was subsequently said to
have incurred the wrath of Robespierre, and Pierre heard
the oft-told story that St. Mery had barely escaped his pursu-
ers when he scrambled aboard a ship minutes before his
enemies would have taken him prisoner. St. Mery later
settled in Philadelphia, where he operated a printing press
and became the central figure around whom other French
refugees gathered in comparative safety to discuss the ulti-
mate and awful fate of Robespierre, Danton and their co-
horts, while sipping vintage Madeira and recalling past
glory.

Pierre was excited when one of his patrons gave him a
copy of St. Mery's book, *Voyage aux États-Unis de L'Amérique,
1793-1798,* in which the Frenchman chronicled accounts of
what he saw, heard and felt in New York, Philadelphia and
other cities in the states he visited. As Pierre familiarized
himself with St. Mery's word picture of St. Dominique, he
again felt a surge of gratitude to the elder Monsieur Bérard
for having encouraged him to learn to read. He smiled often
as he remembered the day Zenobie had brought the
copybook she rescued from an old trunk to the library at
L'Artibonite. That tattered book had prepared Pierre and
his master for the voyage to New York.

Looking back, Pierre recalled his reaction when Mr.
Merchant insisted that he begin his apprenticeship by doing
nothing but cutting the children's hair. In time he came to
recognize that, too, as a blessing. He had listened carefully
to the children's English prattle. Because they spoke with
simple directness, without the embellishments adults are
inclined to add, he had soon been able to converse with his
little customers. Coupled with the habit of thinking about
what he was going to say before he spoke, Pierre was soon
conversing in simple English. Yet as long as he lived, Pierre
was always more comfortable when using his native tongue.

Pierre was often amused when he heard his relatives,
Old Cabress and Célie, gossiping about French planters and

their slaves whom they heard had escaped to New Orleans, Charleston or Baltimore.

Then there were still other times when he came home after a hard day's work to find 105 Reade Street full of refugees from St. Dominique. Mademoiselle Bossard and Madame Dessource, he noted, would dart from one guest to another plying them with questions about St. Dominique. But their sister Madame Bérard showed little interest unless Monsieur Gabriel Nicolas was present. It was then that Pierre would drink a strong cup of coffee, put on his red jacket and bring out his fiddle to entertain the guests.

The slaves grumbled among themselves about the extra work, but they made sure Pierre was nowhere around when they voiced their dissatisfaction.

Pierre had cultivated a warm friendship with the captain who had given him that first letter from Jean Jacques Bérard after he went back to St. Dominique. In the spring of 1794, this seaman friend told Pierre that the burning and looting on the island appeared to have subsided. He said it was rumored that Louverture realized the plantations were the backbone of the economy and had offered some of the planters the opportunity to return to their habitations, providing they did so under the conditions he proposed. He also was said to have forced many of the slaves to return to the land they had fled. Toussaint Louverture knew the expertise of the planters was needed in extracting the sugar from the cane, refining it and transporting the product to market and wharf. These favored planters were expected to share their profits or else be prepared for what Louverture considered appropriate action.

Pierre was told that Louverture traveled from town to town punishing laziness and theft, encouraging the establishment of schools and attempting to instill a sense of the dignity of labor for the good of one's country. Toussaint Louverture's genius for organization, his skill as a statesman and a punishing schedule—whereby day and night often merged when he was still in the saddle, as he exhorted his countrymen to accept the system of the proportional wages and disciplinary laws he had imposed—bore fruit.

In Louverture's favor was the story that he was indeed the grandson of Gao-Guinou, who some slaves said had been an African king before his capture by the slavers. Others said Gao-Guinou was an African prince who had been sold into slavery by a treacherous and jealous king. Louverture's bearing, in spite of his small frame, his organizational ability and the vision of a solvent economy, which he shared with all who would listen, gave credence to this claim of kinship with the revered Gao-Guinou who was said to have been on one of the first slave ships to arrive in Hispaniola.

Napoleon, later to admit the error of his strategy, allowed Louverture to build up the economy until trade on the island attained one-third of the pre-Revolutionary figure. It was no secret that Louverture wanted to retain cordial ties with France, and he attempted to wipe out the Spanish domination in the eastern part of the island but failed. Louverture's acceptance of planters who agreed to his terms led many Frenchmen to return to St. Dominique.

Among those who made the return voyage to the island were Mademoiselle Adeline Bossard and Madame Marie Anne Dessource, sisters of Madame Bérard. They took Pierre's aunt, Marie Bouquement, with them. Pierre had tried to dissuade the two sisters, but they were determined to go back to Dondon and neither Pierre nor Madame Bérard could change their minds.

Madame Bérard was more dejected than ever after her sisters and Marie Bouquement left. Rosalie alternated between weeping over the possible fate of her parents and being elated over her romance with Jean Noel. Pierre was saddened to note that Old Cabress, usually loquacious and cheerful in adversity, grew silent and withdrawn after months passed and there was no news from Marie Bouquement. Célie and Jerome spent most of their time at

Pierre's shop, but when he came home they were invariably in the kitchen telling Rosalie and Old Cabress the latest gossip they had picked up about St. Dominique.

Pierre continued his practice of going to daily Mass at St. Peter's, and each morning he begged God to help him shake the gloom of his homelife and greet his patrons cheerfully. He finally decided to encourage Madame Bérard's fantasy about going back to St. Dominique after the French put down the revolt of the slaves. Then with the help of Monsieur Gabriel Nicolas, who was a constant visitor, Pierre insisted that Madame Bérard resume the small parties—even though he knew he would still have to supply the finance. Again Pierre found himself hurrying home after a day's work, loaded with flowers and delicacies which he arranged; then putting on his red jacket and alternating between being a butler and supplying the music with his old fiddle.

During this period young Juliette-Noel began adding her infectious good nature and artistic homemaking skills to Pierre's effort to bring some happiness to 105 Reade Street again.

With Marie Bouquement away, Old Cabress and Rosalie were glad to have Juliette's help. Pierre found himself looking forward to seeing Juliette in the kitchen when he came home.

In spite of Pierre's many dramatic efforts to keep his young mistress from dwelling on past sorrows, he began to get the impression that she was thinner each day. When he styled her hair he was especially disturbed by her pallor.

Pierre felt impelled to confide his fears to Monsieur Nicolas, who was a constant visitor. In turn, the Frenchman told Pierre that he would like to propose marriage to Madame Bérard but hesitated to do so because of his meager income.

"God will open a door for you," Pierre heard himself assuring the courtly gentleman.

"Do you really think it possible that she would accept me?" Gabriel Nicolas was begging Pierre for encouragement.

In spite of contemplating another mouth to feed, Pierre summoned enough enthusiasm to murmur, "All things are possible with God."

It was hard for Pierre to keep his old fiddle under his chin in the midst of some of the parties he arranged for Madame Bérard, with the cooperation of Monsieur Nicolas and Juliette, who helped out in the kitchen. The conversation invariably revolved around how Napoleon was going to send soldiers to take over St. Dominique, and they could all go home and live in luxury once more. Sometimes as Pierre listened he wondered what he would have done if Maurice and Berto had forced him to make a choice between the slaves or his young master. Then there were the times when memories of Maurice and Berto and even memories of his parents seemed hazy.

Pierre had shopped for the house after Mass and returned to 105 Reade Street before going to his first appointment the day the French Consul brought Madame Bérard the document to be signed which would give Marie Bouquement her freedom. The paper, dated January 20, 1796, stated Marie Bouquement was freed, and stated she was liberated "in recompense for the attachment she has shown us since the troubles that have afflicted St. Dominique, and we release her from all service due us." It had to be signed by all three sisters, and Madame Bérard's signature was the last to be affixed.

Pierre became apprehensive after the consul left. Later that day he went to the waterfront. Luck was with him, and he found a sailor he knew who had sailed out of Cap Français recently. The seaman told Pierre there was little likelihood of Madame Bérard's sisters ever reaching Dondon from the Cap as there was still some fighting in that area.

Pierre's fears proved to be well founded. Adeline Bossard and the widowed Marie Anne Dessource were not allowed to go back to Dondon. The realization that their parents had most likely been killed, together with the fact that the bitter cold winters of New York had lowered their resistance to disease, resulted in what became fatal illnesses for the sisters. Marie Bouquement, who could not leave the Cap to search for her own child, nursed the two French-women until death ended their sufferings.

The Bossard family had been well known in St. Domin-ique, and Marie Bouquement found a former associate of Monsieur Bossard's who had managed to survive. The man assisted her in making the final arrangements for the burial of the two women she had nursed from infancy and agreed to notify Madame Bérard of their deaths. He advised Marie against trying to go to Dondon or L'Artibonite, but his warn-ing fell on ears that refused to hear. Marie wanted to find her daughter Adéle and to see Zenobie and the family at L'Artibonite.

When the letter announcing the death of her sisters reached young Madame Bérard, she refused at first to be-lieve the contents. She kept insisting it was all a mistake until Pierre brought her a letter from Marie Bouquement giving details which compelled her to accept the fact that her sis-ters were indeed dead.

The death of Adeline Bossard and Marie Anne Dessource also had an unfortunate effect on the slaves. Rosalie was fearful for her Aunt Marie and her relatives at L'Artibonite. Pierre could see that Old Cabress was showing signs of mental strain from so much sorrow and uncertainty. Célie went about her tasks at the shop each day, but she was either silent or tearful at home.

Pierre increased his visits to the wharf and questioned every sailor he could coax into conversation. He succeeded in learning that Marie Bouquement was still in Cap Français. Though she had made several attempts to get to L'Artibonite and Dondon, she had always been turned back. As soon as he shared this information with his mistress, she began what was a series of letters begging her old nurse to return to New York. In spite of all that had happened, Madame Bérard assured Marie Bouquement that she needed her in New York so they could prepare to return to St. Dominique as soon as the French troops arrived.

Pierre's young mistress delighted in reading him the letters she wrote his Aunt Marie, and he made sure that they were posted or given to sailors who manned ships that were stopping at St. Dominique again.

Pierre had just entrusted one of Madame Bérard's letters to a sailor who said his ship was bound for St. Dominique, the day the first letter was handed to him addressed to "The Citizen Toussaint, residing in New York." Joyfully he recognized his grandmother Zenobie's familiar scrawl.

Zenobie knew Marie Bouquement was at Cap Français, but there was no way for her to get to her. All was lost at Dondon and nobody seemed to know anything about Adéle, Marie's daughter. Zenobie and her family had been permitted to remain at L'Artibonite. Though she assured Pierre of her affection and the affection of the entire family for him, the letter had a plaintive note. He immediately answered and told her he would send a box of gifts as soon as he could find a ship that would stop at St. Marc, since he knew it was impossible for any of them to get through to Cap Français.

Madame Bérard's letters to Marie Bouquement begging the old nurse to return to New York, and Pierre's letters to Zenobie and the boxes of gifts that the other slaves also contributed to, helped to lift some of the gloom which had been hanging over 105 Reade Street. When Pierre was busy, the boy Jerome went to watch docking ships, and in his halting English asked what ports of call they had visited and where they expected to stop on the next voyage. Jerome brought Pierre a letter from Zenobie telling him that his sister Marie-Louise had left L'Artibonite along with his older brother. Though Pierre's mother and father were still with Zenobie, the old woman admitted that most of the other slaves had scattered after Jean Jacques' death. Zenobie told Pierre that his island home was now being called "Haiti," the name the natives had first given the island. Cap Français, she wrote, had been renamed Cap Haitian. Pierre imagined he could see the old woman struggling with her emotions as she wrote. No doubt his mother would be nearby giving her messages to relay. Pierre had never ceased to be puzzled as to why he had been the only one Zenobie had taught to write.

There were times when Pierre had difficulty deciphering Zenobie's scrawl. He came to understand that the more cryptic the letter the more emotionally involved the old woman was, as in one letter when she wrote: "Your mother had a baby. The baby is dead." Another time she wrote that his grandfather and his father were jealous because the last box he sent contained no gift for them. This was one of the few references ever made to a grandfather who must have performed his biological function and then accepted the dominance of the matriarch Zenobie as the lesser of other evils. Once and awhile the proud Zenobie asked Pierre for things like a pair of scissors, a pipe or calico for a dress Pierre's mother Ursule needed.

Madame Bérard continued to write letters to Marie Bouquement, begging her to come back to New York, as the young Frenchwoman became obsessed with the idea that Marie was her second mother and only her presence would be proof that she still loved her.

Pierre, too, felt that his Aunt Marie's search was futile. Knowing Adéle, he reasoned that she had tried to protect the Bossards when the rebellious slaves destroyed their home and was either killed or maimed during the fighting. His young mistress' melancholia gave him much distress. He told Monsieur Nicolas that he feared for her sanity.

Pierre had exhausted every effort he could make or every trick he could dream up to cheer the grieving young Frenchwoman. He hunted for rare flowers and fruits to give her, but his labors seldom earned more than a wan smile. He created new styles for her hair and wrote out invitations to friends for small parties, then delivered them and rushed home from his work to serve and entertain. Rosalie continued to disapprove of Pierre's efforts to assuage their mistress' grief, but Juliette-Noel seemed to know when Pierre would need a cheerful aide and always managed to appear at the right time. The only other ally was Gabriel Nicolas.

Months had passed without a letter from Marie Bouquement, and Madame Bérard had reached the stage of depression where she ate almost nothing. Pierre prayed harder than ever and reminded himself each day that he could not become discouraged, for discouragement was the devil's most effective tool. Yet the well-intentioned Pierre had begun to wonder what he could do next.

It was a fairly pleasant night in early February 1801. Pierre was weary, but when Rosalie opened the door at 105 Reade Street he was shocked to hear a babble of French interspersed with laughter.

"The French," Rosalie hissed, "have arrived at Le Cap and they," she pointed toward the guests, "are all celebrating."

CHAPTER 8

A Mixed Blessing

In the days following the news that the French had arrived in St. Dominique, which the natives now called Haiti, Pierre learned enough about what had happened to piece together a tapestry of events. Toussaint Louverture, with the title of Governor-General of Haiti, had persisted in believing that his island government could become an independent French colony. He was said to have drafted a constitution which insured autonomy for the island over which he would rule as Governor-General for life, and sent the document to Napoleon, who had already reconquered Austria.

Many Frenchmen believed that Napoleon considered all of Hispaniola to be a field post from which to launch his plan for Louisiana, which would block further expansion by the United States. Napoleon did not intend for an ex-slave to interfere or alter his plan.

It was rumored that Napoleon's animosity against Louverture had been building up for years. When Louverture sent his envoy to deliver the constitution, addressed to Emperor Napoleon I, court attachés said the Frenchman was furious over the idea of a black man daring to challenge him at a time when so many favorable events had created an advantage for him.

The blockade which the British had maintained in

the Atlantic had kept Napoleon from moving against Louverture earlier. But in October 1801, the French had signed the first documents for the Treaty of Amiens. France had also settled certain differences with the United States, where George Washington had turned over the reigns of government to John Adams before Washington died in 1799. Then Adams had gone back to Massachusetts after Thomas Jefferson, the Southerner, had become the third president of the United States in March 1801. Napoleon and his advisors reasoned that Louverture would get no support from a government to the north of Haiti headed by a slave-owning president. Napoleon decided this was his time to move against the black upstart.

A French fleet under the command of General LeClerc, husband of Napoleon's sister Pauline, was reported to be anchored off the coast of Cap Français in early February. This report had spread throughout the French colony in New York and had accounted for the refugees' glee.

That night Pierre simply listened to his sister's explanation for the happiness of the guests at 105 Reade Street, but appeared to ignore her inferences. As usual he determined what service was to be used and how and when refreshments would be served. Then he put on his red jacket and took out his fiddle. He deliberately kept his music soft so that he might better hear the grandiose plans of the people he would entertain. The Frenchmen were making preparations for their return to St. Dominique, where they said they would reclaim their wealth.

Pierre stifled the desire to groan aloud when he heard the Frenchmen describe the way Toussaint Louverture would be captured and the slave revolt would immediately collapse. While Pierre did not rule out the possibility of Louverture being captured, he knew from what the sailors had told him that men like Boukman, Dessalines and Christophe would not give up their fight for freedom unless they were subdued by trickery.

Whenever Pierre thought of the revolt, he remembered Maurice and Berto and wondered if they were still alive. Pierre thought that it would be years before there would be a semblance of peace in the land he had once called home. Yet he continued to coax soft melodies out of his old fiddle as he listened to the refugees who insisted it would only be a matter of months—maybe a year—before they would return to their lush island home and reclaim their wealth.

One morning not long after the news of the French fleet being anchored off the coast of Cap Français had given the refugees renewed hope, Pierre rushed from Mass at St. Peter's to 105 Reade Street for a hasty breakfast before going to his first appointment. In the kitchen he found a weeping Claudine Gaston, Juliette's mother, who asked if she could speak with him in private. Claudine, he soon learned, had overheard her master discussing the possibility of selling Juliette to a visiting southern planter who had expressed a desire to buy the slave girl. Pierre calmly questioned the distraught mother until she recalled the price that had been mentioned.

"I have heard that your master, like many of the French refugees, is in desperate circumstances. Give me a few days and I will be in a position to make it possible for you to purchase your daughter's freedom. But you must not delay making the offer," Pierre cautioned. "Waste no time in stating your intentions, but try to stall until I have the money in hand."

The relieved woman threw her arms about Pierre and expressed eternal gratitude.

"You must promise that our transaction will remain secret," Pierre insisted. "I would never want your daughter, who you must know I admire, to feel obligated."

"As you wish," Claudine promised and wiped away her tears before they went back to the kitchen where Rosalie had set out a roll and coffee for her brother.

As Pierre hurried toward Broadway that day, he reminded himself that he had just made a promise which would postpone the day when he would have enough money to buy Rosalie's freedom. Yet the thought of Juliette being sold into slavery miles away filled him with anger. He reasoned that he had no other choice.

Within a fortnight the transaction between Claudine Gaston and the man who owned Juliette had been completed. Pierre for a change was having a leisurely evening meal when Rosalie opened the door for the excited Juliette, who had come to share her joy with her best friend. As the two girls entered the kitchen, with Juliette still reciting the details of her master's surprise that her mother had enough money to buy her freedom, Pierre observed the dour expression on Rosalie's face and suspected that she was envious of her friend. Rosalie felt the intensity of her brother's gaze and quickly veiled any ugly feelings with a tearful embrace. Pierre listened to Juliette's recital of the events, then asked to see the papers of manumission. Juliette proudly displayed the document which made her a free woman.

Pierre read each word as if the entire matter of Juliette's freedom was a complete surprise to him. Old Cabress merely grunted and continued to move back and forth to the stove. The girls watched Pierre as he rose quietly before he spoke.

"May I flatter myself to say that I am the first to kiss the hand of Mademoiselle Noel—freedwoman?" Pierre bowed as Juliette extended her hand with graceful dignity.

From that day on Pierre knew that he had two goals. He was determined to buy his sister's freedom, but above all else he wanted to make Juliette his wife.

Madame Bérard continued to grieve, and Pierre continued to encourage the attentions of Monsieur Gabriel Nicolas. Rosalie had become even more resentful of her brother's generosity and, in the absence of Marie Bouquement, more outspoken. She made another special effort to gain the support of Juliette as it became more obvious every day that her brother was in love with her friend. However, Juliette's respect and admiration for Pierre was so great she was not inclined to criticize him. Rosalie finally hit upon one incident that forced Juliette to question Pierre in a matter that had nothing to do with his support of the Bérard household.

Around the turn of the century a law had been passed which declared the children of slaves freed after they reached a certain age. The black population of New York was jubilant. They saw this as one more step toward emancipation, and a triumphant parade was planned for July 5, 1800. Pierre had been asked to lead the parade, which was past history by the time Rosalie heard the story.

"He refused," Rosalie told Juliette later. "Not only that, but Pierre said he could not take part in the celebration. We all know he is always lending people money who are trying to buy their freedom, yet he refused to take part in that celebration."

Juliette did ask Pierre why he had refused the invitation to lead the parade.

"I am still a slave. If and when I am freed, I will owe my freedom to my mistress and not the state. What has been said is true; I do not take part in political demonstrations, debates or celebrations. But there is a reason," Pierre declared. "The price I have seen men pay who asked for nothing more than their freedom is a memory I will live with forever. I pray that my presence in this country means I made the right decision. Only God can answer that question. But as long as my countrymen—here and in my home—are dying for the right to be free, I cannot parade or celebrate. I cannot!"

The intensity of Pierre's reply made Juliette wish she had never questioned Pierre about his refusal to head the parade. Years were to pass before she understood his reference to memories of the price men had paid for freedom.

Rosalie soon understood that Juliette would never openly question Pierre's behavior. Without an ally, Rosalie kept her resentment to herself. It would not be long before she would be the wife of Jean Noel, she hoped. Yet Pierre had long since become the father figure to Rosalie, and though she curbed her tongue, she still resented her brother's support of a Frenchwoman who refused to grant him the gift of freedom.

None of Pierre's acquaintances dared ask how he felt about being a slave or supporting his mistress, though it was discussed in polite circles. If he had been asked, Pierre might or might not have told them that he had never felt enslaved because he had never been subjected to the horrors of slavery he had observed during the months before he had agreed to come to New York. He only felt compassion for the lonely woman who was considered his owner. Though she had never been robust, he had been compelled to watch his young Madame grow thin with each of her many sorrows. Her increasing pallor worried Pierre to the extent that he instructed Rosalie, when laying out dresses for her mistress to wear, to choose only those of colorful materials.

Gabriel Nicolas continued to confide in Pierre. Though the Frenchman still earned a living of sorts in the orchestra pits of the few theaters now in New York, his income barely covered the cost of his lodging and an occasional outing. Pierre had encouraged Monsieur Nicolas' frequent visits not only because the Frenchman's presence cheered Madame Bérard, but also because he knew Gabriel Nicolas needed and appreciated the meals which were the result of Old Cabress and Rosalie's efforts and Pierre's selective shopping.

Pierre became even more discriminating in his dealings with merchants. He was forced to get the best bargains for his money because he had started another fund to purchase Rosalie's freedom. Each time Monsieur Nicolas bemoaned the fact that he was in love with Madame Bérard but could not ask her to marry him because of his financial condition, Pierre reminded him that God would open a way. He had decided that the money for Rosalie's freedom would provide funds for this couple if only he could persuade Monsieur Nicolas to propose.

Early in 1802 Gabriel Nicolas finally told Pierre he was going to propose marriage to Madame Bérard. When he told Pierre he was taking the young woman to the theater that evening, Pierre rushed home during the day and instructed Rosalie to lay out an attractive pink gown for their mistress to wear that evening. He made sure that the Frenchwoman's pearl necklace and earrings were on her dressing table. All that day, as Pierre walked from one appointment to another, he was thinking of how he could style Madame Bérard's hair so as to create an illusion of fullness which would offset the sharp lines he had observed.

On the way home that evening, Pierre stopped in a flower shop and bought two flowers. One was a deep pink rose, not yet fully opened. The other was yellow and he made sure it was equally beautiful.

As Pierre styled his mistress' hair piling pouf on top of pouf, but leaving enough loose hair around her face so he could frame it with soft curls, he hummed a French song he knew she loved. Looking in the mirror, he saw a slight smile on the usually sad face. Then Pierre fastened the pink rose in the crowning pouf and handed Madame Bérard her hand mirror. The Frenchwoman clapped her hands much as she might have done during her early days at L'Artibonite when she was so young and happy.

Pierre knew Juliette would be in the kitchen, and he hoped she would get the opportunity to see his work when Monsieur Nicolas called for Madame Bérard. He had a surprise for Juliette, too.

When Rosalie announced Monsieur Nicolas, Pierre was helping Madame Bérard fasten the clasp on her pearl necklace. He handed her a small beaded bag and stood aside, marveling at the grace with which she gathered up the satin folds of her gown to descend the stairs. Pierre could see the handsome and expectant Monsieur Nicolas at the foot of the steps, his hat in a hand framed by lace cuffs on a shirt Pierre knew the French refugee must have bought in Paris during his more affluent days. Then Pierre saw Rosalie hand Monsieur Nicolas a heavy silk wrap which he draped about the frail shoulders of the woman he hoped to marry.

Juliette was not the only one who rushed out of the kitchen to get a glimpse of Madame Bérard as Monsieur Nicolas helped her into the carriage he had hired. Old Cabress waddled into the parlor behind Juliette and Rosalie as they hid behind the lace curtains and watched until the horsedrawn carriage disappeared up Reade Street. Rosalie and Old Cabress insisted that Madame had not looked so happy since Monsieur Bérard went back to St. Dominique.

Pierre stood and listened to the slave women who, he knew, were excited by the scent of romance. Juliette was the first to see him.

"Her hair was beautiful, Pierre! You must have worked for hours. And that rose—where did you find a blossom so perfect?" Juliette asked as Pierre laughed and ran up the steps to his room.

Old Cabress and the girls had returned to the kitchen for another cup of coffee when Pierre rejoined them. He stood in the doorway and listened to their chatter for a few seconds, then cleared his throat to attract their attention.

"Madame Bérard looked as if she had come alive again," Juliette spoke directly to Pierre.

"You asked about the flower I placed in her hair," Pierre smiled as he drew a velvety yellow rose from behind his back. "Here is an equally perfect blossom for an equally beautiful lady," and he handed the long-stemmed rose to Juliette.

While Juliette divided her adoring glances between Pierre and the yellow rose which she pressed to her bosom, Rosalie and Old Cabress exchanged knowing looks. They were surrounded by romance.

Later Pierre walked Juliette home and then took his place in the parlor to wait for his mistress when Célie and

Jerome, arm in arm, let themselves in. Pierre was glad he had not made a light in the room as he would not have wanted the young couple to think he was spying on them. Yet he was mildly surprised as Célie and Jerome had given no previous indication of being attracted to each other even though they worked in Pierre's shop each day.

Pierre waited until he was sure Célie and Jerome had gone to their respective rooms before he went about the business of making a light in the parlor. He must have dozed off because he awoke with a start when he heard the clop-clop of the horses' hooves as the carriage stopped in front of the house. It was now Pierre's turn to peer through the lace curtains, and he was impressed by the gentle manner in which Gabriel Nicolas helped Madame Bérard from the carriage. Pierre waited until he knew the couple was directly outside before he opened the door.

"Dear, dear Pierre. You did not have to wait up. Rosalie had put a key in my bag," Madame Bérard smiled warmly.

"I am delighted that Pierre waited up," Monsieur Nicolas said. "I want Pierre to be the first to know that you have done me the honor of consenting to be my wife."

"I am honored to be the first to know of this happy circumstance." Pierre bowed and quickly ascended the stairs, leaving the couple alone.

As Pierre stood outside the room he shared with Jerome, he was shocked at his own reaction to all he had witnessed that night.

"When," he shook his head, "when will I ever be in a position to ask Juliette to be my wife?"

The colony of French refugees in New York was overjoyed at the announcement of the engagement of Madame Bérard to Monsieur Nicolas. The young woman had suffered more than her share of sorrow, and they all hoped that the impending marriage would offer some happiness. There was a round of parties at 105 Reade Street and elsewhere. Pierre was delighted to see the young Frenchwoman taking periodic interest in her surroundings. But there were days when she confided in him that she would never be truly happy until his Aunt Marie returned.

"She is all I have left in this world." Madame Bérard would usually end these fits of despondency by asking him to write his aunt and beg her to come back to New York.

The spring of 1802 was a time of budding trees and flowering romances. Rosalie and Jean Noel were very much in love, according to Rosalie. Pierre had some doubts about his sister's suitor, who seldom visited her at 105 Reade Street but found many occasions to invite her to the homes of his friends. Pierre refrained from criticizing Jean because he was aware that he was a distant relative of Juliette's. Célie and Jerome seemed determined to keep their relationship a secret, but Pierre had intercepted one or two glances that indicated their feelings for each other. Madame Bérard and Monsieur Nicolas were planning a summer wedding, the young woman persisting that Pierre's Aunt Marie should be present when she married. Pierre was working harder than ever as he wanted to save up enough money to buy Rosalie's freedom as soon as possible after Madame Bérard married. Yet Pierre's fatigue after a long day's work seemed to vanish when he came home and found Juliette in the kitchen with Rosalie. Often Juliette had prepared a special dish for him, and Pierre began to beg God to help him achieve both his goals—freedom for Rosalie, and Juliette for a wife—if and when he, too, was free.

In early June of that year, the French refugees went wild with joy when they learned that General LeClerc had captured Toussaint Louverture and sent him back to France. It would only be months before they would all be ready to go back home, they said.

Pierre got a different story from the sailors who told him that LeClerc had tricked Louverture into signing a treaty and conferring with one of the French majors, only to enable one of LeClerc's aide-de-camps to arrest the Governor-

General, tie his hands and lead him to the harbor at Les Gonaives where he was put aboard the frigate Creole. Toussaint Louverture's wife and family were likewise captured and put aboard the vessel La Guerriere. Both ships sailed immediately for France.

Pierre was terribly confused by stories the sailors brought back about former slaves fighting with the French, then against the French, and sometimes fighting among themselves. He prayed night and day that his loved ones were safe.

As the summer months passed without any word from Marie Bouquement, Madame Bérard was inclined to listen to Monsieur Nicolas and Pierre, who both told her she should proceed with her plans for the wedding. When Madame Bérard agreed, Pierre had only one reservation: July was coming to an end and for years New York had been plagued by an epidemic each August that was called by various names but always resulted in hundreds of deaths. Pierre listened as Madame Bérard made plans for the August event and prayed that this would be the year the plague would pass New York by.

Madame Bérard and Gabriel Nicolas were married at St. Peter's on August 11, 1802. Fr. Matthew O'Brien performed the ceremony and recorded it in the church records. There was much merrymaking at 105 Reade Street that day. As Pierre moved among the guests, smiling as always and catering to their every wish, he was conscious of the way Rosalie's eyes followed him as she ostensibly busied herself with serving the many French refugees who came to congratulate the newlyweds.

Pierre chuckled to himself. "Rosalie is probably feeling sorry for me," he thought, "because she doesn't think I realize this wedding means another mouth for me to feed."

When the series of festive events had ended, Monsieur Nicolas assured Pierre that as soon as he and his new wife went back to St. Dominique and reclaimed their property they would make sure that he, Pierre, was repaid for all he had contributed toward the upkeep of the household.

Pierre and Rosalie were aware of Old Cabress' failing health. The slave woman's gait was so slow it was obvious that walking was painful. Madame Bérard-Nicolas insisted that Old Cabress was grieving for Marie Bouquement. She begged Pierre to write his aunt once more and tell her it was urgent that she return to New York.

Pierre wrote a number of letters to Marie Bouquement begging her for news of his family and urging her to return to New York. He consoled himself in the hope that one or two out of all the letters he entrusted to sailors would reach his aunt.

Marie Bouquement did return to New York, but Pierre's aunt had never succeeded in getting to L'Artibonite or Dondon. She found no trace of her daughter Adéle and finally decided she must have died with the Bossards. The return of Marie Bouquement had a curious effect on Madame Bérard-Nicolas. The young Frenchwoman alternated between tears of joy over the return of her old nurse and indulging in reminiscences of her childhood and the early years at L'Artibonite, which left her morose and withdrawn. Monsieur Nicolas was patient and oftimes aroused her from these moods with stories of his experiences at the theater where he worked. One of his companions, Brillat-Savarin, was an excellent musician whose many escapades, coupled with the capacity to devour enormous amounts of food, provided Monsieur Nicolas with many a humorous tale which he used in his attempts to dispel his new wife's despondent moods.

Pierre was grateful for the presence of his Aunt Marie and Monsieur Nicolas. The demands of his work were now such that he had little time for his mistress, other than to shop for delicacies which might arouse her appetite or dream up attractive hairstyles which appealed to whatever vanity was left in the young woman.

More and more Pierre found himself being requested to serve people who were prominent in local as well as international circles. He had become a great favorite with all of the Schuylers. Angelica Schuyler Church's daughter Catherine, later to become Mrs. Peter Cruger and one of New York's most beautiful hostesses, introduced Pierre to her wide circle of friends. The Bancels, former members of Louis XVI's guard, continued to conduct a French school. In addition to cutting the children's hair, Pierre was asked to dress the children for parties and sometimes instruct them in the proper decorum for the occasion.

Pierre often wondered if his patrons had forgotten he was a slave, as he sometimes found himself being called upon to advise these prominent persons on matters of the strictest confidentiality. It was ironic to be engaged in an industry where his services were sought by persons from the highest walks of life, to be consulted even on matters of state, and at the same time to be the property of the family he was supporting. Over and over Pierre reminded himself that his saving grace had been the fact that he had never felt enslaved. He was not unmindful of Rosalie's resentment of the state of affairs, but he hoped to purchase her freedom before that resentment turned to bitterness.

Pierre was saddened by the report of Toussaint Louverture's death as a prisoner in April 1803 at Fort de Joux in the Jura mountains. During the months which followed this sad news, he was to hear much about the insurrection on the island now called Haiti.

Then came the report that yellow fever had aided the slaves by depleting the French forces to the extent that LeClerc was defeated before he, too, succumbed to this disease. Then, Pierre learned, Dessalines had proclaimed Haiti an independent nation on January 1, 1804.

The defeat of the French plunged the refugees of New York into a state of despair. Their hopes of returning to their island home and reclaiming their wealth were gone.

Pierre's Aunt Marie and Monsieur Nicolas tried to reassure Madame Bérard-Nicolas that there was still a glimmer of hope as they had heard the slaves were fighting among themselves. But this young woman was slowly losing the desire to live in a world which she decided held only sorrow for her.

Pierre felt helpless when he saw the sadness in his young mistress' eyes, though he could not pretend to be sorry about LeClerc's defeat. He never came home without stopping at a bake shop to select sweets which he thought might make up for the large portions of food the Frenchwoman left on her plate. He was pleased when he discovered that Rosalie, in her own way, was also concerned about the health of Madame Bérard-Nicolas. He had noticed the way his sister hovered over the young woman when serving her meals and how she so attractively arranged the pastries he brought in that Madame Bérard-Nicolas would take one of the cakes from the tray, though she seldom took more than one bite.

Pierre and all of New York were soon to be distracted by another tragedy of national import.

CHAPTER 9

Pierre and History in the Making

Pierre was admiring the trees along Broadway one warm July morning in 1804 as he hurried to his first appointment. The spectacle of the abundant foliage on the trees which had been brown and bare so long during the severe winter turned Pierre's thoughts toward the recurring pattern of his own life. Once more he found himself living in two—now maybe three—worlds. His services were being sought by the wealthiest ladies in New York, who showed him great deference. He was the main support of his owner and her slaves. Yet he, Pierre Toussaint, was still a slave. The lush greenness of the trees reminded him of the mysteries and beauties of the universe and injected a glimmer of hope into his state of being.

Pierre became abruptly aware that crowds of people were beginning to line the street. Some of them were weeping and others appeared to be engaging in animated debate. Pierre slowed his gait. Then he heard the name of Alexander Hamilton mentioned. In a few moments he had heard the sad story of how Hamilton had died as a result of a duel with Aaron Burr, the vice-president. The handsome statesman's wife, Elizabeth Schuyler Hamilton, was a sister of his friend, Angelica Schuyler Church, and the sister-in-law of Mary Anne Schuyler, wife of General Schuyler's son, Philip

Jeremiah. Pierre realized that the crowd appeared to be looking and moving in the direction of Robinson Street, where the home of John Barker and Angelica Church stood. Pierre followed at a discreet distance and watched as the family left the Church residence and the Alexander Hamilton cortege began making its way through Beekman (then Pearl Street), and down Broadway to Trinity Church.

Pierre was glad that he was tall enough to peer over the heads of most spectators and see that the hat and sword of the handsome Hamilton rested on the top of his coffin. There were two white-clad black men leading Hamilton's gray horse, who walked as if he was expecting to feel the weight of the graceful figure of his master any minute, turning his head expectantly from side to side.

Pierre could not force himself to leave this crowded scene until after he had seen Elizabeth Schuyler Hamilton, who rode in the carriage following her husband's body. Though she sat erect in her widow's black, Pierre thought she looked as if she was dazed by the unfortunate circumstances which led to the duel at Weehawken, where Aaron Burr's bullet cut short the life of one of America's most brilliant statesmen and left her bereft.

Pierre shook his head as he tore himself away from the crowd. Like Pierre, Hamilton had begun life in the West Indies. His star had loomed so bright in the Union sky, nobody would have predicted this end to his colorful career. Then Pierre began to remember that he had heard bits of gossip about the bad blood between Hamilton and Burr. He even recalled that Hamilton was said to have been responsible for the deciding vote in the national election of 1800, when the federal electors would have been tied at thirty-six votes for Jefferson and the same number for Burr, if Hamilton's entreaties for Jefferson had not influenced the one delegate from Delaware, who had cast a blank ballot, giving Jefferson the election.

There had also been whispers that Hamilton had disclosed Burr's alleged scheme to run for governor of New York and then lead New York and other nearby states into secession. It had been no secret that Hamilton considered Burr a dangerous man, but the duel had not been anticipated. Now the city and even the country was in mourning. Pierre had no idea that the fabric of his life would be so interwoven with that of the Hamiltons and the Schuylers that it would provide a historical story for generations to come.

The unexpected death of Hamilton started Pierre thinking about his own life. He began to speculate as to how long Juliette would wait for him. She was free; he was still a slave. Would he ever be free? Would Juliette wait, he wondered? He was thirty-eight years old and Juliette was only eighteen.

The jostling crowd reminded Pierre that he was already late for his appointment. He knew that his patron would most likely be so involved in discussing Hamilton's death and the probable whereabouts of Aaron Burr that she would pay little attention to his polite excuse for being tardy.

Pierre almost broke into a trot. He did not want to run too far behind schedule, as he wanted to find time during the day to visit the waterfront in the hope that there just might be a ship in port that had brought a letter from Zenobie. Even if there was no letter, he might still find a sailor who could fill him in on the latest developments concerning Dessalines' efforts to carve a republic out of the government the French had abandoned. His visits were seldom fruitful, but Pierre had learned that patience and persistence were of absolute importance. Otherwise he would not have heard that Christophe, later to declare himself King Henry I, was setting up schools throughout the island. When the sailors insisted that Pétion was ruling the southern part of Haiti, Pierre was so confused that he began to dread these visits to the wharf. Yet he could not stay away for fear he would miss a letter Zenobie had sent or some stray bit of information relating to L'Artibonite.

Pierre's persistence paid off, and one day a sailor handed him a letter from his grandmother. After walking a few blocks, Pierre decided he had better read the letter before he took it home. Zenobie told him that his sister Marie-Louise and his older brother had escaped to Cuba. She also told him about French planters he knew who had succeeded in going to Cuba, a number of whom took their biracial children with them.

It pained Pierre to note the simplicity of his grand-mother's request. Her old scissors were now rusty and she needed a new pair. His mother, she said, needed cotton thread and his father would be happy to receive a pipe. Pierre wondered why his grandmother did not refer to Jean Jacques Bérard's death, then he realized that there must have been letters to him that had been lost. It was obvious to him that while Zenobie had mourned and buried the dead—for Marie Bouquement had learned that Jean Jacques died and was buried at L'Artibonite—the old wo-man was now engaged in a struggle to keep the living alive and healthy.

Pierre would share his letter with Rosalie and his Aunt Marie. When he made a package, the women would add an item or two before he took the box and entrusted it to some sailor into whose hand he placed a coin of appreciation and gave instructions as to who might keep the box for his rela-tives in St. Marc or at the Cap. It was a chance he had to take.

Months later Pierre might learn that his father had been at the old wharf in St. Marc soon after the ship dropped anchor. That made him know that his people were confi-dent he would honor their small requests. One sailor re-ported seeing Pierre's mother Ursule, who had ventured into St. Marc on a donkey. Pierre lay awake many a night thereafter trying to formulate a plan for getting his relatives to New York. Any longing he knew was for a wife named Juliette and his relatives so far away.

As if Pierre did not have enough financial obligations, his friend and spiritual advisor Fr. Matthew O'Brien approached him about the necessity to raise funds for the new St. Patrick's Cathedral to be built at Prince and Mulberry Streets. Fr. O'Brien asked Pierre to assist him in the fundraising effort for this worthy cause. The priest had heard of the esteem in which most of New York's prominent families held Pierre. He was sure that many of them would attend the musicales and other fund-raising activities for the building if they knew their presence would please Pierre.

It was not easy then for Catholics in New York to enlist the aid of prominent New Yorkers. Aside from the French refugees, most of whom retained a genteel if sometimes shabby appearance, the Catholic Church in New York was considered the refuge of poor Irish and German immigrants, who were despised and looked down upon by the early Protestant New Yorkers.

This attitude toward the Catholic Church was largely responsible for the bits of gossip Pierre's sharp ears picked up in early spring of 1805. New York society was astonished to hear that Elizabeth Bayley Seton was frequenting St. Peter's on Barclay Street, some whispered, for the purpose of embracing Catholicism. The widow Seton was the daughter of Dr. Richard Bayley and Catherine Chariton. Her mother's brother, Dr. John Charlton, was known to be New York's most prominent society doctor. Elizabeth Seton's grandfather, Charlton, had been the Anglican rector at St. Andrew's for nearly thirty years. Her late husband, William Magee Seton, had been the son of William Seton, Cashier of the Bank of New York, the state's first such financial institution. The elder Seton was a friend and confidant of Alexander Hamilton, the John Jays and the prestigious Livingston family. William Magee Seton had died in Italy in 1803. So Elizabeth Bayley Seton was by birth and marriage connected with some of New York's most affluent and outstanding families. But New York society was shocked to think that one of their own gentlewomen would seek religious consolation in a church of "unkempt immigrants."

Pierre was most likely pained but also amused by some of the talk he heard about Elizabeth Seton. He had long since concluded that his color often faded under the bright light of admiration which so many of the ladies felt for him as the hairdresser skillful enough to execute a flattering hairstyle which would transform them for an evening's sally. But he was forced to decide that many of them must have also forgotten that he heard Mass each morning at St. Peter's, the church they said Elizabeth Seton was frequenting. His own spiritual advisor, Fr. Matthew O'Brien, was said to be "enticing" Mrs. Seton to forsake her Episcopalian church and accept the Catholic religion.

One or two ladies did remember that Pierre made daily visits to St. Peter's, but when they extended conversations in the direction of asking him if he ever saw Elizabeth Seton at church, he changed the subject.

From time to time, Pierre did see ladies kneeling before the Crucifixion by the Mexican artist José Marie Vallejo on the main altar. But Pierre had refrained from asking Fr. O'Brien about his recent convert. He felt Mrs. Seton was entitled to her privacy, and it was enough for Pierre to know that another soul sought spiritual consolation within the confines of the church to which he made his way each morning and visited later whenever time and circumstance permitted. As in the case of Toussaint Louverture, about whom Pierre heard much but never met, he knew who Elizabeth Seton was but neither Pierre nor Mrs. Seton were conscious of having met. Neither of them was aware of the respective roles they were to play in the history of New York.

In spite of all the precautions Pierre, Marie Bouquement and Monsieur Nicolas took, Madame Bérard-Nicolas somehow managed to acquaint herself with the details of General

LeClerc's defeat. She knew how his forces had been depleted by the ravages of yellow fever until there were scarcely
two hundred of them left to sail back to France. They were
surprised when the French woman even knew of the fighting
between black and biracial troops and the rivalries which
existed between their leaders. Pierre suspected that his mistress had been clever enough to wheedle this information
out of Old Cabress, but they did not question the old slave.
They were more concerned with Madame Bérard-Nicolas'
declarations that there was no longer any reason for her
existence.

Monsieur Nicolas, Pierre and his Aunt Marie refused to
succumb to the gloom which might have pervaded the
household. Instead they made all manner of brave efforts to
distract the grieving woman. Pierre's attempts to whet Madame Bérard-Nicolas' appetite were futile. But she sometimes smiled when Pierre and Monsieur Nicolas took out
their fiddles and played a duet of old French songs. Pierre
always took the lead as he was the more familiar with the
young Frenchwoman's favorites.

Between keeping his appointments, supervising Célie
and Jerome at the shop, overseeing the housekeeping at 105
Reade Street and lending small financial support to the
many people in need who sought his aid, Pierre had little
time to worry about whether Juliette would wait for him, or
matters concerning New York as a whole.

Slowly, however, he became aware that many of the ladies he served became momentarily silent when he entered
their sitting rooms or the chambers where he styled their
hair. This, he noted, was especially true when there were
more than two present at the time of his appearance. There
was always the exception, and always some garrulous lady
who would not be silenced by the frowns of her friends.
Once more Pierre began to hear the name of Elizabeth
Seton mentioned, and he was to learn that the fashionable

Setons were ready to do battle on every available front because, they claimed, Elizabeth had influenced her sister-in-law Cecilia to follow her into the Catholic Church.

As preoccupied as Pierre was with the state of young Madame Bérard-Nicolas' health and his inability to save enough money to buy Rosalie's freedom, he might have forgotten about the Setons if he had not begun to notice a resentment toward Catholics in general. It was so subtle that he sometimes thought his imagination was out of control.

Then came the Christmas Eve of 1806. (The date of this occurrence could not be verified at St. Peter's.) He knew then that he had not been imagining that there was an anti-Catholic attitude among many of New York's citizens. Pierre was horrified by the mob which gathered outside St. Peter's and heckled the Catholic worshipers. It was only after a councilman lectured the mobsters that they dispersed. On Christmas day the Irish retaliated by throwing a ring of defense around the church. Fighting broke out; one man was said to have been killed and several injured. It was only after Mayor De Witt Clinton made a personal appearance on the scene and issued a proclamation banning attacks upon Catholics that peace was restored.

Pierre was glad he had made it a custom not to work on Christmas day because he did not feel he could fashion any fancy hairdos or make polite conversation in view of what had happened. He was glad he had not recognized any of his white friends in the mob which had heckled the worshipers at St. Peter's on that black Christmas Eve.

The day after Christmas, Pierre was relieved that his patrons avoided mentioning the Christmas Eve riot or the death and injuries which followed. If the conversion of Elizabeth Bayley Seton and her sister-in-law had contributed to the anti-Catholic feelings which had surfaced in New York, Pierre knew the poor Widow Seton's personal life must have been a nightmare.

In the meantime there were more homeless black boys whose plight was brought to his attention. He would take them to 105 Reade Street and make sure they were fed and sufficiently clothed to protect them against the weather, which all of the Haitians found discomforting. Then he would give them chores around the house until he could find a job for them in some of the homes he visited. If the boys had no place to sleep, he would provide a pallet for them in the kitchen until other arrangements were made. Pierre often wondered why there were so many homeless black boys and so few homeless black girls. But the girls would have presented a different problem, and Pierre was grateful that it was only the orphaned boys he had to provide for.

The females who did appeal to Pierre for help were usually French refugees whose pride prevented them from accepting public charity. The tactful manner in which Pierre had protected Madame Bérard's reduced circumstances gave courage to other French ladies who found themselves destitute, and they found occasion to pen Pierre plaintive notes begging his understanding of their plight and whatever help he could give them. Sometimes they asked for money, other times for firewood, food or a position. Whatever the request, Pierre found a way to honor it.

It was difficult for Pierre to come in after a day of walking from one appointment to another in order to prepare New York's society matrons and their children for fashionable social functions and find Madame Bérard-Nicolas, whom he loved as if she was his own flesh and blood, pale and listless, half reclining on a settee in her dressing room, with a notebook and a pencil on her lap. Increasing illness had impaired her vocal chords to the extent that she could barely whisper and wrote notes to those with whom she wished to communicate. Pierre had failed in his attempts to titillate her appetite, and even the duets he and Monsieur

Nicolas played seemed to be having no effect. Then Pierre hit upon the idea of reading from a book of French fables. He alternated with the sermons of Massillon and Boussuet, which he had read years ago at L'Artibonite when the elder Monsieur Bérard had first given him the opportunity to read all the books in the Bérard library. Oftimes Elizabeth Bérard-Nicolas would fall asleep as Pierre read to her. Monsieur Nicolas would assist the ailing woman to her bedroom where Marie Bouquement would undress her and sit with her until she fell asleep.

One night when the young Frenchwoman seemed especially feeble and withdrawn, Pierre continued to read as he stole occasional glances at her. Suddenly Pierre was conscious of the great effort Madame Bérard-Nicolas was making. Though she was propped up by pillows she seemed determined to sit upright.

Pierre glanced at his Aunt Marie, who was never too far away, but Marie thought it a good sign for the ailing woman to try to summon whatever strength she could, and refrained from helping her. Pierre saw his young mistress grit her teeth as she reached for her pad and pencil because the effort to sit up had left her too weak to even whisper. He watched her as she wrote a note and handed it to him.

"Promise me that you will always watch over Memin," she said, using her pet name for Marie Bouquement.

Pierre struggled to remain calm as he assured the ailing woman that he would always care for his beloved aunt. He knew then that Elizabeth Bérard-Nicolas had decided she was closer to the next world than to the one in which she had suffered so much sorrow.

Marie Bouquement came to the couch and with Pierre's help assisted the young woman to her boudoir.

"I must pray that her end will be peaceful," Pierre thought as he closed the door softly to go to his own quarters. He was surprised to find Rosalie standing in the hallway.

"How—how is Madame?" Rosalie asked.

"I do not think she will be with us long," Pierre admitted.

Rosalie wept softly for a few moments before she put a hand on her brother's arm. "She can't die yet. I know she can't!"

"What do you mean?" Pierre asked. "She is dying in front of our eyes. Her voice is gone and if our aunt did not put on her fanciest dresses you would see her body has wasted away."

"She can't die yet. I know she can't—she just can't!" Rosalie insisted and ran up the stairs before Pierre could question her further.

In spite of Rosalie's insistence that Madame Bérard-Nicolas could not die, the young woman's condition deteriorated daily. Each evening Pierre sat on one side of the bed and Monsieur Nicolas on the other. Marie Bouquement was in and out of the sick room. Sometimes she insisted on brushing the sick woman's hair or changing a peignoir. Pierre's heart ached for his aunt as he knew how much the sick woman meant to her. He prayed for strength so that he might comfort his aunt and his sister when the end came as he realized that Rosalie loved the dying woman in her own way in spite of all she had said. L'Artibonite was a bond they could not deny.

Early one evening Pierre read to Madame Bérard-Nicolas until she fell asleep. He watched the changing expressions on her face as he realized she must have been dreaming. For a few moments he saw a smile wreath the drawn face as the woman's breast rose and fell in a steady rhythm. Pierre decided she was dreaming of Dondon and L'Artibonite and the beauties of the love which had surrounded her then. For a second Pierre thought he heard her humming a tune, then suddenly she sat up in the bed, looked around her and sank back among the pillows in obvious disappointment. There was only Pierre and Monsieur Nicolas in the room, and Pierre decided she had been dreaming of other loved ones. He was about to call for Marie

Bouquement when the sick woman reached out and pulled at her husband's sleeve.

"At once," she whispered. "Get—get a lawyer—Pierre's papers."

Marie Bouquement rushed into the room and seeing the effort it required for the woman to even whisper, tried to quiet her.

Monsieur Nicolas promised her he would get a lawyer the next day if only she would rest.

"Now—get a lawyer now," the woman insisted. "I've waited too long already. Pierre—my beloved Pierre—must—must—be—free."

Monsieur Nicolas went in search of a French lawyer, whom he knew would have the necessary papers and could draw up the document in conformity with French laws. Pierre sent Rosalie to St. Peter's to get a priest while he knelt on one side of the bed and prayed as Marie Bouquement cradled the sick woman in her arms.

When Monsieur Nicolas returned with the lawyer, a priest, one Fr. Brun from St. Peter's, was already in the sickroom. He had brought Pierre's good friend Jean Sorbieu, also a parishioner at St. Peter's, to act as a witness after Rosalie told him that Madame Bérard-Nicolas wished to free Pierre before she died.

The document was drawn up as Marie Bouquement fought back her tears and rocked the dying woman in her arms much as she had when Elizabeth was a child. Monsieur Nicolas dictated while his wife whispered and nodded her consent. The document which set Pierre free read: "I, the undersigned, Elizabeth Bossard, wife of Monsieur Gabriel Nicolas, declare with the consent of Mr. Nicolas, my husband, that my intention is that Pierre Toussaint, my slave, shall be and live free of all servitude, and I consent that he enjoy liberty like any other freedman, that this present act be given all the public authenticity that it may have. Made at New York, July 2, 1807."

The witnesses who signed were: Marie Bouquement, Jean Sorbieu, Monsieur Nicolas and Fr. Brun. The document ended with formal certifications affixed by the French Chancellor, Jean Baptist Anne Marie Lombart.

Marie held the dying woman up as she reached for Pierre's hand.

Pierre was moved by the manner in which his former mistress tried desperately to thank him.

"I have only tried to do what I thought was right," he protested.

"There is no reward on earth for what you have done," Marie Elizabeth Bossard Bérard-Nicolas whispered as she motioned to Marie Bouquement to remove a locket which contained a miniature of herself from around her neck and handed it to Pierre to keep as a souvenir.

"Memin," she was now barely audible, "Pierre, you must always take care of her. Wherever you go, will you take her with you?"

Pierre assured the dying woman he would always look after her beloved Memin—his Aunt Marie Bouquement—who was still fighting to control her grief.

Monsieur Nicolas kissed his wife and motioned to Marie to ease her down on the pillows. Marie Elizabeth asked to be left with the priest.

Pierre found Rosalie in the kitchen, sobbing with her head on the table. Célie and Jerome sat looking at her with their arms around each other. Even in his grief Pierre noted that this was the first time Célie and Jerome had ever let him see any sign of their devotion to each other.

Rosalie looked up as Pierre tried to console her. "I knew—I just knew she could not die until she set you free," the girl sobbed. "You are a good man—like no other man in this world—and you have earned your freedom."

It was not long before Marie Bouquement came and told them that her *"petit enfant"* was dead. The old woman sat rocking with her arms folded as if she was once more hold-

ing the baby who had grown up to be Marie Elizabeth
Bossard Bérard-Nicolas.

Pierre knew there was no consolation he could give
Marie Bouquement, his sister or Monsieur Nicolas. Instead
he went to his room and fell on his knees to thank God that
he had been in a position to keep the dead woman from
ever knowing want. Then he thanked God for having given
her the courage to grant him his freedom at last.

CHAPTER 10

Ides of August

Life at 105 Reade Street underwent many changes. Célie and Jerome disappeared soon after Madame Bérard-Nicolas' funeral. Though Jerome had been abandoned and nobody could or would lay claim to him, Célie, a slave, was still the property of the Bérard-Nicolas estate. However, Monsieur Nicolas and Pierre agreed that it would have been useless to look for the girl, even if they had been so inclined. The fact that the two had disappeared so quickly, leaving no trace of their whereabouts, was proof that this action had been planned well in advance of their actual leave-taking.

Rosalie explained that Célie had changed after the relationship with Jerome had ripened. Where the two girls had previously shared confidences as well as fears, Rosalie said Célie had suddenly begun to avoid being alone with her. When Rosalie spoke to her about the change, Célie countered by saying it was difficult to have a conversation with Juliette-Noel around so much and that she felt left out of Rosalie's plans.

Marie Bouquement persisted in reminding Pierre that she did not wish to burden him. After a few weeks of listening to the same speech, Pierre was wise enough to realize that his aunt needed to be gainfully employed and made sure his patrons were informed that he could supply an expert seamstress or nurse whenever an emergency arose. A woman who had once been Monsieur Nicolas' slave was found to serve as a cook. Then Rosalie, with the help of the homeless boys Pierre brought in from time to time, took over the role of housekeeper.

Pierre was not unaware of Rosalie's wish that he would marry Juliette without delay, now that he was free. Juliette and Pierre had developed the ability to identify and respect the hopes and aspirations of each other. Old Cabress was so feeble she just puttered around the house. Juliette understood that Pierre would not take this step toward his own happiness until he had first purchased Rosalie's freedom from Monsieur Nicolas.

Though Pierre had admitted to Juliette that he was saving in order to build up a purse for Rosalie's freedom, he had cautioned her not to mention this plan to his sister. Marie Bouquement, too, was aware of Pierre's intentions, more because she understood her nephew so well than because of anything he had said to her. Yet Marie prayed that Pierre would not deny himself the joys of a happy marriage too long.

Pierre still haunted the waterfront and depended on sailors and dock hands for news of his island home. Now he also worried about his sister and brother in Cuba, to whom he sent packages whenever he found a friend or sailor traveling in that direction. He was overjoyed the day his patience paid off and he received another letter from Marie-Louise.

The letter from Marie-Louise (as it appeared in *Pierre Toussaint* by Arthur and Elizabeth Sheehan) acknowledged a letter from Pierre and two packages of tobacco. Marie-Louise wrote:

> I thank you. I am going to pass your letter on to Toussaint [Pierre's older brother]. He is twenty-five leagues from here, but I have learned that he is well. When you wish to write him, always send your letter

through me. I am thankful for the news you send me of my son Victor. If you can get his address in Paris, write to him and reproach him for giving no sign of life. I have no news of Antonie [her daughter]. We must hope that one day I will have the happiness of seeing you again. I miss Jeanne and Saint [most likely pet names for Rosalie and Marie Bouquement]. I advise all three of you to go on with your good behavior so that you will be worthy of Madame's kindness. Mr. Pacaud [who must have been her husband] greets you. We are very miserable here and live with great difficulty. I wonder when we shall get out of this sad position. I wish you good health and am always

Your good sister,
Marie-Louise.

P.S. I have no news of Tonette and *Grandmère*.

Marie-Louise had not known of Madame Bérard-Nicolas' death when she wrote. Pierre duly informed her of the death of *"Madame"* and his freedom. He also told her of his desire to go back to L'Artibonite and bring the remaining family to New York. Later Marie-Louise wrote Pierre and argued against his plan to go back to their home, telling him of confusion and violence he might encounter. She had located their brother in La Trinite but was sorry to tell him that she had received news that Zenobie and Ursule were in great need.

Pierre knew that Jean-Jacques Dessalines, who had declared himself emperor, had been assassinated in ambush in 1806. The mighty Christophe then took over the reins of government and set about building stronger fortresses, schools and palaces, two of which became architectural wonders of the world. Pierre heard that Pétion was still holding forth in the southern part of the island.

One of Pierre's friends, Jean-Baptiste Nelson, who did return to their home, wrote that someone reported to him that he had seen Ursule in Port-au-Prince. Pierre felt helpless to do anything for his family but send letters and packages to them and pray that they reach their destination. His own anguish was lessened when Juliette and her mother reminded him that they had received no word from or about any of their relatives since they were brought to New York by the master for whom they still worked as freedwomen.

Requests for Pierre's help continued. In addition to pleas for food, clothing or firewood, he found himself serving as a nurse to lonely, deserted souls who were ill, oftimes dying. Though the priests at St. Peter's came and went, they all soon knew they could depend on Pierre to assist with the destitute ill and did not fail to call on him.

August was a month all New Yorkers approached with prayers and trepidation. It was the month of the plague. New York's water system, laid in 1776, consisted of a network of pitch-pine timbers. Though it was general knowledge that the system was far from adequate, no steps were taken to remedy the situation. Pigs and other animals roamed the streets. Housewives closed their shutters to avoid the sight and smell of servants going to the river to empty nightpots. Some said the plague was cholera. Others said it was yellow fever. One of Pierre's patrons told him that a few years back the plague had claimed the life of the well-known Dr. Bayley, father of Elizabeth Bayley Seton, the young widow who had shocked Protestant New York by becoming a Catholic. There were still those who insisted that "dirty immigrants" had brought some strange disease to this country.

Pierre stopped in St. Peter's frequently. As requests for help with the stricken poured into the rectory, the pastor, Fr. O'Brien, turned to Pierre. Yet the August after Pierre had received his freedom was a time when Rosalie and his Aunt Marie had hoped he would not expose himself to the plague. Already people had begun to flee to higher ground up around Greenwich Village.

They could hear guns booming, and the wheels of the hearses announced their approach. Some said the firing of gunpowder destroyed germs. There were those who went around wrapped in long cloaks which they had soaked in vinegar. Others resorted to smearing themselves with tar, niter and garlic.

Rumors abounded the day Pierre's Aunt Marie had rushed home early to wait for her nephew and beg him not to take unnecessary risks. Already she had been told that the plague had claimed a life. When she heard a knock at the door, the old woman felt a degree of relief. That, she hoped, would be Pierre.

Marie Bouquement knew Rosalie was also concerned. Though she had discouraged all of Rosalie's attempts to criticize Pierre, Marie knew that they were as one in the hope that Pierre would at long last have a chance at the happiness of marriage with Juliette. Without discussing it, the old woman and her niece had only to look at each other to know they were both secretly hoping that Pierre would not insist on nursing the plague victims this year.

Marie continued to sew on the garment she was making as she heard Rosalie run down the stairs to open the door. She listened for Pierre's voice. Instead she heard Juliette's cheerful greeting.

Marie strove hard to hide her disappointment from the lovely girl who glided into the kitchen where Marie was working and planted a kiss on each of the older woman's wrinkled cheeks.

"What a lovely kerchief you are wearing on your head," the woman said. "It matches your dress, and I'd love to know how you drape it so becomingly."

"That is my secret," Juliette teased. "Your nephew has already complimented me several times. And what is the garment you are sewing, may I dare to ask?"

"It is a shirt for Pierre—as if you did not know," Marie laughed.

"Why not a dress for yourself?" Juliette asked as she examined the garment Marie was making.

"I promise you," Marie's needle was still, "I promise you I

will make a dress to wear to the wedding—yours and Pierre's."

It was then Juliette's turn to blush and fumble for words. Rosalie was enjoying it all until she heard a loud knock at the door. She recognized it as her brother's manner of notifying them that he would soon use his key if nobody opened the door for him.

"He is here," Rosalie hissed. "He will have the latest news."

"What news?" Juliette asked. "Are there new developments?"

"Patience!" Marie whispered as she rose to meet her nephew.

"Is it true?" the old woman asked. "I've heard rumors."

"I'm afraid we are in for another bad spell," Pierre admitted. "They are putting up the barricades. On my way home I passed a building they said was empty, but I heard a woman scream. I must go back there after I make sure I have in my bag everything I might need."

"I do not understand," Juliette said. "I stopped to talk to a group of friends at the market and nobody told me that the plague was spreading."

"We heard there have already been deaths," Rosalie said. "But I don't know why Pierre has to go. There are doctors and nurses. Why does he always have to take this risk?"

"There are not enough doctors and nurses," Pierre commented sadly. "And some of them have themselves fallen victims to this sickness."

"What about you?" Juliette asked quietly. "What—what would we do without you, Pierre?"

"Didn't you hear that the plague does not strike us?" Pierre laughed at his own sarcasm.

"I know a few of *us* who were buried last August," Marie said quietly.

"We have to take it—" Pierre began his usual affirmation when Rosalie interrupted.

"You think of everybody but yourself—and—and those who love you," the anxious girl sobbed. "You took care of Madame all of those years, and now that you are free you're still acting like you are some white man's slave who has to go out and nurse all of the—the relatives he left to die." Rosalie was so agitated Juliette put her arms about her to reassure the girl.

Pierre's Aunt Marie continued to sew without looking up from the garment. He stood in front of the old woman for a second before he spoke. "I must wash up before I go out. Please be so kind as to get the satchel I keep in the hall closet. I think most of the supplies I may need are in the bag. I will bring the prayerbook with me when I come downstairs."

"Do you have to go? I'm sure Fr. O'Brien is doing all he can," his aunt said.

"He is only one man—and a priest, not a nurse."

"Neither are you," Rosalie persisted in spite of Juliette's efforts to quiet her.

"*Ma chérie,*" Pierre gently pushed Juliette aside and kissed his sister's forehead, "I forgive you for your anger as I know you speak from a heart overflowing with love and concern for me. And there is some truth in what you say. I have never truly felt I was a slave to any man or woman, but I am a servant of the almighty God who made us all. When one of his children is in need, I am glad to be *his* slave. And as for me not being a nurse, have you already forgotten about *Grandmère?* Do you not remember how she nursed everybody—as well as the animals—at L'Artibonite? Do you not remember the small patch where she grew herbs from which she made medicines for the sick? Or have you forgotten how Ursule nursed everybody when the sickness came to L'Artibonite while Zenobie was traveling? You helped, too, when even our own brother was bathed in the sweat of his fevered body."

Pierre's effort to console Rosalie only made her weep

harder. "I—I could not bear for anything to happen to you. You are all I have," she sobbed.

"Shame on you," Pierre chided. "You have our aunt here and Juliette," and he left the kitchen to prepare for what he knew he must do.

The three women were standing by the front door when Pierre came down the steps. His aunt handed him the satchel which he opened and examined before he added the prayerbook.

"I will walk you home before I go back to Maiden Lane," he told Juliette when he noticed the frightened expression on Marie Bouquement's face.

"I've heard there was a death there, and that the people have all fled," the old woman whispered.

"I heard a scream and a plea for help as I passed what was supposed to be an empty house with barricades all around it. That is why I must go back."

"They will jail you for climbing over the barricades," Rosalie moaned.

"Then Fr. O'Brien will get me out of jail," Pierre smiled as he held the door open for Juliette. He cast a reassuring glance at his aunt, whom he knew would spend the next few moments lecturing Rosalie on her lack of faith even though she knew better than the girl the risks Pierre would be taking.

For a while Pierre and Juliette walked in silence. "I wish I could go with you. To help—if you need me," she said.

"Knowing that you will be waiting and praying will make me take every possible precaution," Pierre assured her.

Once Pierre saw Juliette open her door he hurried without looking back. Remembering what Rosalie had said, he grew even more serious. "If only they knew how much love there is in my heart for all of them," he mumbled to himself and then laughed at the thought that a possible passerby might have thought him already delirious.

When he reached the house where he had heard the

woman screaming, Pierre looked around to see if there was anyone else in the apparently deserted street. Then he quickly jumped over the barricade and went in the house to search for the woman, praying that he was not too late.

A surprised Pierre found a weary, bewhiskered and grateful Fr. O'Brien praying with the woman. He could smell the fever as she tossed and turned, and Pierre immediately went in search of water. Cold compresses on her head seemed to give the woman some relief. Then Pierre glanced toward Fr. O'Brien, whom he knew had had little sleep since the plague struck. Exhaustion soon overtook the priest, who was already half asleep, his prayerbook on the floor.

Pierre took out his own prayerbook and read until the woman, too, dozed. Then he prayed that God in his wisdom might spare her life. He washed his hands carefully, emptied the basin of water and awakened the priest, who anointed the woman before they went out into the darkness and jumped the barricades.

As they walked toward their homes, the two weary men were silent. Pierre still had a few blocks to go after Fr. O'Brien left at St. Peter's. Rosalie's outburst had more of an effect on him than he had realized at the time. Then Pierre stopped in his tracks, smiling as old memories cast a different light on Rosalie's concern. "I sometimes forget that Rosalie, too, is the grandchild of the clever Zenobie. She knows I can never fully enjoy my freedom until she, too, is free. She has heard me say I would hope her to be a free woman when she marries that young Noel. It was vain of me to think that love for her brother is her only concern. But I must take the necessary steps to secure her freedom as soon as possible."

After Rosalie's initial outburst that first August following Pierre's freedom, his sister refrained from comment when he went out with his bag to care for the stricken. He figured that Juliette and his Aunt Marie, without a doubt the two women who knew him best, had told her that only death or imprisonment would prevent him from ministering to the victims of the plague. But when Pierre realized that he was saying more prayers for the recovery of the stricken than prayers for the dying, he conferred with Fr. O'Brien and they agreed that this August's plague had run its course.

Then Pierre remembered that as far back as 1793 he had heard about two black men in Philadelphia, Richard Allen and Absalom Jones, who had recruited nurses to care for the victims of the plague. These two men, he heard, had even volunteered to remove the bodies of those who perished from the disease. But after the crisis had passed the white community expressed the unified opinion that blacks were immune to the disease which had felled such large numbers of Philadelphia's citizens, and little gratitude was shown for the services the black men had rendered.

"If only they knew how many black men's eyes I have closed in death," Pierre thought, "they would never bless us with this false immunity."

Pierre was amused when he remembered the number of times he had seen men entrusted with carrying out the law which forbade citizens to cross the barricades during the crisis, turn their heads when he jumped over the hobby-horses which had been set up to keep people away from the contaminated victims. Yet whatever immunity God had granted him was not taken lightly, and he said many a prayer of thanksgiving.

Pierre had neglected his patrons during the most crucial days of the plague. Going over his books, he discovered that he needed to start collecting monies due him if he planned to buy Rosalie's freedom any time soon.

"Madame," he might say, "did I remember to thank you for the last token of esteem your servant brought to my shop?"

That graciously asked question never failed to remind delinquent patrons that Pierre's bill was past due. But when he observed the signs of genteel poverty materializing in homes where the abundant life had previously been evident, he made his usual rounds without pressing for his fee.

Each week—even day by day—brought Pierre closer to realizing his determination to purchase his sister's freedom, though there was no day when he did not also look forward to making Juliette his wife. During this period Juliette detected a sense of expectancy in Pierre and assured him with a smile here and a nod there, or sometimes when they parted at night with a kiss and crossed fingers, that she understood.

Pierre's working hours were so extended that his courtship of Juliette was more or less confined to her presence at 105 Reade Street, when he came home for a late dinner and he would walk her home. The night he told her he would most likely be coming home early the next day and would be pleased if she could arrange to be there, Juliette felt fairly certain she knew his reason for making this request.

Rosalie was giving the cook final instructions for the evening meal when she thought she heard a knock at the door. It was so early she wondered who could be calling at this hour. Rosalie was just beginning to wipe her hands on her apron as she heard the heavy old knocker again. When she opened the door to see Monsieur Nicolas and Pierre waiting to enter, Rosalie made no effort to hide her amazement. The men ignored the astonished expression on the girl's face and swept past her, but before Rosalie could close the door she saw Juliette running up the steps.

"Am I too late?" Juliette was panting.

"Late for what?"

"Pierre asked me to meet him here, but I had to go on an errand for my mother," Juliette explained as she followed Rosalie into the kitchen.

Rosalie was in the process of talking with the cook, who had been one of Monsieur Nicolas' slaves, when Pierre and Marie Bouquement appeared. Pierre guided Rosalie to an empty chair without saying a word. Then he handed her a long, official-looking envelope. As soon as Rosalie saw "Empire Français" on the envelope, she started crying.

"Open it first," Pierre said quietly. "That is a document to be preserved. It should not be stained with tears."

Rosalie obeyed her brother's suggestion and dried her tears with the tail of her apron before she opened the envelope.

"I don't understand all of these words but I know they mean I am free!" the girl cried. "Oh, Pierre, I know you must have sacrificed so much to pay Monsieur Nicolas for my freedom. Jean will not be marrying a slave. There is nothing to hold our wedding up now. And I owe it all to you."

"You owe me nothing," Pierre protested as Juliette and Marie Bouquement, who both knew how many times during the intervening years Pierre had thought he had enough money to purchase Rosalie's freedom when the needs of the household or a plea from some unfortunate soul had depleted his savings, exchanged glances.

"Would you be so kind as to read it to me—aloud?" Rosalie handed the document to her brother.

When Pierre had finished reading the document which the French Consul had drawn up for Monsieur Nicolas in return for Pierre's savings, he politely informed his sister that he was a hungry man. Marie Bouquement set the dining room table for Monsieur Nicolas while Juliette began finishing the meal Rosalie and the cook had started.

Rosalie did not move. "It's not right. It's just not right!" she blurted.

Juliette smiled when Pierre demanded that his sister explain herself.

"I think I know my friend better than her own brother," Juliette laughed.

"You bought my freedom and I am going to marry the man I love, but what about you and Juliette?" Rosalie demanded.

This picture by Nathaniel Fish Moore is the only photograph known
to have been taken of Pierre.

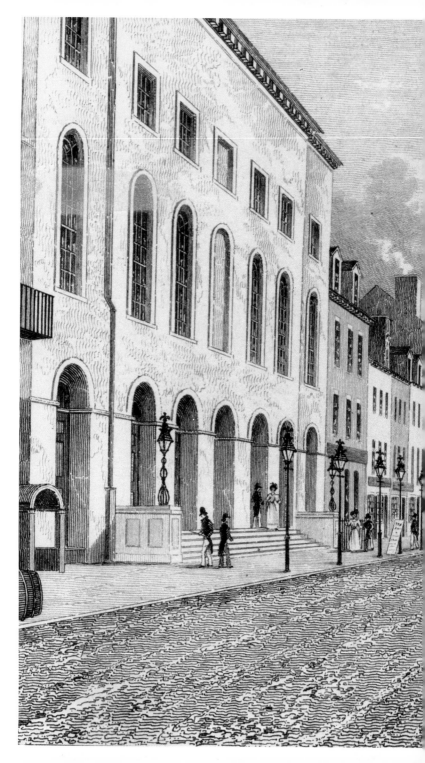

ark Theater with St. Paul's Chapel to the right. Pierre always
remembered passing St. Paul's Chapel on Lower Broadway that
first day in New York when he had to walk from the wharf to the
house that Jean Bérard had rented on Reade Street.

Pierre was a constant visitor to the wharf at the foot of Wall Street during his first years in New York. The men shown in the picture to the left are in front of a popular coffee house.

© Collection of The New-York Historical Society

H. Fossette.

E   SLIP.

(treet)

Baron Hyde de Neuville, who settled in America after he fled from
France and Napoleon's displeasure. His wife, the Baroness de Hyde,
was a famous painter, and this photograph was made from a watercolor
executed by the Baroness. For a short time Baron de Hyde conducted
a French school but later turned it over to Victor Bancel. Pierre was
often asked to come to his school to cut the hair of the pupils and to
instruct them in manners and dancing.

Marie Elizabeth Bérard-Nicolas, Pierre's young mistress, who had been the wife of Jean Jacques Bérard, Pierre's master and friend. The profusion of curls in the hairstyle the young woman was wearing when this picture was taken demonstrates the care and concern Pierre showered on her. She gave Pierre his freedom on her deathbed.

College Place and Murray-street.

The home of J. C. Stevens at College Place and Murray Street later became a part of the original Columbia University campus. John C. Stevens was a partner in a quarry business with Philip Jeremiah Schuyler, the son of General Schuyler and husband of Mary Anne Sawyer Schuyler, one of Pierre's closest friends. After the steamboat became a reality, the Stevens family set up a ferry service between New York and Hoboken, where they turned part of their country estate into an amusement park known as the Elysian Fields, where the sports of baseball and cricket were introduced to New Yorkers.

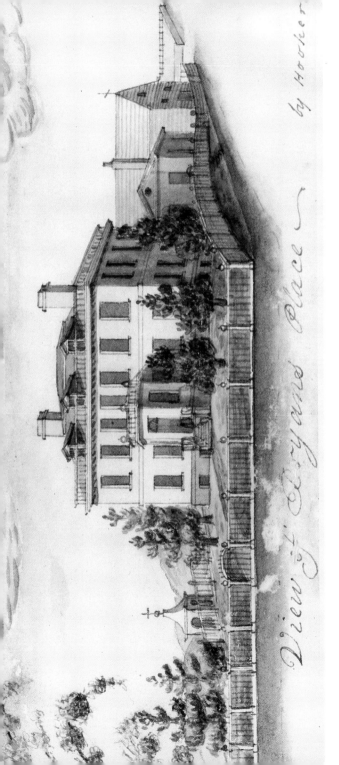

View of Schuyler Place ~ by Hooker

The Philip Schuyler home, near Albany, NY, was a gathering place for the children and grandchildren of General Schuyler, a hero of the Battle of Saratoga. They always remembered General Schuyler's appraisal of Pierre: "I have known Christians who were not gentlemen, gentlemen who were not Christians. I know one man who is both, and that man is black."

Philip Jeremiah Schuyler, son of the famed General Schuyler and husband of Mary Anne Sawyer Schuyler. Philip often said that his wife and sons turned to Pierre whenever they needed a solution to a problem. The photographs of Philip J. Schuyler and his beautiful young wife were taken from paintings by the celebrated artist, Gilbert Stuart.

Mary Anne Sawyer Schuyler, wife of the son of the famous General Schuyler, was one of old New York's most renowned hostesses. Her sister, Hannah Sawyer Lee, wrote the first book ever published on Pierre's life. Mrs. Schuyler often referred to Pierre as "my saint Pierre." He spent much time devising hairstyles to shift attention from the full face of his loyal friend, when he dressed her hair for the evening. The Schuyler home was Pierre's last stop of the day. Mrs. Schuyler's sons, husband and entire family shared her admiration for this gentle black friend.

George Lee Schuyler, the son of Philip Jeremiah and Mary Anne Schuyler. Along with his brother, Robert Lee Schuyler, he was appointed executor of Pierre's will. Pierre had known the boys from early childhood and their correspondence with him has been preserved. George Lee married Eliza Hamilton, the daughter of James, Alexander Hamilton's third son.

Pierre's wife, Juliette Noel. After he married her, Pierre knew more happiness than he had thought was possible on this earth. Juliette not only encouraged Pierre to continue his many acts of charity, but she took an active part in his endeavors. Their home became a cheerful gathering place for Pierre's friends and patrons.

Euphemia, the child of Pierre's sister, Rosalie, and Jean Noel, was born on September 16, 1815. When Pierre's sister asked that he name the baby, he gave her the name of the saint of the day. When Rosalie's husband abandoned her and her child, Pierre took them to his home, where Rosalie later died. Pierre then adopted Euphemia and she added another ray of happiness to his life and Juliette's life.

Pierre often took little Euphemia here to the Battery to enjoy the invigorating cool breezes from New York Harbor. By the time Euphemia could toddle, her antics delighted the many people who gathered about the waterfront. Pierre insisted that the sea breezes were beneficial to Euphemia's health. To the right can be seen the famous Castle Garden.

The first St. Patrick's Cathedral at Mott and Prince Streets. Pierre was a conscientious fund raiser for this effort on the part of the Catholics of New York, who at that time were mostly immigrants or the children of immigrants. Pierre was buried in the cemetery at Old St. Patrick's Cathedral.

© Collection of The New-York Historical Society

St. Peter's Church, at the corner of Barclay and Church Streets, as it looked in 1831. Pierre attended Mass here every day. A plaque has been placed on the front wall of the church in his memory.

© Collection of The New-York Historical Society

Cardinal John O'Connor (second from right) is shown after officially opening the cause of Pierre Toussaint. Left to right are: Msgr. Robert M. O'Connell, vice postulator; Msgr. Michael J. Wrenn, President of the Historical Commission; Rev. P. Carlos Lizarraga, C.P., postulator; Cardinal O'Connor and Bishop Norbert M. Dorsey, member of the Historical Commission.

John Cardinal O'Connor turning the first spade of earth at Old St. Patrick's cemetery in preparation for the exhumation of Pierre Toussaint's remains.

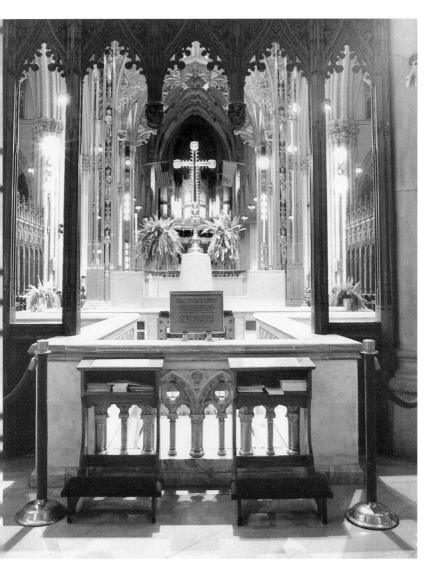

The Pierre Toussaint prayer kneeler, next to that of Terence Cardinal Cooke, behind the main altar of St. Patrick's Cathedral.

Pierre Toussaint's prayer kneeler, behind the main altar and opposite
St. Mary's Chapel at St. Patrick's Cathedral.

Close-up of the prayer on the Pierre Toussaint prayer kneeler at St. Patrick's Cathedral.

CNY/ Chris Sheridan

Following the ceremony at St. Patrick's, Waldemar Roebuck, director of the Pierre Toussaint Guild, and Ellen Tarry, author, are shown at the last resting place of the remains of Pierre Toussaint.

Haitian choir and worshippers at St. Jerome Catholic Church in Brooklyn sing praises in honor of Pierre Toussaint.

Fr. Guy Sansarique, pastor of St. Jerome Church, Brooklyn, (right front) and Msgr. Robert M. O'Connor, vice-postulator (rear), are shown in procession before a Mass honoring Pierre Toussaint.

Fr. Guy Sansarique, pastor of St. Jerome Church, Brooklyn, (right front) and Msgr. Robert M. O'Connor, vice-postulator (rear), are shown in procession before a Mass honoring Pierre Toussaint.

Young girls from St. Jerome's Church shown in procession at the concert in Pierre's honor at St. Paul the Apostle Church. Their grace and native attire add to the beauty of the occasion.

Haitian choir and worshippers at St. Jerome Catholic Church in Brooklyn sing praises in honor of Pierre Toussaint.

Pierre pulled Juliette away from the stove where she pretended to be busier than she really was, and placed an arm around her shoulder. "Juliette and I will take it as God sends it and I hope it is his will that we, too, will be man and wife before too long."

"There you go again," Rosalie began to cry, "putting everything on God. And you know you are not getting...."

"Don't you dare remind me that I am getting older," Pierre shook his finger in mock seriousness.

"I think we have had enough of the *whys* and *whens*," Marie Bouquement said as she rejoined the group. "Pierre has already said he is hungry, and if you really appreciate all he has done for you," the old woman looked at Rosalie, "you will feed your brother."

"Agreed!" Pierre laughed and opened the kitchen door to Monsieur Nicolas who had come to offer a bottle of wine for the celebration.

Pierre paused with his head still bowed after he said grace over the delayed meal. For the first time, he had said a prayer exclusively for his own happiness—his and Juliette's.

CHAPTER 11

A Touch of Fulfillment

Pierre found it delightful, in the days which followed Rosalie's freedom, to watch Juliette and his sister as they went about the happy task of preparing for Rosalie's marriage to Jean Noel. Yet Pierre had some reservations about the prospective bridegroom. He remembered how his sister, upon seeing the document which declared her freed from slavery, had said there was nothing to prevent her marriage to Jean—now that *she was free.* Rosalie's brother could not help wondering about this strange, shadowy young man who avoided him. Jean was a member of the Noel family that had settled in Baltimore after they fled St. Dominique. Though Pierre was not clear as to the exact relationship between Jean and Juliette Noel, he was reluctant to damage his rapport with Juliette by criticizing Jean. It was obvious that Rosalie and Juliette were oblivious to the misgivings Pierre was having about the approaching nuptials. So he remained silent.

On May 21, 1811, one week after Rosalie became a free woman, she married Jean Noel at St. Peter's Church.

Though Rosalie's happiness was apparent to friends and relatives alike, her leavetaking from 105 Reade Street, where she had grown from little more than a girl to a married woman, was tearful. Juliette and Pierre attempted to assure

her that they all would exchange frequent visits. But Pierre
had the distinct feeling that the bridegroom was impatient
with his new wife's insistence on turning back several times
to embrace her brother or kiss her Aunt Marie, Old Cabress
and Monsieur Nicolas' cook.

"Now you are really free," Marie Bouquement told her
nephew afterward.

"I wonder," Pierre frowned.

"Pierre!" the old woman spoke sternly as Juliette
dropped her eyes.

"If you mean I am free from financial responsibilities,"
Pierre smiled, "you are right. But I have little left to offer my
own bride other than my love and devotion. I will speak to
Madame Claudine and inform her that it is my ardent desire
to marry her daughter, Juliette—if she will give her permission."

"She will—oh, I know she will!" Juliette declared.

"I was afraid both Claudine and I would be dead before
you came to the conclusion that God would give you
permission to seek your own happiness," the old woman
commented before she left Pierre with Juliette, who was
beaming over the strange, anti-climactic proposal for which
she had waited so long.

Pierre could not refrain from thinking about all the
changes which had taken place since Madame Bérard-
Nicolas' death. He was free and in turn so was Rosalie, now a
married woman as well. Pierre wrote the family at L'Artibonite of events as they transpired, but for some time he
had not even had a scrawled note from Zenobie.

Pierre had heard that Christophe had lost hundreds of
men in a battle with Pétion on the island now spoken of as
Haiti. Fr. O'Brien had been replaced at St. Peter's by a
Jesuit, Fr. Anthony Kohlmann, who besides becoming pastor
had been made vicar-general, to act until such time as New
York should be given a bishop. In the meantime Pope Pius
VII was still at Savona, where he had been spirited by

Napoleon's emissaries who had arrested the Holy Fr. because he had dared to excommunicate the Emperor. The Pontiff refused to name any new prelates or perform other expected duties until he was given his freedom. So Fr. Kohlmann was vicar-general for a bishopless diocese. In addition to his priestly duties, he also had to raise money for the construction of the new cathedral to be built at Prince and Mulberry Streets.

After Pierre spoke with Claudine Gaston, Juliette's mother, who had also waited a long time for this conversation, he shared with Monsieur Nicolas his intention to marry Juliette. The Frenchman was delighted and asked Pierre if he would permit him to serve as a witness at the ceremony.

Pierre expressed his preference for the third floor quarters at the Reade Street house. Though the Frenchman had the money from Rosalie's freedom, Pierre had always been the one who paid the rent to Abraham Bloodgood, the owner. Since Pierre had supported the household as long as Gabriel Nicolas could remember, the Frenchman could not have denied Pierre any part of the house he wanted. The first floor was taken up with sitting rooms, parlor, dining room and kitchen. Monsieur Nicolas, Marie Bouquement, Cabress and the cook occupied the second floor. He knew that Pierre had chosen the third floor to save Marie Bouquement and Old Cabress from having to make the effort to climb the steps.

Juliette, too, understood why she was to live on the third floor of the house where her husband would be paying the rent. As soon as the date for the wedding was set, she busied herself with making the quarters to which she would come as attractive and cheerful as she could.

Marie Bouquement was happy to become a part of Juliette's decorating team, and her handy needle-stitched draperies and coverlets enabled Juliette to transform the third floor into a bridal chamber. This marriage was an answer to the old woman's prayer that God spare her to see

Pierre happily married. In a way Juliette had taken the place of the daughter Marie had left in St. Dominique whose fate was still in doubt.

Marie and Juliette tried to involve Rosalie in planning for Pierre's wedding, but Pierre's sister seldom had much time to spend with her relatives or her friend Juliette. They had discovered that Jean Noel was intensely jealous and never wanted to find his wife out when he came home.

August 5, 1811 was to be the happy day. There had been no sign of the plague so far. Marie Bouquement had already reminded Juliette that she, too, had better pray that the plague was either late or did not strike this year. "Otherwise," the old woman teased Juliette, "you might be standing at the altar waiting for a groom who has turned nurse."

It was as if God was smiling on the patient Pierre and his understanding bride as there was not even a cloud in the sky to mar their wedding day. Fr. Kohlmann presided over the ceremony at St. Peter's. Gabriel Nicolas, Pierre's close friend Jean Sorbieu, along with Jerome Willagrand, John Benjamin, Donatien Cilardy, Bernard Etienne and all of Juliette's friends and relatives were present. Rosalie and Juliette's mother wept throughout the ceremony, but Marie Bouquement's radiance was only surpassed by that of the bride; God had answered her prayer and she was at peace with the world.

Pierre's aunt and Juliette's mother had made all the arrangements for the reception at 105 Reade Street. From the time Monsieur Bérard had gone back to L'Artibonite, it was the first party there that Pierre did not finance out of his savings and provide the music for as well. The women, with the help of Monsieur Nicolas, made sure that Pierre and Juliette's reception was as beautifully appointed as had been the many parties he had arranged for Madame Bérard and her sisters. Monsieur Nicolas, who contributed a part of his dwindling reserve, also provided the music.

Pierre had cautioned his relatives against mentioning his

marriage to any of his patrons, but Marie Bouquement knew there were a few ladies she often worked for who would have been hurt if they had not been told. Juliette was wise enough to know that many of the useful gifts which Pierre's Aunt Marie displayed so proudly had been the result of the old woman's guidance to the donors.

Juliette was so beautiful in her bridal white that her groom found it hard to gaze other than on her radiant face. He, too, in his dark suit with the white shirt and ascot his Aunt Marie had made, was an imposing figure.

The novelty of a party not of his giving threatened Pierre's usual composure. It was almost as if he never expected to be happy after having seen and shared so much sorrow. Juliette, however, had never had the slightest doubt that she would one day be Pierre's wife. Her dream had come true, and the bride gently placed her hand on Pierre's arm to remind him that the guests were waiting for them to lead a dance.

Rosalie, too, exuded the joy she felt over her brother marrying her best friend. The girls embraced each time they were near each other, and Rosalie said she hoped Célie would hear about the wedding—wherever she and Jerome had gone.

Pierre noted that Jean Noel stayed to himself when he was not with his wife or Claudine. At the height of the festivities, Juliette and Pierre, hand in hand, passed Rosalie and Jean as Rosalie was telling her insistent husband why she was not ready to go home. Juliette flinched and that was the only time during that happy day that anyone saw what might have been interpreted as a frown on Pierre's face.

Gifts arrived at the Reade Street house for weeks after Pierre's wedding. Pierre was still inclined to be concerned lest his patrons think he had expected these presents.

His Aunt Marie replied to his remarks on the subject by borrowing one of his pet phrases. "These gifts," she insisted, "are only *small tokens of esteem* from your patrons."

"My patrons pay me for services I render. Why should they also send gifts? And just who informed them?"

"No patron can pay you for all the things you do for them," the old woman declared. "You dress and style their hair, you cut their children's hair and teach them manners, as well as French and French songs. You find servants for your precious patrons and present them with poseys on anniversaries, birthdays and special occasions. Can't you learn to receive sometimes instead of always having to give?"

Juliette was surprised at the manner in which Marie Bouquement took Pierre to task and waited expectantly for her husband's reply.

The stern expression on Marie Bouquement's face vanished as her nephew enveloped her in an embrace before he spoke. "Give Pierre time," he teased. "I am forty-five years old with a wife twenty years my junior and patrons who shower me with gifts. I am not experienced at accepting so much love and generosity at one time."

Pierre sometimes felt like pinching himself to make sure he was the happy man who approached his home each night to an attractive young wife awaiting his return after a long day, with the aroma of an appetizing meal permeating the house, once the door had been opened for him. Pierre teased Juliette by telling her she had spies posted along the way so she knew just when he would be arriving. The truth was Juliette had waited so long for Pierre that she had become familiar with his habits and could almost time his arrival. Sometimes in the midst of a meal Pierre would sample some dish which evoked memories of his childhood. He had reason to suspect that his aunt shared her culinary secrets from Zenobie and Ursule with his bride. He had begun to learn how to receive as well as give, so he refrained from asking his wife how she became an expert on ways to appeal to his appetite.

Juliette began to invite Pierre's friends into their home. She had decorated the third floor quarters so tastefully that even Monsieur Nicolas and Marie Bouquement sometimes wondered if they were in the same rooms. Pierre was not unmindful of the fact that Juliette always managed to include some friend who had fallen on hard times among any guests she invited.

In small ways Juliette relieved Pierre of responsibility for the house. Since their courtship had been forced to thrive on their goings and comings, she had come to know many of the merchants with whom he shopped. Pierre had never stopped to consider how closely he had to budget his time in order to obtain provisions and supplies for the Reade Street house and attend his shop. Now Juliette anticipated their needs and begged his advice on how and where she should obtain them.

Once or twice Pierre chanced to pass the Oswego on Broadway near Maiden Lane while Juliette was shopping. He watched from a distance as his young wife accepted the freshest produce at prices which she found acceptable. Pierre was impressed by the pretty picture she made as she bargained with the storekeepers. Her attire was always as cheerful as her smile, which he decided sprang from the well of kindness which dictated her pleasant disposition.

Marie Bouquement did what she could to help the young bride, but the old woman's physical condition limited her ability. Like Claudine, she was so pleased with this marriage that the two older women talked of little else beside Pierre and Juliette and how they both hoped that God would bless the union with children. Old Cabress, who had become more withdrawn, only shrugged her shoulders and sucked her teeth.

However, there was one small concern. Rosalie did not visit the Reade Street house as much as her aunt and her friend had expected. Juliette suspected that Rosalie's infrequent visits were the result of her husband's jealousy. Juliette then began stopping by the place where Rosalie lived when she was fairly certain Jean Noel would not be at home. When Pierre came home, Juliette would regale her husband and Marie Bouquement with some silliness she and Rosalie had discussed or some memory of past events which they had resurrected. Pierre, who knew his wife so well, decided that Juliette was making an effort to prevent him from feeling hurt because weeks passed between his sister's visits. He also suspected that Juliette felt certain loyalties to Rosalie's husband, who was a member of her family.

Pierre would have been even more concerned if he had known that Juliette always carried a dish of food when she stole a visit with Rosalie. Marie Bouquement observed the circumstances of Juliette's friendship with Rosalie and added one more petition to the litany she said each night.

Then Pierre seemed to find more homeless black boys than ever before. He would bring them home and make a place for them to sleep in the cellar until he could find someone who would hire them or take them on as an apprentice. When a new boy showed up before the older ones had been placed, Marie Bouquement teased Juliette by telling her that the boys smelled her good cooking and waited outside for Pierre so they could tell their sad stories, having heard that Pierre never turned a hungry boy away.

Pierre's business continued to prosper. He kept one boy as an apprentice and another to take messages and run errands. Though hairstyles changed from the elaborate powdered poufs and twists piled high on the ladies' heads that Mr. Merchant had first taught Pierre to execute, he had been quick to learn to style the wigs and perukes which became so fashionable at the time of the French Revolution. He foresaw that the day of the wigs would pass and studied whatever periodical he could find, besides listening to women who had returned from distant travel. Pierre's uncanny ability to anticipate the new hairstyles, some of which he actually created out of necessity, won the continued acclaim and demand of New York's most fashionable ladies.

Few if any other black men were welcomed into the

homes that Pierre frequented. The wealthy French ladies patronized him as much for the pleasure of listening to his polished French, which the Bérards had taught him, as for the fancy hairstyles he created to enhance each face and personality. Most of the ladies would have been even more pleased if Pierre had dropped a morsel of gossip now and then. But he remained a master of evasion when he knew one patron was curious about another's affairs.

The Schuylers, Hamiltons, Crugers and the Churchs, as well as the LaFarges and Binsses regarded Pierre more as a confidant. When a child was awkward, Pierre was sent for to cut his hair and then instruct him in the proper decorum for the social event he was to attend. When a servant was taken ill, a message was dispatched to Pierre's shop. He found a replacement and sometimes suggested a remedy until a doctor could be found.

Juliette was pleased that Pierre's patrons sought his aid in finding servants. Otherwise she and Marie Bouquement would have been cook and waitress to a small army of homeless black boys. Though Pierre had advised them to keep the boys busy, there was only so much to be done in one house. On the occasions when Pierre had an urgent request for a butler or waiter, he would rush home and instruct the most likely candidate, then apologize to Monsieur Nicolas when some strange black boy served his evening meal in order to gain the experience Pierre would have to vouch for.

Before Pierre and Juliette could celebrate their first anniversary, the country was once more at war with England. The year 1812 also produced more unemployment which meant Pierre brought more homeless boys to 105 Reade Street. After several victories by the British, New York was in a panic, and feverish preparations were begun to prepare for an attack. Pierre added his boys to the crowd of men, women and children who worked day and night to rebuild gun emplacements along the Battery, which had been unused since the Revolutionary War.

Pierre had to admit that he worked almost as hard at dispensing advice as he did at his trade. It was common knowledge that he never turned anyone away without a kind word or a dole. Yet there were times when even Pierre's resources were taxed. The homeless black boys could be housed, clothed and fed, but the genteel white ladies who were forced to shed the last vestiges of pride and appeal to Pierre for help presented a different problem, as he often confided to Juliette.

One French lady was advised to accept a small number of students to whom she would teach French. Then there was another lady who had been making clothes for her entire family as their resources dwindled. Marie Bouquement had been ailing and was unable to go to the homes of Pierre's patrons for whom she had been sewing. So Pierre notified those patrons that he would deliver any garments they had in need of altering to an excellent seamstress, as one way of launching his needy friend on a new career. Juliette aided her husband in all of these charitable schemes. Sometimes she even suggested solutions.

Then came the first sadness; Marie Bouquement fell seriously ill. During the happy months following his marriage, Pierre had failed to realize how feeble his aunt had become. Some days she did not leave her room until evening, and Juliette had been reluctant to shock Pierre into recognizing his aunt's condition. Roles reversed and it was Old Cabress who now looked after Marie Bouquement.

Juliette told her mother there was hardly a day when the ailing woman did not persist in talking to her about her relatives back at L'Artibonite, the Bossard family and her lost daughter Adéle. There was also hardly a day when Marie failed to tell Juliette how happy she was that she had married Pierre, and reminded her of his virtues.

Juliette's mother had told her it was often this way near the end of a long life. So in a way Claudine prepared her daughter for the death of this old woman who had prayed that her nephew would marry before she died.

Marie Bouquement died the last week in August 1812. She was buried on August 30 in the "Catholic ground," the new cemetery at Prince and Mulberry Streets where St. Patrick Cathedral was being built.

The war years were busy but happy years for Pierre. He still worried and prayed about his family at L'Artibonite, but he continued to send packages, knowing the chances that they would receive them were slim. He reasoned that whoever received the articles he sent would need them. Though Pierre was now too busy to visit the waterfront each day, he continued the habit of stopping by from time to time for a possible chat with the many seamen he had come to know. His island home had been declared the kingdom of Haiti in 1806 with Christophe ruling as King Henry. Though the seamen continued to tell Pierre about the schools, roads and bridges that King Henry was constructing, they also told him about the many palaces the ruler had built and the battles he engaged in with those who opposed his rule.

Juliette pointed out to Pierre that he seldom came home from one of his visits to the wharf in a happy mood. "You are fortunate," she reminded him. "Other than the cousins who were taken to Baltimore and my restless brother Gaston, my mother and I do not know if we have another living relative."

"Madame," Pierre enjoyed feigning formality with his wife, "you speak much truth—as always. It is not befitting for me to be sad and question the generosity of the same God who blessed me with one of the loveliest ladies in New York for a wife."

Pierre did not stop his visits to the waterfront, but if he was disturbed by the news he picked up from the sailors and dock hands, he kept from Juliette his fears for his relatives' safety. Yet he never ceased to pray for the ones he had left behind. When Pierre decided to make a will it included provisions for any relatives who might survive him.

The British burned the city of Washington in August 1814. Once the report spread that the recently built White

House had been burned, the New Yorkers were convinced that the British fleet would soon sail into their harbor and start a bombardment.

Pierre admonished those who approached him with stories of what had happened in Washington and the fate likely to befall New York, and he told them that they did the citizens a disfavor by creating a mood of gloom and fear. He could not help but think of the stories he had heard about the repressive laws against blacks which had been passed in the federal city since the seat of government had been moved there in 1800.

There was increased excitement in September 1815 when a British fleet appeared off the shores of Baltimore and troops landed. Then came the bombardment of Fort McHenry and the awful *bombs bursting in air* that inspired Francis Scott Key to write *The Star Spangled Banner.*

Juliette had decided she could no longer keep Rosalie's plight from Pierre. Rosalie was expecting a baby and was having a most uncomfortable pregnancy. Jean Noel was lazy as well as jealous. There were many days when Rosalie would have gone hungry if Juliette or Claudine had not brought food to the expectant mother. Pierre had attempted to talk to his brother-in-law, who made no secret of the fact that he wanted nothing from Pierre—not even a job. As was his habit, Pierre included Rosalie's welfare in the petitions he made each morning when he and Juliette went to St. Peter's for Mass. While making his daily rounds, Pierre tried to find delicacies for Rosalie just as he had for his young mistress when she showed little inclination to eat. Juliette became Pierre's emissary, as they had agreed that any confrontation he might have with Jean Noel would upset Rosalie.

Pierre had reached the point in his thoughts concerning his sister's condition where he felt her health and the health of the baby she was to bear were of such importance that he would have to find a way to help her, in spite of her husband. Once he prayed over a situation and gave it sufficient thought, there was no stopping him.

That evening in September when Pierre came home after a long day to discover that Juliette was not at home, he had already decided that they could better care for Rosalie if she was moved back to 105 Reade Street. But the house was empty. Not even the cook nor Monsieur Nicolas, who seemed to be away more than he was at home these days, answered his call.

The house was dark and Pierre realized Juliette had been away for some time, as she never permitted him to come home to a dark house.

Wearily Pierre lighted the lamps and sat at the kitchen table while he pondered his sister's situation and tried to figure how he could persuade her to come to live with him again. He heard the door open and rose to greet his wife. Juliette's face showed the strain of a long, difficult day.

"How is she?" Pierre sensed a certain anxiety in his wife.

"The baby was born today," Juliette slumped in the chair Pierre had so recently vacated and covered her face with her hands.

"What is wrong?" Pierre demanded. "Are they both alive—and well?"

"Barely," Juliette answered. "Rosalie has been sick so long and it was a hard labor. My mother is with her now."

"I must go to her at once," Pierre said.

"It will do no good—she is asleep and needs to rest. You would only disturb her."

"And the baby?" Pierre asked.

"She is so tiny," tears ran down Juliette's cheeks. "The doctor does not have much hope for her."

"Oh," Pierre smiled, "that means it is a girl. I finally have a niece. And the father—is he proud?"

"Nobody knows where Jean is," Juliette admitted.

"How long has he been missing?"

"For days. I know I should have told you before," Juliette admitted, "but each day we would hope to have some news of him."

Pierre put a reassuring hand on his wife's shoulder. She had begun to sob from fatigue as well as relief that she was no longer keeping a secret from her husband. "As soon as Rosalie can be moved we must bring her and the baby here," he said.

"And you are not angry with me?" Juliette asked.

"How could I be angry with one who has been an angel of mercy to my sister? And the baby's name?" Pierre asked.

"I forgot to tell you," Juliette smiled. "Rosalie told me to tell you that she wants you to choose a name for her daughter."

"Today is the Feast of St. Euphemia," Pierre heard himself saying. "So the baby will be called Euphemia."

Pierre was suddenly filled with a longing to see this newborn baby on whom he had conferred the name of the day's saint. At the same time he felt a need to cherish and protect the child whose father had abandoned her and the woman who had mothered her. He had never realized before how much he had wanted a child of his own. Now a jealous, lazy and shiftless man had given him a child, and he was filled with a happiness he had never known before.

"My joy has conquered my hunger," Pierre joked. "A strong cup of coffee with a roll and whatever fruit we have in the house will serve as supper for little Euphemia's uncle. I can tell that her aunt is too weary for heavy food." Pierre went about brewing the coffee and hunting for rolls to make a light meal, while his weary wife watched him with relief.

Pierre sniffed the aroma of the coffee he drank and spread preserves from a jar he remembered his Aunt Marie had made the year before.

"I'm hoping this coffee will revive you," he teased his wife. "We must set about the business of preparing a room for our sister and our niece. I will move them as soon as the doctor permits me."

CHAPTER 12

A Small Miracle

Weeks passed before Rosalie was strong enough to be moved. There was still no news of her husband. Pierre had conferred with his friend, Dr. Francis Berger, who emphasized the fact that whatever hope there was for Rosalie's recovery and the survival of her baby depended on nursing care and nourishment. The doctor admitted to Pierre that Rosalie was in the advanced stages of tuberculosis and that there was a possibility that she had transmitted the disease to the baby.

"Is there any hope for my sister?" Pierre asked.

"I have done all in my power," the doctor admitted. "It is unfortunate that Rosalie's condition was not brought to my attention earlier. As for the baby—I am amazed that she is still alive. Pierre, you have helped so many others; I wish I could do more for you."

Pierre was to remember the doctor's words several times on the day they were moving Rosalie and the baby to the Reade Street house. Rosalie's eyes were closed and she was either coughing or gasping for breath. The baby was so still; Pierre kept praying that God would give him a chance to make them both comfortable before either of them were taken from him. Once they were safely settled and Rosalie opened her eyes and smiled at Pierre he felt a surge of hope.

He knew Juliette and her mother would nurse Rosalie. From then on it was the baby he worried about, prayed for, and attended during every moment he was in the house.

Pierre had a shop at 56 1/2 Chapel Street. Most New Yorkers traveled about the city in their carriages or on horse-drawn trams, which attracted customers by the tinkling of the bells around the horses' necks. But Pierre, as a black man, was not allowed to ride the trams. He had to walk from one appointment to another. Yet when Juliette or some friend complained about this situation, Pierre reminded them that he met many friends on foot that he might not have seen if he had been permitted to ride the trams.

Dr. Berger was surprised that Rosalie and the baby continued to cling to life. Once or twice the doctor stopped by the Reade Street house when Pierre, with the baby bundled in blankets, was starting out for a walk. He explained to the doctor that it had been his experience that fresh air was the best possible remedy for one so young who had trouble breathing. The doctor could only shake his head as he watched Pierre make his way toward City Hall Park where he would sit and croon to the tiny baby until she fell asleep.

Rosalie, too, had confounded the doctor. Though she was in the advanced stages of incurable tuberculosis, she continued to fight death. Some nights neither Pierre nor Juliette dared sleep for fear Rosalie would not be alive when they awoke. But the young mother pulled through each crisis, and with the first gust of strength asked about her baby. Then there were the other nights when Juliette sat by Rosalie's bedside while Pierre hovered over the baby. Pierre still went to early Mass at St. Peter's each morning. Juliette could not go with him until weekends when her mother came and sat with the two patients.

After the winter winds had blown all the leaves off the trees at City Hall Park, Pierre would sit in the warm kitchen with little Euphemia and sing French lullabies to her. Sometimes he said his evening prayers with the sleeping child in the crook of his arm. Over and over he begged God to spare her life, always aware that it would be a miracle if this frail child lived.

Juliette was delighted with the change which had come over Pierre. He had never expressed his longing for children, and yet, she reasoned, the longing must have lain dormant for years. He never came home without bringing something for the baby. He brought gifts for Rosalie, too, but Pierre's overriding concern for the baby was apparent to all who knew him. Rosalie, too weak to properly express her gratitude, could only smile with appreciation for the love and care her brother lavished on her child.

Claudine Gaston had written the Noels in Baltimore, but nobody seemed to know what had happened to Jean, Rosalie's husband. The sick woman's fierce desire to live until she knew her baby was out of danger appeared to overcome the heartbreak of being abandoned. There were times after a fit of coughing when Juliette thought she saw sparks of determination in Rosalie's eyes.

"Sometimes it's as if her body has given up and only these eyes are alive," Juliette told Pierre one night. "They are always watching. But she listens, too. If the baby whimpers, when I go back to her room she manages to ask how she is."

Rosalie understood that the baby was kept away from her most of the time for the baby's protection. Though Pierre and Juliette took every precaution, neither of them could bring themselves to deny her the joy of seeing Euphemia once each day.

By the time Christmas came, Pierre was telling himself that Euphemia was his small miracle. Juliette's mother remembered broths and other concoctions they gave babies of Euphemia's age back on the island. Pierre encouraged them to try anything he was told would make Euphemia strong.

Pierre's patrons had also heard about Euphemia, and they expressed their appreciation for Pierre by sending Christmas gifts for the baby. Though Pierre had previously insisted that his patrons paid him and had no need to make gifts, he beamed each time Juliette showed him some present which had arrived for the baby.

Monsieur Nicolas was seldom at 105 Reade Street. A group of religious activists had succeeded in closing the theaters and thrown many musicians out of work. When the slave who had been his cook disappeared, Pierre and Juliette suspected that the Frenchman had sold the woman to obtain money. They also suspected that he avoided the house because of the nature of Rosalie's illness, but was reluctant to offend Pierre.

Friends who called to wish the Toussaints holiday greetings told Juliette they had not seen Pierre so happy since the day of his wedding. The baby was in his arms or on his lap whenever he was in the house, and he gave a meaning to each gurgle or grimace the infant made. When Euphemia began to smile Pierre was ecstatic. Juliette was watching him from the doorway to the kitchen the first night he tickled the baby under her bony little chin and she laughed. Then Pierre began talking to Euphemia in a mixture of French and English, which was as close as he could come to baby talk.

"I do believe the dignified Monsieur Toussaint is addressing his niece," Juliette teased.

"She actually smiled at me," he insisted.

"After you tickled her under her chin," Juliette reminded. They both laughed in relief.

Pierre was suddenly silent as he looked down on the small child. He was remembering the long-ago sea voyage which brought him from St. Dominique to New York. They had encountered one storm which tossed the ship from side to side. But it had finally subsided without any more warning than when the first spray flooded the decks and sent all the passengers to their cabins and staterooms, where they had huddled in fear. Pierre remembered how he held Rosalie and Célie, trying to quiet them as he silently asked God to hold the winds and calm the waves. That prayer had been answered and now the baby was smiling up at him, even though Dr. Berger had said it had little if any chance to live.

Later that night Juliette watched him as he knelt on the prie-dieu outside the room where they slept. She knew he was thanking God for sparing little Euphemia. Pierre was so happy she could not find it within her soul to wonder why God had not blessed them with a child of their own.

In January news of Andrew Jackson's victory at New Orleans reached New York. Already Pierre had heard some of his patrons say the war was over since a treaty had been signed. But all sorts of rumors—some of victory and some predicting doom—persisted until February. The Treaty of Ghent had indeed been signed two months before between the British and the Americans. But it was not until a sloop, the *Favorite*, sailed into the harbor bringing the treaty that New Yorkers finally heard they were no longer at war. Then bedlam did reign!

Pierre, who had come home early, heard the din and walked over as far as Broadway. He saw crowds of people marching with lamps, torches or whatever illumination they could find to light their way as they celebrated the end of this disastrous war.

Pierre hurried back home to assure Juliette that the noises they heard were sounds of celebration instead of doom. People were dancing in the side street, and Pierre had a hard time disengaging himself from one merrymaker who had imbibed more than his share of spirits.

Though Juliette had remained in the hallway between the room where Rosalie lay glassy-eyed with a consuming fever and the room where Euphemia was asleep, Pierre slowly explained the jubilation over the end of the war. Then he watched her throw off the tenseness of the protective figure she had presented when he returned.

Soon after the war ended, Pierre had occasion to remember the day he started down Broadway and saw the Alexander Hamilton funeral procession. This time New

York was paying the last tribute to Robert Fulton, who had earlier made history with his steamboat. Pierre remembered the rivalry between Fulton and the Stevens family, all of whom were friends of the Schuylers. He heard the guns booming as the cortege made its way to Trinity Church.

In the face of death Pierre usually looked back and weighed the blessings God had bestowed on those who peopled his world. Just this past spring, Bishop Jean Louise Lefebvre Cheverus of Boston had dedicated the new St. Patrick's Cathedral at Prince and Mulberry Streets, still an area considered a wilderness by most New Yorkers. Bishop Cheverus, later destined to be elevated to an even higher office in the Church, had been a spiritual father to the Native Americans in Maine and a servant and advisor to the poor Irish immigrants of Boston. Pierre, who had worked so hard to help raise funds for the construction of the new church, thrilled at the sight of the ecclesiastical splendor and beauty of the ceremony of dedication. As happy as Pierre was about the new church, he knew that the bishop they had been expecting for so long, regardless of who he was, would have to depend on all the Catholics of New York to support the new cathedral. Pierre also knew that meant he would have to help.

It was during the period when little Euphemia's life was still uncertain that Pierre heard Napoleon had met his waterloo and been banished to St. Helena. Pope Pius VII had returned to the Vatican and appointed a Dominican, John Connolly, to be the first bishop of New York. Yet months were to pass before the new bishop arrived. Fr. Anthony Kohlmann, the pastor at St. Peter's, returned to Georgetown University where he had previously served on the faculty. Fr. Charles D. French was Pierre's new pastor. Archbishop Carroll of Baltimore—which had become the first Catholic diocese in America—had died in December shortly after he had the joy of knowing that Pope Pius VII had assigned a bishop to New York.

Pierre decided he had much for which to be grateful. He was resigned to the knowledge that Rosalie was dying but hopeful that Euphemia would survive. He was glad that this first winter of Euphemia's life promised to be reasonably mild. Pierre looked forward to the approaching spring when he could take the baby to City Hall Park or even walk all the way down to the Battery.

Pierre had a special problem. He had a hard time keeping track of his age. There had been so many changes in his life it was difficult for him to realize that he was slowly approaching the half-century mark. Nobody but Rosalie and Juliette even suspected Pierre's true age. Even Old Cabress, who had appeared to become more alert since the death of her friend Marie Bouquement, was not sure. He was still tall, erect and always well groomed. It was not unusual for people who passed him on the street to turn around for a second to look as they speculated about the identity of the imposing-looking black man.

Stories of Pierre's charity and good works were spreading. His patrons made no secret of the many extra services he rendered for which he refused recompense. He only asked that he be remembered in their prayers. Pierre had more work than he could handle alone. He had trained a couple of his homeless boys to cut the children's hair and assist him when he went to a household where a number of ladies insisted that he fashion a series of his flattering hair styles for them.

Each morning at Mass, Pierre gave thanks for the delayed beauty which now cloaked his everyday life. He was well aware of the suffering of other men of his race and the efforts they were making to throw aside the yoke of slavery. Being more humble by nature than his imposing appearance indicated, Pierre reasoned there was only so much he could do. He determined to use whatever talents he possessed to the best possible advantage in the world around him. He substituted good works for the open confrontations he continued to avoid.

Euphemia was the focal point of Pierre's concern. Juliette had concluded that their childlessness had been preparation for nurturing this little one. Though Rosalie was only clinging to a weak spark of life, a sort of euphoria settled over the Toussaint household. Juliette's mother Claudine looked forward to joining them each evening when her work was finished.

Then one stormy night when Euphemia was almost seven months old it looked as if Pierre's dream would be shattered. Euphemia began choking and the effort to breathe caused convulsions. Juliette closed the door to Rosalie's rooms so she would not hear the baby. Pierre sent one of the boys for Dr. Berger.

It was late and the storm was raging when the doctor opened his door and saw the little black boy standing on his steps, water dripping from his clothes.

"Which one is it?" The doctor knew the boy had been sent by Pierre.

"The baby," the sleepy boy mumbled and shivered.

Dr. Berger hated the thought of going out in the storm. But there was no way he could forget the many times there had been nobody to attend his patients but Pierre.

"Run ahead and tell him I will be there as soon as I can dress," he advised the boy. "If Pierre refuses to give up, I can't either," he told himself.

When Dr. Berger reached the house, he found the door open and Pierre standing inside out of the rain. "Come, there is not a moment to lose," he urged as he took the doctor's coat and led him up the steps to the gasping child.

Juliette, sitting beside the child's cradle, stood when the doctor entered the room. "If you could just help her to breathe," she begged.

"Get another pillow for her head," the doctor ordered as he opened his bag and prepared to examine the child who was struggling for breath. He shook his head as he eased the bony little body from side to side.

Juliette stole a glance at Pierre, whose face was like a mask. She knew her husband was probably praying, but watching the doctor as he worked over the frail little body only filled her with fear.

"I can remember the day she was born," Dr. Berger frowned. "I never thought she would live the night through. Now it is how many months later?"

"Euphemia will be seven months old in a few days," Pierre spoke up before he went to get another pillow to put under the baby's head.

Dr. Berger watched Pierre as he propped up the child. "I wish I could give you some hope," he said. "But there is nothing I can say or do. Children born of tubercular mothers seldom survive. You must prepare yourselves...."

"There must be something you can do, Dr. Berger," Pierre insisted.

"I have long since done all I could. Each time I have been here to see Rosalie I have marveled that either of them was still alive."

"I do not believe she will die!" Pierre persisted.

"Look at this tiny body," the doctor pulled back the covers. "You say she is seven months old, and I've seen babies who had more flesh on them when they were born."

"Her mother was always small," Pierre would not give up.

"My good man," Dr. Berger put a hand on Pierre's shoulder, "I'm afraid you will have to accept the inevitable."

"I will accept God's will, but I do not believe Euphemia is going to die."

The doctor sighed. "Few men have your faith, Pierre. Perhaps that is stronger than any medicine. Now, how is Rosalie?"

"I will take you to her," Juliette offered. "I closed the door to her room so she would not hear the baby. But Doctor, I must insist that you have a cup of coffee before you go out in that rain again."

Juliette preceded the doctor to Rosalie's room and lighted a lamp so he could see his patient.

"Why are you awake?" the doctor asked as he lifted the wasted arm to feel Rosalie's pulse.

"Why—why are you here?" she managed to ask. "Is she—my baby all right?"

"You didn't tell me why you were awake," the doctor evaded Rosalie's question as a torrent of rain beat relentlessly against the window pane.

Rosalie managed a wan smile and pointed toward the window, indicating the rain had kept her awake. Dr. Berger teased Rosalie about staying in bed so much and talked about people they both knew in order to take Rosalie's mind off the reason for his visit.

Later as the doctor sat in the kitchen enjoying the coffee Juliette had poured in a huge mug, he heard Juliette, who had gone back upstairs, chuckling outside the door. Dr. Berger looked up expectantly when she entered the kitchen.

"What is it?" he asked.

"Euphemia opened her eyes, and Pierre insists she smiled at him," Juliette was smiling, too. "He says the baby knows that prayer is more powerful than your medicine."

"For his sake," the doctor shook his head, "I hope he is right. There is almost nothing else I can do—except go out in this rain again."

The next day the baby showed no signs of the illness which had sent her into convulsions the night before. Pierre went around smiling and sniffing the air. The sun was shining and except for the wet cobblestones, the streets gave little evidence of the thunderstorm and rains which had broken window panes and showered riverlets on the sidewalks.

"Spring is here!" Pierre insisted. "I can smell it. In a few days it will be warm enough for me to take Euphemia to the park."

From the time of Euphemia's recovery, Pierre believed

that the little girl's welfare and education were all a part of God's plan for him.

While Pierre was marveling at the wonders of another spring and thanking God each day as he emerged from the house and saw the green buds on the trees, he received a note at his shop from a Madame Brochet asking him to come to the City Hotel. Pierre knew most of the French families, but he could not recall anyone named Brochet. But for that note he would have been on his way home. The thought of little Euphemia, who had shown signs of recognizing him, made him impatient. He toyed with the idea of sending one of the boys to tell the lady he was busy and could not come on such short notice. The name of Brochet continued to puzzle him. Could this be some French lady from his island home who had made her way to New York?

Pierre was familiar with the City Hotel. Each year he styled the hair of New York's most socially acceptable ladies for the dances given by the City Assembly at this hotel, to which only New York's elite were invited. Though City Hotel had been the scene of many of New York's most famous entertainments, it was also headquarters for important foreign visitors.

Pierre, whose curiosity had been aroused, made a quick compromise. He had brought a bright red ball for Juliette to hang over Euphemia's crib because he insisted the child was too long to continue sleeping in a cradle. He would hurry by 105 Reade Street, leave the ball with Juliette for the baby and then go to the City Hotel to see who this Madame Brochet was.

However, Pierre could not resist the temptation of showing the baby the red ball. It did attract Euphemia's attention, and that made him even more reluctant to leave home again. The thought of disappointing some French lady who must have been recommended to him forced Pierre to tear himself away from the child and make his way toward City Hotel.

Pierre turned at Broadway and walked south. To his left he saw the beautiful new City Hall, now nearing completion. Even detractors who had complained about the site being on the outskirts of town had to admit that the almost-completed edifice was stately and beautiful.

Many of them still complained that a half-million dollars was too much to pay for this building designed by the architects John McComb and Joseph Mangin.

Even the new City Hall could not take Pierre's mind off Juliette and Euphemia as he walked toward City Hotel, which stood next to Trinity Churchyard. Still, there was a softness in the air which he found delightful. He would finish whatever task awaited him and hurry back home.

Pierre was well known to the desk clerk, and when he handed the man the note a porter was instructed to show Pierre to Madame Brochet's suite. A maid opened the door and announced that the hairdresser had arrived.

The woman welcomed Pierre in French, and she was so delighted at his reply she continued to talk as Pierre opened his bag, put on a white apron and gave the curling tongs to the maid to heat over a brazier of coals. He placed all the other instruments of his trade on the dresser, then asked Madame Brochet how she wished her hair styled. Once that had been decided, Pierre began his work.

"There are many fine French families here," Pierre told her.

"I am sure. I have met one or two ladies I would have liked to know better. One of them recommended you, and the desk clerk assured me I would be pleased with your service. But one has to be so careful about making new friends. If only my closest friend Aurore could have come with me, things would have been different. But Mademoiselle Bérard—that's Aurore—insisted she could not come at this time."

Pierre quickly pulled the hot tong from a curl. It was too much to expect this woman to know the Bérards from St.

Dominique. If so, who was Aurore? Perhaps the wife of one of the Bérard sons.

"Madame," he managed to say, "Bérard is a name I know well. I was with a family of Bérards in St. Dominique—many years ago."

"Aurore is from St. Dominique—though I hear the slaves call it Haiti now," Madame Brochet said, remembering all her friend had told her about the family and their habitation.

Pierre did not wish to appear foolish and regained his composure before he spoke again. "The Bérard family I knew lived at St. Marc. They had four daughters and four sons. I did not know Aurore Bérard. The daughters of the family at L'Artibonite were Eulalie, Victoire, Felicite and De Pointe, who was my godmother."

"Astonishing!" the woman exclaimed. "Aurore *is* De Pointe. Her father changed her name during the Revolution. He thought De Pointe sounded too aristocratic. The other sisters are all married and living away from Paris."

"Her parents?" Pierre made himself ask, though he felt he knew the answer.

"Dead—long since. Aurore is all alone. She told me how they lost everything during the slave's uprising. I suspect she has money problems."

"Tell me more about her," Pierre begged as he made himself continue to curl Madame Brochet's hair.

Suddenly the woman pushed aside the hand holding the curling tongs and stood up. "You," she said, "must be one of the slaves who came to New York with her brother Jean Jacques to escape the troubles."

"I am," Pierre struggled to control his emotions. "Monsieur Jean Jacques went back to St. Dominique to try to reclaim what he could for the family and died from pleurisy. I remained with young Madame Bérard until her death. She gave me my freedom on her deathbed."

"How extraordinary!" the Frenchwoman exclaimed and began to chatter about her friend Aurore.

"Madame," Pierre implored, "please allow me to finish styling your hair. Then I shall beg of you to give me more news of my godmother and her family."

Pierre imagined he was arranging his godmother's hair and created a style that Madame Brochet proclaimed "magnifique!" when he handed her the mirror to inspect his work.

As Pierre settled down in a chair near Madame Brochet, he kept remembering how he had toyed with the idea of not coming to her hotel. It must have been God's will, he decided, that this meeting take place so he would know where and how the Bérards had fared. If only, he wished, he could find someone who had visited L'Artibonite.

Madame Brochet was also moved by this chance meeting. Though she knew her friend Aurore would be delighted, she was aware of the effect this was having on the black man who had styled her hair as elaborately as any hairdresser in Paris.

Pierre asked about the sons, Lester, Des Glajeux and Du Pithon. Lester was dead, but his wife and son were still in Paris. Aurore did not see much of Des Glajeux, and Du Pithon had married an American girl.

Pierre related the highlights of his life with the Bérards in New York and how Jean Jacques had apprenticed him to Mr. Merchant. He mentioned his aunt, Marie Bouquement, and how she had gone back to St. Dominique with Madame Bérard's sisters but was never able to get to L'Artibonite. He traced the decline of Madame Bérard's health to the death of Jean Jacques, but glossed over the manner in which he had supported his young mistress. They were both overcome by this meeting. Pierre, who seldom showed his emotions, left hurriedly after thanking Madame Brochet for giving him information about his godmother, but not before he had expressed the wish that Aurore might visit New York.

Pierre walked along Broadway like a man in a trance. He was so lost in thought he almost passed Reade Street. Later that night, after he had made sure little Euphemia was asleep, he heard the front door open and, peering over the staircase, saw Monsieur come in. Pierre greeted the Frenchman and asked to speak with him. Juliette, who was in a curious dither, was also invited to join them downstairs in the parlor, where Pierre related the story of his appointment with Madame Brochet and all she had told him.

Pierre's wife and the Frenchman were amazed that a chance encounter would have produced such a pleasant result.

"I am sure you will write Mademoiselle Bérard," Juliette smiled, and Gabriel Nicolas spoke of the Bérard sons he had known during his childhood.

Pierre knelt longer than usual on his prie-dieu that night. He looked in on his sister and covered the one foot little Euphemia always seemed to wiggle out from under the cover. His grateful reverence for God was overcoming, and he had to pray out his appreciation.

It was late afternoon of the next day before Pierre could get to the City Hotel to give Madame Brochet the letter he had written the night before. He had a feeling from what her friend had said that Aurore Bérard was not well supplied with this world's gifts. Pierre chuckled as he thought of how he had sent Rosalie to gather flowers out of which he had made garlands for his little godmother when they were children. He could remember his mother Ursule shaming him when he cried because De Pointe was going off on a ship that would take her to Paris.

"At least," Pierre squared his shoulders as he walked through the door of the City Hotel, "at least she will know her godson is loyal and in a position to share whatever he has with her. Where would I be if her father had not encouraged me to read and write? And her brother insisted that I should have a trade at which I could make a living. Yet little did he know how many my trade would provide for."

Pierre greeted the clerk and asked for Madame Brochet.

"She is not here," the man answered.

"Then I will leave this letter for her to deliver to a friend when she returns to Paris."

"Her ship sailed this morning. She is already on her way to Paris," the clerk announced.

A feeling of deep disappointment came over Pierre. Then he remembered he had been so excited to meet someone who knew the Bérards that he had neglected to ask Madame Brochet when she was returning to France. He consoled himself with the knowledge that Madame Brochet would be sure to tell her friend she had met her godson, now a freedman and a coiffeur in New York.

Juliette, who knew how excited Pierre was over his encounter with a friend of the Bérards, was waiting for Pierre. She saw the letter he had labored over still in his hand but refrained from questioning him until he told her what had happened.

"I am sure Mrs. Cruger or the de Neuvilles will find her for you and deliver the letter," she consoled.

Pierre knew that his young friend Catherine Church, who had married Peter Cruger, would be delighted to deliver a letter for him to Aurore. Baron Hyde de Neuville was now the French ambassador to the United States. The ambassador and his artist wife were friends Pierre valued. He knew he would find his godmother, but he still had a fear that she was lonely and in financial difficulty. He wanted so much to assure her of his love and offer whatever assistance he could.

"It is a matter to pray over," Pierre told Juliette before he went upstairs to see Rosalie and Euphemia. He sat with Rosalie for a while and reminded her of how they had played with his godmother so many years ago at L'Artibonite and how he insisted that she gather flowers out of which he made garlands for the little French girl. Rosalie tried hard to recall, but the memory of De Pointe, who had become Aurore, was like a shadow moving across a blurred screen to the sick woman. She sensed her brother's excitement and hoped he would hear from his godmother.

Pierre remembered Aurore in his prayers each morning during the Mass at St. Peter's. He took Euphemia for walks and sat in City Hall Park. As the weather improved he could pull back the blankets in which he had wrapped the baby, and he found himself telling the child about how George Washington had taken his position near where they sat to bid his weary troops farewell at the end of the Revolution. He'd point down Barclay Street toward the corner where St. Peter's stood, and the child's eyes would follow the movement of his hand.

Now and then people would pass who knew Pierre and stop to ask about the baby or to peer at the tiny face in the middle of so many blankets. Pierre sometimes chuckled at the puzzled expressions he saw on the faces of persons sitting nearby. He was never sure whether they thought him a little crazy when they heard him talking to Euphemia or whether they wondered about a man in his middle years having a young baby. But Pierre enjoyed the outings in the park, and he decided Euphemia was thriving on the fresh air, tenderness and concoctions Juliette and her mother were feeding her.

It was almost three months after Madame Brochet left New York before Pierre had any news of his godmother. The letter, dated November 27, 1815, reads as follows:

> Madame Brochet, on her return to this city fifteen days ago, has given me news of you, my dear godson. I as well as my brothers and sisters are truly grateful for the zeal you have shown in wishing to learn something of us and for the attachment you still feel for us all. After the information Madame Brochet gave me, I don't doubt that you will be glad to receive a letter from me. I write to you both with pleasure, and I am glad to learn that you are prosperous in your affairs and very happy.
>
> As for us, we have never left Paris. Our situation is not

a happy one, for the Revolution deprived us of all our property. My father was one of the victims of that frightful period. After being confined six weeks in prison and, under constant inspection of the government, to their own place near Paris, he and my mother died of grief.

My sisters and brothers are married, but I am not and am compelled to make efforts to live which have impaired my health which is now very poor. Were it not so I might be tempted to take the trip you desire, but I am not the less sensible to the offers you have made through Madame Brochet, and I thank you most sincerely. It is something for me to know that amidst all my troubles there exists a person who is so much attached to me as you are. I wish I could live in the same town that I might give you the details by word of mouth about my family....

Write to me, my dear Toussaint, about your wife. I know you have no children. Do you know anything relating to St. Dominique? What has become of all our possessions and our former servants? Tell me all you know about them. Have you any of your former companions in your city? My nurse Madeline and your mother—are they still living? Tell me everything you know. Adieu, my dear godson. Do not forget to write me and depend on the affection of your godmother who has never forgotten you and who loves you more than ever since she finds you have always preserved your attachment to Aurore Bérard.[2]

Pierre read the letter to Juliette and Rosalie. He refused to comment on the thread of sadness which ran through the letter. "As soon as Rosalie and Euphemia are strong enough, we will all go to Paris and see Aurore and the other Bérards," he declared.

Rosalie and Juliette only smiled as they had both accepted the fact that Rosalie would never be strong again.

---

2. Arthur and Elizabeth Sheehan, *Pierre Toussaint* (New York: P.J. Kenedy and Sons, 1955).

"In the meantime the de Neuvilles will be going to France and we must send a gift."

"I will go shopping tomorrow when my mother stops in," promised Juliette, who was delighted that Pierre had derived so much pleasure from the letter.

This was the beginning of many gifts and letters which Pierre and Juliette sent to his godmother who lived at No. 10 Rue de Tournon, Faubourg, St. Germain.

Aurore had shared the news of Madame Brochet's meeting with Pierre with the other Bérards, and it was not long before a letter arrived from Du Pithon, Aurore's brother. It seemed that other French ladies who had visited New York had also enjoyed Pierre's services, but it remained for Madame Brochet to discover his connection with the Bérard family. Pierre wrote in detail about their arrival in New York in 1787 and Jean Jacques' determination to return to St. Dominique. He wrote what little he knew about their island home, and reluctantly admitted that it had been some time since he had received a letter from L'Artibonite. It was painful for him to even admit not having any knowledge of Zenobie and his mother Ursule. He refused to concede that Zenobie was most likely dead by now. He often thought that Rosalie's defiance of death was an inheritance from Zenobie.

As happy as Pierre was over the letters from the Bérards, these letters produced deep melancholia in Gabriel Nicolas. On the one hand, he longed to be in France with them, but since his finances were such as to make a trip impossible, these missives only reminded him of what his life had been like before the slaves revolted.

The great Protestant preacher John Wesley had many converts in New York, and their zeal resulted in widespread local reforms. Theaters were closed. Dancing and card playing were condemned, and people who had made a living in places of amusement were thrown out of work. As a musician, Gabriel Nicolas could find no employment. The money he had received from the sale of the slaves was gone. His pride would not permit him to live off Pierre any longer, and he left a note informing his benefactor and friend that he was seeking employment further south but would be writing from wherever he settled.

Pierre understood Gabriel Nicolas' reluctance to accept his board and keep, but this was another link to his past which was lost. Though saddened by Monsieur Nicolas' departure, Pierre went immediately to Samuel Bloodgood, the owner of the house, and asked him to draw up papers making him legally responsible for the rent of 105 Reade Street.

Letters from the Bérards were arriving now on a regular basis. Always they begged for news of St. Dominique and friends they had once known. Pierre shared whatever information he had, usually an elaboration of the activities of King Henry I, as Christophe called himself. He gave them names and addresses of the few friends who had remained in New York and told them about the French communities in Philadelphia, Baltimore, Charleston and New Orleans.

Juliette was a shrewd shopper, and she delighted in going from store to store to find useful gifts that some patrons of Pierre who were going to France would deliver to Aurore. She even involved Rosalie in wrapping the gifts, though the ailing mother could do little more than hold a piece of paper which Juliette gave her, or hand her sister-in-law a ribbon for a fancy bow.

As another spring—the spring of 1817—approached, Pierre resumed his visits to the park with Euphemia, who was beginning to prance about, taking high, unsteady steps. Juliette was glad Pierre had not been at home the day Euphemia had made her first attempt to crawl down the three flights of steps at 105 Reade Street. Fortunately the child's crawl had been more of a bounce, and Old Cabress had caught her before she hit the landing on the second floor. Juliette decided God must have left Old Cabress around for some good purpose.

Pierre was delighted with Euphemia's prattle, which was a combination of French and English. When Juliette tired of listening to what Pierre insisted Euphemia had said, she politely asked him if he was willing to repeat that conversation in the confessional. That always stopped him.

Juliette, who attended to all of Rosalie's bodily needs, knew that her sister-in-law could not last much longer. The hemorrhages always seemed to come at a time Pierre was not home. Fortunately Juliette's mother's employer traveled extensively, and that made it possible for Claudine to spend a great deal of time at the Toussaint residence. She had warned Juliette that the hemorrhages were becoming more frequent. Juliette often had to leave the room while her mother stayed with Rosalie as she spat up her life's blood.

One night when Pierre was singing Euphemia to sleep and the child was making mimicking noises which Pierre thought was singing, he heard Rosalie call him in a surprisingly strong voice. He placed the baby in her crib and went to his sister. Juliette had propped the gasping woman up on pillows.

"My—my baby," she managed to say, holding out her emaciated arms.

"Euphemia is asleep," Pierre explained. "I've just tucked her in for the night."

Juliette left the room before Rosalie pleaded for her baby again.

"My baby—my baby. I want my baby!" the woman insisted.

Pierre looked around as Juliette came back with the sleeping child and handed her to Pierre. "Rosalie is dying," she whispered.

Pierre only hesitated a moment before he told Juliette to run downstairs and get one of the boys to go to St. Peter's for a priest. Then he held out the baby to her dying mother.

Rosalie made an effort to take the child, but she was too weak. Pierre placed Euphemia on her mother's stomach, holding one hand under the child as he knelt beside the bed praying silently. Rosalie looked from her baby to her brother who had succored them and smiled before she closed her eyes on the world.

Pierre, who had seen death in so many forms and places, rose and took the still-sleeping baby in his arms. When Juliette returned, he went for his prayerbook so he could read the prayers for the dead—this time for his own flesh and blood. Juliette wept silently as she hugged the motherless child.

When Fr. French came, Pierre explained that Rosalie was dead. The priest anointed her and read the prayers of conditional absolution. Once more Juliette saw Pierre mask his grief as he pulled the sheet over his sister's head, then turned to the priest and made arrangements for a funeral Mass. Juliette marveled at her husband's control as grief for her friend and sister-in-law shook her frame and tears refused to be stemmed.

After the priest left, Pierre took the child from Juliette and encircled her waist with his free arm. "There are only the three of us now," he said quietly.

Juliette stopped crying. "Not as long as Claudine Gaston lives and you keep bringing homeless boys home. You slipped that last one in without telling me," she smiled. "But he was the only one who admitted he knew where St. Peter's was. So maybe he was here for a purpose."

"Like Old Cabress," Pierre added. "But we will not disturb the old woman tonight."

"What about my mother?" Juliette asked.

"She will be here before too long. Someone will tell her they saw a priest go into 105 Reade Street and she will know," Pierre said.

CHAPTER 13

The Paternal Pierre

Pierre's grief over his sister's death was dulled by the outpouring of love and care which he lavished on her child. He hurried home from work each day to take Euphemia for an outing. Some of these excursions took them as far down as the Battery, where he enjoyed sitting on the benches in the park outside Castle Garden watching Euphemia point to ships anchored in the harbor as she squealed with delight. When the rays of the sun grew stronger and the ladies protected their complexions with vari-colored parasols, the little girl went into raptures of delight each time one of them passed. If Pierre had not restrained her, she would have run after each sunshade.

Sometimes Pierre would see a dejected man sitting on a bench, his luggage at his feet, whose appearance signaled disappointment or destitution. Pierre tried hard to make himself immune to the problems of these unknowns, but before he started the homeward trek he had usually become involved to the extent he was offering to help the men find the addresses they had been given or suggesting where they might find a night's lodging until permanent arrangements could be made.

Pierre often wondered if the compliments these men

paid little Euphemia were sincere or if they felt they had to show their gratitude in some way.

Evenings after these excursions Pierre would entertain Juliette with accounts of Euphemia's exploits. "This child is a true artist," he insisted as he told about Euphemia showing him the different ships and trying to grab the ladies' colored parasols. "You should hear her imitate the birds in the park," he would add, "and she has made friends with all of the vendors who sell flowers."

"No wonder I am getting so many bouquets," Juliette would smile.

When Pierre talked about Euphemia imitating the birds in the park, Juliette remembered Marie Bouquement's accounts of how the small Pierre had entertained the Bérards at L'Artibonite by impersonating the actors he had seen at the theater in St. Marc. While Juliette had no doubt that Euphemia was going to be a bright, alert child, her aunt would have been happier if the little girl had grown more robust. Pierre was content to insist that Euphemia sang like the birds in the park and showed an unusual appreciation of movement, colors and the beauties of nature.

Pierre's patrons were delighted with the verve with which he now approached each task. Though still exhibiting the dignity which had become a kind of trademark, he had shed the beginning of a manner of austerity which began to develop during the period when he was supporting the Bérard-Nicolas household and agonizing over when he would have enough money to buy Rosalie's freedom and marry Juliette.

Juliette never criticized Pierre since she always understood what he was trying to do. To her mother's amazement, she never even questioned him when he brought homeless boys to their house. And the night, which was to be the first of many nights, when she heard sounds coming from the basement which told her that Pierre was teaching the boys to play the fiddle, she could only be grateful. She knew the discordant sounds would one day be melodic because Pierre never gave up on any plan he undertook. She also knew that the boy—or boys—who displayed the most talent or the greatest desire to learn would later receive a violin. Then one evening when Pierre had invited friends in, his latest prodigy would be called on to entertain. When one of Pierre's patrons asked if he knew a musician he could recommend, the most promising of the boys would be dispatched.

Juliette might well have been a soothsayer as events transpired just as she had surmised. Soon after one of Pierre's musical discoveries disappeared, another homeless black boy who had to be bathed, fed and tutored took his place. The magnitude of Pierre's charity never ceased to amaze his wife. She was pleased to be a part of all he did, though sometimes she grew weary from the demands.

Juliette was not the only one who marveled at all the things Pierre accomplished in his quiet way. Mary Anne Schuyler, the wife of Philip J. Schuyler, son of the famous General Schuyler of the Battle of Saratoga fame, felt her day was not complete until Pierre stopped by the Schuyler house on his way home. If there was to be entertainment during the evening, she could be sure Pierre would style her hair before she went out. If there was a problem with the servants, she knew Pierre would either advise her on how to handle it or find another servant to substitute. Mary Anne Schuyler made no secret of the fact that she depended on Pierre to turn near disaster into a positive situation. Her sons, William, George Lee and Robert Lee, also went to Pierre with their problems and confidences.

"What would I do without Pierre?" Mrs. Schuyler often asked her husband, also an admirer of the black hairdresser.

Angelica Schuyler Church's daughter Catherine, who

became the famous Mrs. Peter Cruger, had formed a bond of affection for Pierre during her childhood. She still depended on him to style her hair before each of her "at homes."

Pierre was always smiling when he had an appointment at the home of James Hamilton. He knew little Eliza, named for her grandmother Elizabeth Schuyler Hamilton, would be waiting for him. If her hair did not need cutting, she would beg him to sing some French ditty or teach her some dance step he might have to improvise on the spot.

There was hardly a time Pierre styled the hair of his friend Madame Larue, the Frenchwoman, that she did not threaten to return to France now that the Napoleonic Wars were over. The LaFarges, the Binsses, Livingstons, Bancels and so many of the other ladies whose families shaped the history of New York City vied for Pierre's services. Yet he appeared unaffected by the manner in which he, the slave hairdresser, had now become a confidant and advisor. Life was good and Pierre was grateful for small favors.

It could not be said, however, that some few of these lovely ladies were not above trying to elicit news from Pierre about his other patrons. Pierre's habit of weighing each word gave him time to phrase replies when some frivolous matron attempted to trick him into commenting on the current scandal. He might appear deaf to gossip for a while, but eventually he would remind the lady that he was a coiffeur, not a bearer of tales. The manner in which Pierre resisted these efforts to pry information out of him about his patrons was always so deferential and courteous that the ladies never took offense. But sometimes Pierre was glad to escape their questioning.

Yet when he made his last stop at Mary Anne Schuyler's on Canal Street, he never indicated the incidents which had given him concern. Most of the servants in the Schuyler household had ties to Pierre, and when he arrived either the servants or the Schuyler boys greeted him enthusiastically. Mary Anne's husband, Philip Jeremiah, sometimes joked about how his wife saved any problems of the day for Pierre to solve when he stopped in on his way home.

Another of Pierre's patrons was Marie Stevens, the wife of John C. Stevens, son of the Colonel John Stevens who had been first to apply the principle of steam propulsion to boats. When Mrs. Stevens was out of town, she wrote Pierre teasing letters instructing him to write her a strict account of everything that was happening in New York—good or bad. He sometimes shared these letters with Juliette and then told her about the dazzling balls the Stevens gave and the odd manner in which Mrs. Stevens sometimes handed out her invitations.

Juliette had already heard Pierre speak of Mr. Brown, the sexton at Grace Church. Pierre explained that Mrs. Stevens had great respect for Mr. Brown's retentive knowledge of the correct addresses for the socially elite. So she would have her carriage driven to Grace Church, pick up Mr. Brown, and then he would direct the driver to the proper addresses of those New Yorkers whose names Mrs. Stevens had written on the invitations to her ball.

Juliette smiled each New Year's Day when she heard the clatter of horses' hooves as Mrs. Stevens' carriage stopped in front of 105 Reade Street and the lady alighted, left a gift for Pierre with a note of best wishes at the door and then drove away. As she stood behind the curtains in the parlor, Juliette often wondered what would happen if, when she heard the carriage stop, she opened the door and wished Mrs. Stevens a happy New Year. She never acted out her thoughts; she knew Pierre would consider that "too forward."

Yet there had been times when some of Pierre's patrons had occasion to visit his home, and they always commented on Juliette's attractiveness and the colorful clothes she wore. The scarves she wrapped around her head so artistically added to her height and gave her a regal bearing. Though Pierre seldom repeated these compliments to Juliette, she had been told that he once replied to one of his patrons by saying he thought his wife to be one of the most beautiful ladies in New York. This was an extravagant statement, such as few had ever heard Pierre make, but it indicated his love and affection for the woman who had waited so many years for him.

Juliette knew that Mary Anne Schuyler and Marie Stevens were special favorites of Pierre. She delighted in having him tell her the history of the Schuyler family, including the old General's conduct at the Battle of Saratoga, with all the controversies and ramifications. He also insisted that few men had made a greater contribution to the young republic than Colonel Stevens.

Madame Larue first told Pierre that a group of laymen, known as the Roman Catholic Benevolent Society to Provide for Catholic Orphans, founded in 1816, was attempting to establish an orphanage. Leading this group was Francis Cooper, the first Catholic member of the New York legislature. His friends Cornelius Heeney and Robert Fox, former partners of John Jacob Astor, were also members. They had succeeded in gaining the support of the new bishop, John Connolly. He had already written Mother Elizabeth Seton, foundress of the Sisters of Charity of St. Joseph at Emmitsburg, Md., and asked her if she would send three of her Sisters of Charity to New York to set up an orphanage. Madame Larue told Pierre that these sisters had staffed an orphanage at Philadelphia under difficult circumstances, and were considered to be the best possible choice for the New York venture. She said the society had already purchased a house for the sisters on Prince Street.

When Madame Larue told Pierre that she was a member of the women's auxiliary to the society, he congratulated her and wondered why she was telling him so much about this society. He reminded her of all the controversy stemming from Mother Seton's conversion and promised to pray for the success of the society's worthwhile efforts.

Pierre's friend wanted more than his prayers. Madame Larue then reminded him of how he had been taking black orphans into his home for years and insisted that he also had an obligation to inform his patrons of the need to support a home for white orphans. Before Pierre left Madame Larue, he had promised to help solicit contributions for the first home for Catholic orphans in New York City.

That night when Juliette listened to her husband as he described the efforts of the Catholic laity to provide for the homeless white children, she found it hard to understand how he could take on added responsibility.

"You already have your *petit* orphanage here," she reminded.

"I only bring black boys here. There are many homeless white children, and they must be cared for, too. I have already promised to help Madame Larue in any way I can."

Juliette knew that Pierre's many wealthy patrons would gladly contribute to any cause he espoused. "It could have been worse," she thought. "Someone could have told him about a family of white orphans who had no home and I would have to make room for them here."

That August, Sisters Rose White, Cecelia O'Conway and Felicita Brady arrived in New York. They took up residence at the Fox's home, as the house on Prince Street was not ready for them yet. Pierre had already begun to collect donations for the orphanage, and he proudly informed Juliette that James Hamilton had been his first contributor.

Though Euphemia continued to be slight of build, Juliette was delighted when Pierre called her attention to how tall the little girl had grown. He often talked about Euphemia after they had retired, and Juliette always listened when he invariably concluded his discussions of Euphemia by mentioning the power of prayer. He firmly believed that as a result of his petitions Euphemia had outgrown the malady which claimed her mother's life. Juliette, who just as firmly believed that God helped those who helped themselves, listened and made sure the little girl had an egg in her milk each day, though she disguised it with flavoring. She cajoled the child into eating vegetables, and once she discovered that the plantain on which they had all thrived back home was Euphemia's favorite food, she found different ways to prepare this starchy fruit.

Pierre was delighted the first night he came home and found Euphemia and Juliette standing at the door waiting for him in identical outfits that Juliette had made. Thus began a ritual to which he looked forward each evening going home to the tall, slender woman and the tiny girl awaiting his return.

Happy years have a way of passing all too quickly, and Pierre continued to marvel that so much happiness had awaited his middle years. Letters were regularly arriving from Aurore and the other Bérards. Juliette often took Euphemia with her to help with the selection of gifts for Pierre's godmother. Pierre was always surprised at how much Juliette was buying with the money he gave her when he came home to find his wife and Euphemia in the midst of packing neat packages for friends who were traveling, to deliver to Aurore. Juliette taught Euphemia to tie a ribbon bow, and the little girl thereafter insisted that the brown wrapping paper be left off until her "dear uncle" came home and saw the bow she had tied.

Pierre continued the long walks with Euphemia, and she danced about him each time he entered the house, asking him where he was going to take her that day. She had already learned that anytime they went for a walk which took them past St. Peter's on Barclay Street, they would stop for a visit before going home. Juliette noted the prideful satisfaction with which Pierre told her how the little girl took his hand and pulled him in the direction of the church as soon as she sighted the building. Sometimes Juliette heard Pierre laughing as he and the child approached the steps. Euphemia had learned to imitate the vegetable and milk vendors who traveled through the streets announcing their wares in a singsong fashion, and it was music to Pierre's grateful ears.

Once Pierre entered the house, Euphemia was either in his arms, on his knee or dancing about him as he did his chores. It was inevitable that she would begin to recognize names and places. The Binsses often asked him to come to the school they conducted and cut the children's hair. One evening when Madame Binsse had sent Pierre a note asking him to come the next day to cut the hair of a number of the students, Euphemia heard Pierre mention the engagement to Juliette.

"Let me go with you, uncle," she begged. "I could help you like you say the boys from the shop help you."

For a second Pierre allowed himself to think of how proud he would be to take his niece to the Binsse's school. "That would not be proper for a little girl of your age," he answered after thinking it over.

"Am I still a *little* girl?" she asked. "Aunt Juliette says I'm growing like a weed."

"Indeed you are growing," Pierre admitted. "But your uncle cannot take you out to work. Instead he must begin to teach you to read and write."

"I could never read or write as much as you," the child insisted.

"How do you know how much I read and write?" Pierre questioned.

Juliette, who already knew the answer, wondered what Euphemia would say. At first the little girl only smiled and looked at the new slippers her uncle had brought her.

"Euphemia, I asked a question," Pierre reminded her.

"My dear uncle," she began, "sometimes I—I—"

"What is it you are trying to say?" Pierre was puzzled.

"My dear uncle, sometimes after you hear my night prayers I get up and—I peek in your room and take a little look at you while you are sitting at the desk writing. Aunt Juliette knows I love you so much I always want to see you. And," Euphemia was encouraged by the expression of amazement on Pierre's face, "I asked Aunt Juliette if she could write like you, and she said she couldn't—that nobody we know can write like you."

"That is very kind of your aunt," Pierre cleared his throat and spoke loud enough for his wife, who was in the next room sewing, to hear him. "But if you are old enough to offer your services to your uncle and big enough to get out of bed and watch your uncle write, then it is time for you to learn to read and write."

Pierre was not sure whether Euphemia was delighted over the prospect of learning to read and write or relieved that she had not been scolded for getting out of bed at night. But he accepted the warm hugs and kisses the child gave him until Juliette reminded her it was past her bedtime.

Later that night, after Pierre made sure Euphemia was asleep, he discussed the "peeking" incident with Juliette.

"Euphemia does not even talk like a child," he said.

"I wondered when you would notice that. It is because she doesn't have children to play with. She's always around grown-ups," Juliette reminded her husband.

"At L'Artibonite I had De Pointe and Rosalie for play-mates," he said as his mind drifted back, and Pierre began to tell his wife stories of that long-ago childhood.

As he talked, Pierre imagined he was once more on the dusty road leading from the old church in St. Marc, with his mother holding his hand as they trudged along. Then Mass was over and the elder Madame Bérard was getting into her carriage but giving Ursule coins for Pierre to buy pastries at the market place. Pierre admitted that once—and this was the first time Juliette heard this version of the story—Pierre had danced from one stall to the other in the market place until Ursule was tired of looking for him. She eventually sent Marie-Louise and his older brother to find him. But Pierre was enjoying the game of hide-and-seek, and they could not find him. Then when Pierre tired of playing games, he could not find his mother or his sister or his brother. Tearfully, he remembered, he had started the long journey home—alone.

The sun had been high in the heavens, and Pierre had consumed many pastries and confections without bothering to drink from the pump in the square. The road stretched out flat before Pierre, but he could not see his mother. He was hot, tired and thirsty. Tears had begun to fall when he heard a carriage approaching and scampered to the side of the road. Then he saw it was the Bérard's carriage, and he remembered André the coachman pulling on the reins of the horses to make them stop. Then the elder Monsieur Bérard had instructed André to let Pierre climb up and sit beside him on the front seat.

A short distance later the carriage overtook Ursule and Pierre's brother and sister. He could see that his mother was about to turn back to look for him, but Pierre admitted to Juliette that he only waved as the horses trotted toward L'Artibonite.

Pierre managed a shamefaced laugh as he admitted that he had stayed close to his grandmother Zenobie for the next few days after they got back to L'Artibonite.

"And you wonder about Euphemia getting out of bed to watch you write?"

"She is an unusual child!" Pierre said again. "I must make plans for her education."

Later that night Juliette awakened to discover Pierre was not beside her. With half-opened eyes she saw him sitting at his desk writing furiously. She knew he was outlining his plans for Euphemia's education.

Pierre's wife could barely write her name. She read numbers and signs and was good at counting. "He will make sure she has the best teacher he can find," Juliette thought, "but by the time Euphemia has learned to write, her Aunt Juliette will have also managed to scribble a letter or two." She drifted off to sleep knowing full well that Pierre would be reluctant to admit that his wife also needed tutoring, as that would have been an admission he would be loath to make about the one he loved so passionately.

CHAPTER 14

What Is an Orphan?

Pierre was hardly prepared for the announcement Madame Larue made the next time she sent for him to style her hair. For what seemed like years, he had been listening to her talk about returning to France. This time she informed him that she was definitely going home. Before he had fully accepted the fact that he was losing one of his most important patrons, Madame Larue informed him that she expected him to continue soliciting funds for the Catholic orphanage on Prince Street.

"I have been telling Sr. Cecelia how helpful you have been. Just today I told her you will be turning whatever you collect over to her as I will be in France. I will send my donations directly to you. I know I can depend on you. Can't I, Pierre?"

"Yes, Madame Larue. You can depend on me," Pierre heard himself saying, half wondering why.

As Pierre walked home he thought about his last promise. He also thought about the drive he had recently helped launch to repair St. Peter's. He had promised to help raise funds for St. Patrick's Cathedral and make a donation to the school for black boys and girls at St. Vincent's. Now he had agreed to solicit funds for the new orphanage. He had previously thought of this as an effort to assist Madame Larue. It was his responsibility, he had learned.

"It's like the fishes and the loaves," Pierre thought as he turned into Reade Street, anticipating the affectionate greeting he would receive when he reached home.

As soon as Pierre had kissed Juliette and Euphemia, the little girl was in his arms, begging her uncle to take her for a ride on his shoulders.

"Only one ride until we have had our lessons," he warned as Euphemia made a face.

"You do want to learn to read and write?" he frowned.

"Oh, yes, dear uncle! But I want to ride, too," the little girl admitted.

As Juliette set the dinner table, she knew Pierre was going up the steps to bring out the old copy book he had used so many years ago when Jean Jacques Bérard was preparing him for the trip to New York. Already he had taught Euphemia to trace her name. Juliette was pleased when Pierre wrote his name as well as hers and helped Euphemia to copy them. Though Pierre never saw all the papers Juliette worked over with Euphemia, the two females made sure that Euphemia had something to show her uncle each night. Then the little girl almost always got a lecture on L'Artibonite and how Zenobie had first taught Pierre to write his name.

"Why don't they come to see us?" the child would ask.

"There is great unrest and much fighting all around them. It would not be safe for my family to attempt any travel," he answered sadly.

"Uncle," Euphemia rested her crayon on the slate Pierre had given her, "why are the people at your home fighting?"

Pierre wondered how he would explain the upheaval in St. Dominique, now Haiti, to this child. He knew she was totally unaware of the horrors of slavery. Friends of all colors and national backgrounds frequented their home. He sometimes wondered if she realized she was black or the legacy of her blackness. Though he realized he and Juliette had been overly protective, his problem was how to answer the child's questions—and her questions were beginning to increase in complexity.

Once more Euphemia repeated her question while Pierre was trying to decide on an answer.

"You know how I sometimes have to go down to the basement to quiet the boys I bring home because they have nowhere else to go?"

Euphemia nodded and waited.

"Sometimes those boys are arguing and fighting among themselves. It may be because one wants to sleep in a spot where another wants to sleep. Or it may be because one wants to wear a jacket that another boy says belongs to him. They can't agree so they talk loud and sometimes hit each other. And that is the way it is at my home; the men who control cannot agree on who determines what. So they fight."

"I wish they would stop fighting," Euphemia said. "But tonight they are quiet in the basement," she announced soberly.

"I am glad they are," Pierre sighed. "I would not want your lessons to be interrupted."

"Uncle, do you know what *Grandmère* Claudine said about the boys you bring home?"

Pierre admitted that he had no idea what his mother-in-law had said.

"She said it is no wonder they don't have homes because they are all a bunch of rowdies. And if they talk loud while she is here, she goes down the steps to the basement and makes them behave. She says you are too soft with them."

It was a struggle for Pierre and Juliette to keep from laughing at the droll manner in which Euphemia repeated what Claudine had said. After dinner Pierre heard noises that sounded like a scuffle, and he went down to the basement to quiet the boys, determined not to be *soft.*

Madame Larue had already begun to send Pierre her donation for the orphanage from Rouen, France, where she had settled. She had reminded him that he was to report to Sr. Cecelia on the first Monday of each month. Pierre bought a ledger, for this would be the most ambitious solicitation he had ever undertaken. He would keep accounts that the sisters could examine.

Juliette was not unmindful that Euphemia mixed the happenings of the day with her lessons each evening after dinner. But she insisted that the little girl make an effort to comply with whatever small assignment Pierre gave her. Together the two of them would trace their names and Pierre's name over and over again. Juliette enjoyed the child's company, but she often wished there was a school she could attend. Some evenings when Pierre was coaching her, Juliette noted that his eyes were heavy, and she knew he was weary from walking all over New York.

Juliette felt another prayer had been answered the day Pierre stopped in to tell her that Mrs. Ruckel, a gentlewoman of considerable education, had complained to him about her difficulty in finding lodging in homes where there was no objection to the few pupils she had come to her quarters each day. "I was just wondering—" Pierre began and waited for Juliette's reaction.

Juliette decided against indicating to Pierre that she suspected what he had in mind. "And what were you wondering?" she asked after sending Euphemia upstairs to fetch a clean apron.

"I was wondering what you might think about offering to rent Monsieur Nicolas' rooms to Mrs. Ruckel. The last time I heard from him he was with a carnival that was traveling further south, and that was many months ago. The good lady could take more pupils and—and—"

"And she could teach Euphemia as well," Juliette said, and they both laughed at the game they had played with each other.

Euphemia clapped her hands and gave Pierre a big hug when he told her that Mrs. Ruckel, already known to the little girl, was going to come to live with them and would teach her as well.

"Is my dear uncle tired of teaching me?" Euphemia pouted.

Juliette saw the expression on Pierre's face and quickly explained to the child that her uncle was a very busy man, and Mrs. Ruckel would have more time to spend with her.

"Soon you will be writing letters to your uncle telling him about all you have done each day." Pierre was determined that Euphemia would not think he no longer wanted to teach her. "I will still have to supervise your French. Now I must hurry to call on Mrs. Ruckel and tell her she is welcome to move in with us. I have an appointment with Mrs. Cruger, and Mrs. Schuyler will be expecting me later."

"Take me with you," Euphemia begged. "I'd love to see the pretty Mrs. Cruger, and you always talk about the Schuyler boys."

"And who will help me prepare your new teacher's rooms?" Juliette asked.

Pierre smiled at the spectacle of the little girl wringing her hands as she said: "Dear uncle, I cannot go with you as I must help my Aunt Juliette."

"Your Aunt Juliette is fortunate to have so able a helper," he smiled as he hastened his steps so he would have time to visit Mrs. Ruckel before keeping his other appointments. "She does need to be around children, though. That will be one of the benefits of having Mrs. Ruckel live with us."

Then a thought came to Pierre that made him stop in his tracks and lean against the nearest tree. Mrs. Ruckel was white and so were her pupils. What would happen if there was a complaint about a white woman living with a black family? Nobody, Pierre reasoned, had complained when Madame Bérard and her sisters lived there. But, he reminded himself, he had been a slave then, although he was a freedman when he was supporting the household after his owner's death while Monsieur Nicolas lived at 105 Reade Street.

Suddenly Pierre smiled. "O ye of little faith," he chided himself and quickened his pace. He would mention the contemplated arrangement with Mrs. Ruckel to the two patrons he would be visiting. He knew both of the ladies to be sensitive to his status as a freed slave in spite of their obvious admiration. If there was any danger in the plan he knew he could count on a discreet word of warning. Then what would he tell Juliette and Euphemia if the answer was negative, he wondered?

That evening, after a visit at the Schuylers, Pierre hurried home to tell Juliette of his concern. He had changed his mind about visiting the teacher. Instead he stopped in his shop and sent a note to Mrs. Ruckel by one of the boys telling her she might feel free to move to 105 Reade Street at her pleasure.

Juliette and Euphemia were waiting for him, and the little girl insisted on taking his hand. She led him to the quarters they were preparing for Mrs. Ruckel so he could see how she had helped her Aunt Juliette.

After the evening meal, when Pierre was reasonably sure Euphemia was asleep, he spoke to his wife about the fear he had experienced. "I mentioned it casually to Mrs. Cruger and to Mrs. Schuyler," he admitted. "They both thought it a wonderful arrangement."

Juliette paused before she smiled. "I do, too," she said and kissed her gentle husband.

On occasions such as this Juliette found Pierre's modesty puzzling. She knew that in spite of all he had done to conceal his role, people still talked about how he had supported the young Madame Bérard. It was common knowledge that there were always two or three black boys "in residence," as Pierre called it. People saw Pierre going to Mass at St. Peter's each morning, and the pastors made no secret of his donations. The fearlessness he displayed when nursing victims of the plague had been public knowledge. He had helped dozens of slaves to obtain their freedom. Now he was collecting funds for a white orphanage. Pierre was becoming a legend. Yet because he was black he had been fearful of inviting a white woman who needed living quarters where she could also take pupils to live in his house. Though Juliette was patient with Pierre, it was hard for her to understand how he could remain oblivious to the esteem in which he was held.

"God only made one Pierre Toussaint," Juliette reminded herself.

Mrs. Ruckel was still arranging the room in which she received her pupils when Pierre stopped in to give Juliette a note from their young friend Cesarine Meetz. Cesarine, whose mother had been one of Pierre's patrons, wrote to inform them that she was accepting an invitation to visit which the Toussaints had extended some time past.

Juliette had coaxed Pierre into inviting Cesarine. At age sixteen she was already a promising young musician and was now accepting a few students from well-placed French families.

Though by saying she imitated the birds Pierre appeared to dismiss the little songs Euphemia sang so well, Juliette had recognized the promise of a beautiful voice in her little niece. Several times Cesarine had commented on Euphemia's ear for music and expressed the desire to give her lessons. Now Cesarine was coming for tea and Juliette had high hopes.

The many friends who enjoyed the Toussaints' hospitality had lavish praise for their hostess. Since Cesarine's visit was of special importance, Juliette began making preparations well in advance of the day. She was pleased that Euphemia had reached the stage where she was helpful about the house.

Euphemia, now approaching her seventh birthday in 1822, was delighted when she could help her Aunt Juliette lay out the best white damask tablecloths and polish the silver tea service.

Juliette could only smile when she heard Euphemia describe both these days of special preparation and then the event to Claudine when she came to visit. According to the little girl, her Aunt Juliette sat at the head of the table pouring her delicious chocolate out of a shining silver pot. Meanwhile, one of the boys from the basement passed the little cakes Uncle Pierre always brought home from the bakery when he knew guests were expected.

"My Aunt Juliette pours chocolate like a queen, *Grand-mère* Claudine. You should see her!"

"Euphemia," Juliette laughed, "a queen would not pour chocolate. Someone would pour for her."

Euphemia's enthusiasm could not be dampened. "When I told my dear uncle that you looked like a queen, he said you were his queen," and she looked at Juliette's mother for approval.

"Your Aunt Juliette is a gracious hostess," the older woman admitted. "And she tells me that you are of great help to her."

"I just love the days when company is coming," Euphemia declared.

The little girl was unusually elated the day Cesarine Meetz was expected.

"Aunt Juliette," she asked as she brought out the silver trays and bon-bon dishes which had been gifts from Pierre's patrons, "do you really think Mademoiselle Meetz might give me lessons?"

Before she replied, Juliette smoothed the middle crease

out of the tablecloth and reached for the napkins Euphemia had brought. Though Cesarine Meetz had complimented the little girl when she sang the French songs Pierre had taught her, the possibility of lessons had never been discussed in the child's presence.

"Do you want to take music lessons from Cesarine?" Juliette asked.

"More than anything else!" Euphemia answered.

"Then we must ask your uncle's permission," Juliette said, thinking she detected a smile of confidence on the little girl's face. "Your uncle is more concerned about your health and your ability to read and write than about music lessons."

"Mrs. Ruckel says I am a bright pupil, and you already said I am growing like a weed. Remember?"

"We must wait for your uncle's decision," and Juliette asked Euphemia to bring out the hand-painted chocolate cups.

Juliette knew there was no need to continue that conversation. Nothing could be done without Pierre's agreement, and she had other worries at the moment. She was hoping that the boy who was coming upstairs to serve would be properly dressed and would not break her chocolate cups.

It was almost as if Euphemia had read her mind again. "I hope the boy will be clean," the child said drolly.

"Your uncle gave the necessary instructions before he went to the shop this morning," Juliette explained. Then she reminded Euphemia it was time for them to get dressed to receive their guest.

Juliette knew that Claudine would probably arrive as they were dressing and would make sure the table was correctly set and the water and milk were ready for the chocolate. The boy selected to serve would come to the kitchen first, and Juliette knew her mother would give him a thorough inspection.

Juliette dressed Euphemia in a small replica of the garment she was to wear. Then she arranged the child's thick braids so as to form a coronet. Around the circle of braids she draped a branch of artificial blossoms. Juliette assured herself that only a healthy body could support such a thick growth of hair. The young woman became uneasy when she realized she was always searching for signs of good health in this frail child born of a tubercular mother.

Euphemia looked at herself in the mirror and admired the hairdo. "I'm going to tell dear uncle he is not the only one in this house who can style hair," she laughed. Juliette was wrapping two scarves, one blue and one red, around her own head so it looked as if the scarves were braided.

Everything went as Juliette had planned and hoped. Cesarine came and brought a friend who was also a musician. After the refreshments Juliette took her friends to the parlor. The little girl went upstairs to her dolls, since she always insisted on saving a pastry and a half cup of chocolate to have with the many dolls Pierre's patrons had sent her.

The ladies had barely made themselves comfortable when Pierre let himself in quietly and joined them.

"I am so glad you could find time to join us," Cesarine said after she had introduced her friend. "I hope you and your lovely wife have had time to think about my offer to give Euphemia voice lessons."

"I was not aware that you were serious," Pierre admitted. "Euphemia is just beginning to read, and her writing is showing some slight improvement. I would not want to burden her with too many studies."

"Only her mornings are spent with Mrs. Ruckel," Juliette pointed out.

"She really has a beautiful voice," Cesarine insisted. "I could take her three afternoons a week."

"We do not allow Euphemia to go out alone. How would she get to your house?"

"I would come here. This child shows so much promise, I would consider it a privilege to train her."

"That would be an imposition," Pierre objected.

Knowing Pierre's love for music and sensing that he was inclined toward consenting, Juliette spoke up. "I will be glad to take Euphemia to Miss Meetz' home. Just today Euphemia told me she wanted to take music lessons."

Pierre laughed heartily. "Pierre is no match for three ladies—all of whom are very dear to him. If it is agreed that Euphemia is to take music lessons—and something tells Pierre it is—then I suppose that means her uncle must buy her a piano."

Juliette left the parlor so Cesarine and Pierre could discuss the terms of Euphemia's music lessons and she could prepare a fresh pot of chocolate for her husband. In the kitchen Claudine had been joined by Old Cabress, who only sat in a corner and mumbled now and then. Claudine was already preparing fresh chocolate as Euphemia had come down with her favorite doll that she said wanted another cup of chocolate. When Juliette told the little girl her uncle had consented for her to study with Miss Meetz, Euphemia begged to be allowed to take the chocolate to her uncle so she could properly thank him. Juliette smiled as she prepared the tray for the little girl and remembered what Pierre had said about not being a match for three ladies.

Some days later Juliette decided the three ladies had underestimated Pierre. Though he said he had mapped the plan long before the discussion of the music lessons, he informed Juliette and Euphemia that from then on, every Friday he would expect to find two letters from Euphemia waiting for him. One letter would be in English and the other in French. He had already informed Mrs. Ruckel, who was not quite sure that Euphemia was ready for writing a formal letter. However, the teacher was quick to nervously add that Euphemia was among her best pupils.

Euphemia, who enjoyed the idea of having a school in her house—"just like the Bancels' school," she often said— was not overly enthusiastic about the new chore. But she detected the glow on her aunt's face which indicated that this, too, would be a task they would complete together. And so it was that Euphemia and Juliette's days took on an added dimension.

Pierre's collections for the orphans continued to increase. Fr. John Powers, now at St. Peter's, seldom lost an opportunity to thank Pierre for the assistance he was giving the Sisters of Charity and to share his intense desire to raise funds for a larger building to house the increasing number of orphans.

Euphemia's interest in the orphans and her persistent request that she be permitted to invite them to 105 Reade Street for a tea party forced Pierre into another compromise.

"There are now too many children at the orphanage for us to invite them here," he told Euphemia. "I think it might be a good idea for you to visit them."

"But you always said Prince Street was too far for me to walk," Euphemia reminded her uncle.

"By the time your next birthday rolls around," Pierre laughed, "I am sure your legs will be strong enough for such a walk."

"And will we stop at the baker's and buy them some of the little cakes you bring home when Aunt Juliette is having company?"

"We will take them pastries and whatever fruit I can find."

"I can spare one or two of my dolls," Euphemia offered.

"The last time I visited Sr. Cecelia," Pierre said, "I saw a number of little girls. It would not be fair to give one or two dolls and leave the others without."

"Then, dear uncle, you must buy dolls for all of the little girls."

"Suppose some of the little girls need shoes or dresses. Don't you think that would be more important than a doll?"

"But all little girls want dolls," she insisted.

"They must have the shoes and dresses first." Pierre realized he had to be firm with Euphemia.

"As you say, dear uncle." Euphemia knew that when Pierre had made up his mind there was no need to insist. "But I can hardly wait for my birthday to come."

That night as Juliette prepared the little girl for bed, she explained to her that Pierre's patrons were donating money so the sisters could buy shoes, clothing and food for the orphans. She also told the child that Fr. Powers was trying to raise money to build a larger orphanage. "They need clothing and a decent place to stay more than they need dolls," she told Euphemia.

Juliette had heard Euphemia's night prayers, tucked the covers about her to make sure she did not kick them off during the night, and was about to leave the room.

"Aunt Juliette?" Euphemia yawned.

"What is it, Euphemia?"

"All—all little girls want dolls."

"What do little boys want?"

"Don't know," Euphemia said sleepily. "Uncle Pierre will have to ask the boys in the basement."

Juliette tiptoed out of the room and went in search of her husband to tell him about her conversation with Euphemia. "You know she will not let you rest until you find someone to buy dolls for the little girls."

"Euphemia must learn to be more practical," Pierre insisted.

"She's only a child," Juliette defended.

"My dear wife," Pierre embraced Juliette, "your niece has a child's body and an old woman's mind."

"Tonight," Juliette laughed, "Euphemia is my niece."

"She is our child," Pierre declared. "God gave her to us."

"And she is even beginning to look like you," Juliette said.

"That is what people say when we are out walking," Pierre nodded. "I must take time to look in the mirror."

Between daily classes with Mrs. Ruckel, music lessons with Cesarine Meetz and those letters each Friday, Euphemia and her aunt were kept busy. But each night when Pierre came home Juliette told him that Euphemia was counting the days to September 16th.

When Pierre returned from early Mass on St. Euphemia's feastday, his niece was waiting for him and Juliette let her serve his coffee and roll.

"What a pretty dress you are wearing today," Pierre complimented the little girl.

"It is my birthday present from my dear uncle and my dear aunt," Euphemia explained.

"We won't be going to the orphanage until after lunch. Aren't you dressed too early for the outing?"

"Mrs. Ruckel is having a little tea party so all of her pupils can celebrate my birthday," Euphemia explained. "And I begged Aunt Juliette to let me wear my birthday dress. That way she won't have to rush and dress me again when you call for me."

Pierre smiled to himself as he finished his breakfast. "She must have heard me when I left the house this morning," he told Juliette.

"And she came to my room and asked permission to wear her new dress for the reasons she has just told you."

"Of course her dear aunt agreed," Pierre chuckled as he heard Mrs. Ruckel complimenting Euphemia, who had gone to the teacher's quarters, on the pretty dress.

"I would have preferred her to wear something more ordinary looking," Pierre picked up his bag. "The orphans have so little."

"When Euphemia gets through chattering with them and flitting from one to the other, they will lose sight of what she is wearing."

"I suppose my dear wife is right," Pierre called as he hurried out for his first appointment.

Pierre returned soon after noon, just as Mrs. Ruckel's "tea party" to celebrate Euphemia's birthday had ended. Juliette insisted that the little girl take along a shawl as there had been a stiff breeze during the earlier part of the day. Mrs. Ruckel took the opportunity to thank Pierre for accommodating her and told him that Euphemia was an excellent reader.

"I am watching those letters for improvement," Pierre answered.

"But she is so young. Just give her time," Mrs. Ruckel pleaded.

Pierre looked up at Juliette, who was smiling in agreement with the teacher, just as Euphemia came down the stairs with her shawl, thereby ending the subject under discussion.

Pierre had to curb Euphemia's enthusiasm at the baker's shop. He had brought along a basket of fruit and another basket for the pastries. Euphemia soon had her basket filled with the little cakes and looked so wistfully at another display tray that the kind baker, who Euphemia had told about her visit to the orphanage, packed another box of pastries as a gift for the little girl.

Sr. Cecelia was delighted to receive the funds Pierre had collected, and the orphans, many of whom had never seen a little black girl before, were fascinated by Euphemia and everything about her. Pierre let his niece present the fruit and pastries to the sisters, who called the children in and told them Euphemia had brought these gifts for them on her birthday. The children said "Thank you" in unison as the sisters had taught them, and proceeded to devour the gifts.

Euphemia tried to talk with them, but conversation was difficult as most of the children were eating as if they thought the pastries and fruit might suddenly disappear.

"The next time I come to visit," Euphemia told Sr.

Cecelia, "they will talk with me and we will all have more fun. I am taking music lessons, and maybe I can even sing a song for them."

Pierre noticed on the walk home that Euphemia was unusually quiet.

"Now that you have visited the orphans and promised Sr. Cecelia to come again, are you happy, Euphemia?" he asked.

"There were two pitiful-looking little girls who acted as if they would cry any minute. And, uncle, they all ate so fast— as if they were hungry."

"I am not sure the sisters can afford fruits and pastries every day," he explained, but Euphemia still looked worried.

She stopped walking and faced Pierre. "Uncle, what is an orphan?"

Pierre took a deep breath. He had known that sooner or later Euphemia might ask such a question about the orphans and then about why she had an aunt and uncle instead of a mother and father.

"Euphemia," he began, "an orphan is a child who has no mother or father."

"But," Euphemia frowned, "don't they have an uncle?"

Pierre thanked God for the blessing God had sent him on St. Euphemia's feastday eight years earlier. Walking along as the child skipped in front of him apparently forgetting she had asked a question he would have found difficult to answer, Pierre prayed for the wisdom to guide this child through the years ahead.

CHAPTER 15

The Shadow of Things to Come

Pierre often wondered how he had lived without Juliette and Euphemia. And yet Pierre had to admit that during what others might have called a sterile period in his life, he had not been conscious of being unhappy. While he had grieved over his relatives at L'Artibonite, there had been so many others depending on him that he had not taken time to examine his personal life. Now that he knew this great happiness, his heart overflowed with gratitude.

Pierre was especially pleased that Euphemia was brought into contact with other children through Mrs. Ruckel's classes. Juliette had a brother who now and then also visited with his small son, Gaston. More and more some few of Pierre's patrons with young children found excuses to arrange for Euphemia to meet their offspring. Pierre was almost certain that Euphemia talked with the boys from the basement when they came upstairs.

Pierre's niece struggled with her letter writing chore. Sometimes these letters were little more than a nursery rhyme he or Juliette had taught her. At other times the little notes reflected things Euphemia had done during the day. Now and then secret yearnings emerged.

One of the earliest letters she wrote made Pierre aware

of Euphemia's longing to know more of the children of the patrons he visited. The desire to please her dear uncle was also reflected.

Pierre's patrons were pleased that he had acquired a wife and the niece who was more like a daughter because the two provided these ladies with a way to make gifts to Pierre without risking his displeasure. Still, the families like the Schuylers, Churches, Crugers, Hamiltons and LaFarges made sure that they selected a good book, a warm scarf, a cravat, or maybe a dress shirt brought back from Paris for Pierre's Christmas remembrances. But Pierre's most cherished gift at Christmas 1822 was a letter from Euphemia which read:

New York, December 25, 1822

Dear Uncle,

I am very pleased to have it in my power to write It is the first time and I hope you will bear with me you cannot expect much I must say the time I have been at it I ought to do better How foolish are children they think what is for their good but I hope my dear uncle will not get out of patience with me I mean to try this next year to improve both in my music and my writing I do not say only but I mean to do so and Miss Mettze I hope will not have any reason to complain of me I mean to be in the year very industrious and try to please everybody and I hope I shall keep my resolution.

Adieu, Dear Uncle
Your foolish little niece
E. Toussaint

P.S. I wish you the compliments of the season and many happy returns of the same.

Pierre read the letter over and over. He felt that even his gift to Euphemia of the long-awaited piano was inadequate to express his appreciation, and he complimented her effusively.

Only Juliette and maybe Mrs. Ruckel knew how much labor had gone into that one little missive. Juliette had been tempted to try to write a greeting also then decided against it. Later when Pierre spoke to her about Euphemia's letter, she was glad she had refrained.

"I can't begin to tell you what memories Euphemia's letter brought back," he declared. "I kept thinking of Zenobie and how much we all owe her. But Juliette," he whispered, "would you please be so kind as to ask Mrs. Ruckel to instruct Euphemia to use a period at the end of a sentence?"

When Juliette conveyed the message to the teacher, she suggested to Mrs. Ruckel that the two of them might confer from time to time on Euphemia's progress.

"Few of my other students would even attempt a letter. And most of them are older than Euphemia. But the good Mr. Toussaint expects a great deal from the little girl," observed Mrs. Ruckel, who was also anxious to please her landlord.

Juliette had a discarded and smudged copy of the letter. "You might take this old letter and show her how much better it would read after she used periods," Juliette suggested, hoping that she gave no indication she was almost as ignorant of how to use periods as Euphemia was.

Pierre was delighted with the letter Euphemia wrote in French. "And look at this script," he said as he showed the letter to Juliette again.

"What about her periods?" Juliette smiled.

"With that fancy script and all of the flourishes," Pierre admitted, "I hadn't paid much attention to the periods."

Juliette beamed as her husband read Euphemia's letter over and over and declared the French was near perfect. Juliette and Euphemia had copied part of the letter from the copy book which had once belonged to Jean Jacques Bérard.

Pierre was more concerned when Euphemia wrote on another occasion:

Dear Uncle

I would certainly like to see Mrs. Cruger and her
children I have got a picture that I think looks very much
like Mrs. Cruger I should like to see that young lady that
wrote me that letter and Miss Caroline and Eugenere and
their mama and papa but I never expect to have that
pleasure dear uncle there is a looking glass curtain at the
theater and if I am a good girl I want to know if you will
take me to see it

adieu dear uncle
Your dutiful niece,
Euphemia Toussaint

Though Pierre was proud of his niece, he had no intention of taking her to visit the Crugers without a special
invitation. He was black and so was his niece, and he never
forgot it. Mrs. Cruger, who had loved Pierre as long as she
could remember, was hesitant to extend such an invitation,
knowing how proudly correct Pierre was and not daring to
have him think she was being patronizing. Many months
were to pass before Mrs. Cruger took matters in her own
hands and called at 105 Reade Street when Pierre was out.
She was received graciously by Juliette and delighted by
Euphemia, who entertained her with a song she had recently
learned. Pierre was surprised but not displeased when
Juliette and then Mrs. Cruger told him about the visit.

Though Euphemia's letters were stilted, they still expressed her childish desires.

On January 6, 1823, Euphemia wrote:

Dear Uncle

I am very much pleased to think I can write a few
lines to you I am very sorry I cannot write a long long
letter. I hope Mrs. Ruckel will not have occasion to find
fault with me I will be very glad if you will give me the
cravat you promised me to make my doll a frock I hope
my next letter will be better.

Juliette was evidently teaching Euphemia to sew, for on January 8, 1823, the little girl wrote:

Dear Uncle

I want to ask you if I can invite two or three girls to come and see me in the course of a few days as it will be my doll's birthday and you promised to buy me some calico for curtains to my doll's bed but I would rather you would get me only enough for a frock no more favors at present dear Uncle

your affectionate niece
Euphemia Toussaint

Pierre, in affectionate moods, often softened Euphemia's name by calling her "Euphemie," and as she carried the Toussaint name instead of that of her father Jean Noel, she sometimes signed her letters "Euphemie Toussaint." The letters written in French were almost always signed "Euphemia Toussaint."

Pierre's friend, Jean Sorbieu, a witness when Pierre and Juliette married, was one of a number of refugees who had returned to France at the end of the Napoleonic Wars. Sorbieu had been a planter in St. Dominique and never really adjusted to life in America. So he moved his family to Rouen, France, and Pierre knew that each letter he received would contain praises for France and criticism of America, especially the Church in America, now beset by ethnic controversies involving the clergy.

It was an especially cold night when Pierre came home with a letter from his French friend that he had not had time to read all day.

Euphemia was practicing a new piece of music, and Juliette was trying hard to make the wood-burning fire in the dining room send out more warmth. Pierre held his hands to the feeble flame, then took the poker from Juliette and prodded the smoldering wood until there was enough warmth to dispel the chill in the room.

"Look what came today," he held up the letter from Sorbieu.

"You miss him, don't you?" Juliette asked.

"His letters make me think he is here in person and I am still listening to his gentle but obvious criticisms of America and the Irish clergy," Pierre admitted.

"Was he ever really happy?" Juliette questioned.

"He inherited his father's habitation in St. Dominique when he was very young," Pierre explained. "Though he was wealthy he yearned for that which he did not have—the companionship of young men of his own age. He would often ride over to L'Artibonite even before Monsieur Jean Jacques came back, and find excuses to talk with me or beg me to get out the fiddle and play a tune for him. He has always been seeking—" Pierre was remembering his friend when they were both young.

"He seems to have found what he was seeking in France. Do you think it is so much better over there?" Juliette asked.

"I sometimes wonder," Pierre admitted. "It would be good to be near Sorbieu and Madame Larue. And then there is my dear godmother. I detect a certain loneliness in her letters. I wish I could comfort her."

"Why don't we go to her?" Juliette asked.

"Would you really like to?" Pierre was glad to discuss a subject he had already given much private thought.

"Would I like to go to France? Of course I would," Juliette answered. "But how would you make a living there?"

Pierre held up his hands. "With these," he began and suddenly shuddered.

"What is wrong?" Juliette was troubled by the sudden change she had seen come over Pierre.

"I—I suppose I am tired. Madame Toussaint, you must know your husband is no longer a young man."

"That is why we should decide soon if you are going to France to be near Mlle. Aurore."

"Why don't I write and ask her if she would like us to come to France?"

At this point in the conversation, Euphemia danced into the room. "Dear uncle, are you going to France?" she asked. "Will you write me when you get there? Then I will write you and all my letters will be in French."

"If I go to France, my little Euphemia will go with me," Pierre promised.

"Then I could play with Caroline and Eugene Sorbieu. And I could help Aunt Juliette make a dress for Mlle. Bérard."

"Not so fast," Pierre took the frail child in his lap. "I must first write and determine if we are needed."

Later that night when Euphemia was asleep and Pierre sat at his desk adding up the collection he had made for the orphans, Juliette leaned over his shoulder and asked: "Why did you suddenly look so worried when I asked you how you would make a living?"

Pierre closed the ledger. "When I held up my hands I thought of something that happened before I left St. Dominique. A friend—a dear friend—vowed to kill the man who was responsible for the death of the woman he loved—with his two powerful hands—which he held out to me in anger. The simple gesture of showing you my hands which I would use to provide a living brought back the old memories."

"Forgive me for questioning you." Juliette was alarmed at having Pierre recall painful memories.

"I have never told the full story to anyone. Perhaps it is time for my wife to know what manner of man she has married."

"As if I did not already know," Juliette assured. The memory of Maurice and Berto, the secret meetings they took him to and their flight into the mountains before Monsieur Bérard brought him to New York came back to Pierre with such force that he was glad to unburden himself to his wife. Then Pierre described his own misery during the time he knew the slaves were plotting a revolt against the French planters, and he had to face Monsieur and Madame Bérard every day. Then there was the incident with Ducheine and Caradeux and finally that scene when Maurice had held up his hands, with fingers spread, and vowed to kill the man who had killed his *"femme."*

Juliette could not keep from crying. "And I thought I knew all about you," she lamented. "Everybody thinks you were always pampered and sheltered by the Bérards."

"I was sheltered," Pierre's voice was hoarse, "not only by the Bérards, though. Zenobie and Ursule forbade me to associate with the other slaves. Yet as I examine my feelings for Euphemia, I realize that they thought they were protecting me as I think I am protecting our child. It took Maurice and Berto to open my eyes to the plight of my people. And I was not sure about what Pierre would do.

"But I never revealed what I had heard at the secret meetings—not to anyone—until tonight. Now I suppose everybody involved is dead. May they all rest in peace, for each of them thought they were doing what was right—even Maurice and your poor Pierre."

Pierre's confession gave Juliette a better understanding of her husband. In the days which followed, she did everything possible to assure him that there was no reason for him to continue nurturing the sense of guilt with which he had lived so long. In the course of these verbal exchanges, Pierre came to realize he had done all he could at the time.

The letter regarding the proposed trip to Paris was written to Aurore Bérard.

Then Juliette became engaged in even another charitable project. Juliette's cousin, Fanny Montpensier, lived in Baltimore. For some months she had been writing the Toussaints about the condition of Haitian slaves in that city. Many of the blacks had been abandoned by their owners who had suffered financial reverses. The slaves were then unable to provide clothing, shelter and food for their children. The Sulpician Fathers had been conducting Sunday Mass and catechism classes for these children for some years. But everybody agreed that they needed a school since many of these hungry, ragged children roamed the Baltimore streets during the day. Fanny and three other young working women from the island now called Haiti were assisting the priests in their efforts to care for and educate these unfortunates. Juliette's cousin shared her great concern with the Toussaints who responded with donations and gifts.

Pierre, who had become even more aware of the needs of children because of his love for Euphemia, encouraged Juliette to purchase clothing suitable for the children Fanny Montpensier described. There was a constant stream of priests visiting between Baltimore and New York. For one reason or another most of them called on the Toussaints, sometimes for the practical purpose of finding lodging at 105 Reade Street during their stay in the city. The Toussaints found this a convenient way to send packages to Juliette's cousin for the children.

Pierre was delighted with Euphemia's progress as a letter writer. Cesarine Meetz was still giving the little girl voice lessons, but Pierre arranged for her to go to a Mrs. Rochefort for piano lessons.

Pierre found that he had less and less time for instructing Euphemia and engaged the services of a Mr. Gentile, who came to the Toussaint home for the purpose of teaching Euphemia French.

In spite of Pierre's efforts to keep Euphemia occupied with lessons in English, French and music, her letters reveal that there were times when she behaved or misbehaved like any other child. No doubt Mrs. Ruckel had given Pierre a report on Euphemia when the little girl wrote:

New York, January 10, 1823

Dear Uncle

I do not know what to write I have nothing to tell you
except Mrs. Ruckel tells me I have behaved something
better this week I hope it will give you pleasure to hear it.
Dear Uncle how glad I shall be when summer comes to
go with you and take walks and I know if I am a good girl
you will take me but I hope there will be no fever to
prevent me from having pleasure

your affectionate niece
E. Toussaint
Dear Uncle

P.S. I hope you will not forget the cravat

Another letter indicates that Pierre had permitted
Euphemia to write some of his patrons, among whom was
Miss Sarah Anne Moore, sister of Nicholas Fish Moore, presi-
dent of Columbia College. Miss Moore was also related to
Clement Clark Moore, the author of *The Night before Christmas*.

Dear Uncle

I believe that you will have a funny letter because all
what I have in my head I put it in Mrs. Moors letter but I
hope next week it will be better than this week Dear
Uncle I will thank you very much if you will give me a pair
of scissors

adieu Dear Uncle
Euphemie Toussaint

In spite of Pierre's love and assurance, Euphemia must
have had periodic yearnings about her mother. The following letters indicate this.

New York, October 8, 1823

Dear Uncle,

I am reading a story about a little boy whose name
was Jack and a gentleman named Mr. Glover one day as

he was going to take a ride and he heard a noise and he went to see what was the matter with the little boy and he went close up to him asked him what was the matter he told Mr. Glover that they put his mother in there he said she promised she would come again but she did not keep her promise

Adieu Dear Uncle
Euphemie Toussaint

In March, 1824, Euphemia was still thinking about the little boy named Jack whose mother had died. She wrote:

Dear Uncle

I read a story about a little boy whose name was Jack he had the misfortune to lose his mother before he had reached his fifth year and Mr. Glover was passing by a burying ground he heard the voice of this little boy and Mr. Glover went up to him and asked him what was the matter he said he was calling his mother who they had laid there yesterday. she told me she would come back again but she did not keep her promise. [Note: Euphemia used periods in two places.]

Adieu Dear Uncle
Euphemie Toussaint

By April of that same year (1824) Euphemia's thoughts were again turning toward emulating her elders by entertaining her little friends.

New York, April 2, 1824

Dear Uncle

I am very much obliged to you for them books you gave me when will you think of your promise I only want two or three of my friends with Mrs. Bennets and Mrs. Mitchels children

Adieu Dear Uncle
Euphemie Toussaint

In 1825 when there was a spate of balloon ascensions, these were also reflected in Euphemia's letters. Already Lafayette had returned to America as an elderly hero and had his parade up Broadway. To the once dashing general was given the honor of cutting the rope which permitted New York's first passenger balloon to rise into the skies over the Battery. Euphemia must have seen the balloon which went up that year from Castle Garden for she wrote her dear uncle:

"Did you see the balloon that went up Thursday afternoon at four o'clock? Poor Mrs. Joseph could not see it at all. Everybody saw it but her. She is in pain with her eyes. I think it is a great misfortune to have weak eyes but we must take it as God sends it."

The Toussaint home was a barometer of social events, especially of those events related to Catholic activity. For not only did Pierre attend the ladies of the most prominent families in old New York, he also waited on most of the French ladies who found time to visit the city. Euphemia usually knew what events were underway and what was anticipated. More than once Pierre had to admit that his niece listened well.

The orphans had outgrown the original building on Prince Street. Fr. John Powers was still trying to raise funds for a new building. Clement Moore, the author, had discovered Lorenzo Da Ponte in a Broadway bookstore. This talented musician who was also an ex-priest was said to be a friend and former collaborator of Mozart. The man was destitute and Moore, who took him to his home, was able to persuade a group of his friends interested in studying Italian to engage Da Ponte as a tutor. Though this only provided a meager living for Da Ponte, who had been a favorite at the court in Vienna as the author of the librettos for *Don Giovanni* and *The Marriage of Figaro,* he did meet members of the most prominent New York families.

A number of Pierre's patrons studied Italian with Da Ponte, and it was only natural that the musician would hear of Pierre and Fr. Powers' efforts to raise money for a new orphanage. A Mr. Dominick Lynch, Jr. became interested in the project, and Da Ponte persuaded him to sponsor the Garcia Singers, already famous throughout Europe, in a New York appearance for the benefit of the orphanage. Da Ponte finally convinced Signor Garcia, the leader of the group, that this would be an excellent opportunity to be the first to present Italian opera in New York.

Euphemia must have heard some of the plans unfold since she wrote:

"I have heard that the Italian opera singers have arrived and you said that when they come you would go to the theater. I hope I shall be able to go and see them. I should like to see them very much indeed. I have heard that they cannot speak any other language than Italian."

The Garcia Singers did come to America. Maria Felicita Garcia, the leader's daughter, was the prima donna. She later married and became famous as Madame Malibran.

The benefit concert given by the Garcia Singers at the new St. Patrick's Cathedral was a tremendous success. Pierre assisted Fr. Powers as ticket taker. He and Juliette evidently took Euphemia since she wrote on November 25, 1825:

"When we were at the opera a few nights ago I think that young lady sang 'home sweet home' so sweetly that I should be very much pleased if you would be so kind as to get it for me and I will try to imitate her as much as I possibly can not only in song but in all."

Euphemia did not know that the choir members at St. Patrick's were so unimpressed by the Garcia Singers that they resigned en masse. But Fr. Powers and Pierre were happy because the concert had been a financial success. Soon afterward Fr. Powers was able to build an orphanage that would accommodate 150 children.

In October 1826 Bishop John Dubois, who succeeded
Bishop Connolly, was consecrated and Pierre did not take
Euphemia. Later she wrote: "Have you seen the new bishop?
I have not seen him yet. I believe I will go to see him some
day at church."

Juliette's mother Claudine Gaston had a son Joseph who
had children, for in one letter, written May 13, 1825,
Euphemia said:

Dear Uncle

I begin to think that Gaston and me will soon be able to
play the jou jou very well indeed and then I hope that you
will give a party and a large one too that will be some
recompense for the pains we have taken to learn it.

Adieu Dear Uncle
Euphemie Toussaint

Pierre's own happiness only caused him to double his
efforts to help those less fortunate. An increasing number of
priests appealed to him for help of one sort or another. The
boys in the basement came and went—but they always left in
a better condition than when he first gave them shelter.
People from all over the city appealed to him for aid, knowing that he would always help in whatever way he could.

Evenings after Euphemia was asleep, it was Pierre's pleasure to point out to Juliette the familiar phrases in
Euphemia's letters such as "We must take it as God sends it,"
or "God knows best."

Pierre was pleased at the concern Euphemia showed for
others. A Mrs. Danenberg appears to have been one of
Euphemia's favorites, and in November 1825 she wrote:

Dear Uncle

I have heard that Mrs. Danenberg was very sick indeed her daughter came hear for you to go for Doctor
Berger but you was not at home and I sent Peter [most
likely one of the homeless boys] with her for him I feel

very sorry for her and I hope she will soon be better I think that she is a very good lady Dear Uncle I think that your promise is a long time comming I hope that you have not forgotten it a reddy I love to make you think of your promise,

Adieu Dear Uncle
Euphemie Toussaint

As much as Pierre loved Euphemia, there were times when he had to scold her for some childish prank. This was indicated in the letter she wrote, saying:

Dear Uncle

I am very sorry that to please you I did not wish you a happy birthday as I had not a clear heart to wish it to you I feel very angry with myself to think that I had occasion to make you angry dear uncle will you be so kind if you please to forgive me this once and wait until New Years and then I hope I will be able to wish you a happy New Years and feel happy myself allways and learn well.

Adieu Dear Uncle

The two letters each week continued, and Pierre noted Euphemia's improvement in French as well as in English. She had a new French teacher, and Mrs. Ruckel admitted she was an excellent English student considering her age. Needless to say none of the other students came near to matching her skills in letter writing or reading.

The following letter shows how Euphemia had progressed.

New York, June 13, 1828

Dear Uncle

I take this opportunity to write you to tell you that Mr. Genvere says that I have but two weeks to read French as well as any one I am so pleased to hear it that I will study as much as I can I have changed my verbs I am now learning the four conjugations that is not difficult for when you know the first the rest are nothing. Dear Uncle do you know what part of the country Mrs. Bancel is gone and if she is going to stay all summer will you be so kind as to excuse me for having so short a letter this week for I began to compose it very late I hope that next week I will make it up.

Adieu Dear Uncle
Euphemie Toussaint

Pierre continued to extend himself so as to help all who appealed to him for advice or material assistance. Juliette, who had already written a number of short letters to her Cousin Fanny in Baltimore—as a result of studying along with Euphemia—admitted to herself that she, too, had every reason to be happy. Yet she experienced a strange sense of uneasiness whenever Euphemia complained of being tired. She attempted to discuss Euphemia's recurrent spells of fatigue with Pierre.

"She is exceptionally tall for her age," Pierre told Juliette. "What you consider weariness is just growing pains."

Juliette was not satisfied with her husband's explanation of Euphemia's listlessness. She had observed the child on several occasions when she was making a determined effort to fight off the fatigue which seemed to overcome her near the end of each day.

Pierre's complacency made Juliette doubt her own best judgment. Perhaps, she decided, there was really nothing to worry about.

CHAPTER 16

Events Force Change

Pierre began to think more and more about the manner in which he was preparing Euphemia for life. In contemplating the kind of life the little girl would have, he pondered his own situation. Though he was black, through an odd set of circumstances he had been accepted into the homes of New York's most prestigious families—because they needed his services. With his French patrons, his fluency in his native tongue and the impeccable manners which were the result of the training Zenobie, Ursule and the Bérards had begun when he was a toddler, he had many assets. Then Jean Jacques Bérard had taught him enough English before they came to New York to enable him to manage the household affairs at 105 Reade Street. Through perseverance he had mastered the new language, though he would never entirely lose his French accent.

In looking back over the years, Pierre could not forget how perplexed he had been when Monsieur Bérard had told him he had made arrangements for his apprenticeship with Mr. Merchant.

"God must have been in that plan," Pierre smiled as he thought of the benefits derived from his profession.

In spite of all this self-examination, Pierre was not sure

what would be the best preparation for Euphemia. A black girl in New York faced a doubtful future.

Sometimes as he was curling the hair of one of his more garrulous patrons who was discussing the plight of the immigrants, Pierre had to steady the hand with which he held the hot tongs when the lady said: "At least the blacks are fairly clean. But these Irish and German immigrants—they are all so dirty and ragged."

Pierre thought about the condition in which he found some of the homeless boys he took to 105 Reade Street. He smuggled them into the basement and gave them a basin of water, soap and a towel with the hope that neither Juliette nor her mother Claudine would see them or get a stray whiff of the scents coming from their unwashed bodies. Now it was the white immigrants who were the social outcasts. Yet these same white immigrants were taking jobs formerly held by freed black men.

As Pierre walked home from one of his appointments, it was not unusual for some black man or woman to approach him with a story of how they had lost a job because a white immigrant agreed to do the same work for cheaper wages. Pierre always listened. In many instances he advanced a small loan. At other times, when he knew the person to be industrious and trustworthy, he was in a position to direct them to the home of one of his patrons who might need domestic help.

At times like this Pierre thought of Euphemia. "I am not educating her to be a maid or a charwoman," he would mutter. "What else is there for her? She will not know want as long as I live, but I will not live forever."

One night in the privacy of their quarters, Pierre confided his fears to Juliette.

"She could be a teacher," Juliette said, after giving the matter some thought.

"And where would she teach?"

Juliette reminded him of the African Free School, which

had been founded in 1787 by the New York Manumission Society. Pierre then remembered he had heard that John Jay, later governor of New York, had been the first president of the society.

"I once heard you say Alexander Hamilton was the secretary. I know how you respected Mr. Jay and Mr. Hamilton."

Pierre smiled. "You, too, listen well."

"You've been a teacher to all of us," Juliette insisted. "How else would we know what is happening in New York? There is hardly a night when you come home that I don't learn something that I didn't know before. Yet there are times when you don't see the end of your nose."

"Pardon?" asked the startled Pierre, who was not accustomed to the critical note in Juliette's voice.

"You are worrying about Euphemia's future—years from now. But you never noticed that in that letter you read yesterday from cousin Fanny, she mentioned that she had received my letter—not yours. That was the first letter I ever wrote and you—you never said a word." Juliette burst into tears.

Pierre embraced his weeping wife. *"Ma chérie,"* he was the French lover once more. "Stupid! Stupid Pierre!"

The weeping woman shook her head violently. *"Vous habile*—you are clever—and sometimes forgetful—but never stupid!" Juliette smiled as she wiped away the tears.

"Fanny's comment did not escape my eyes," Pierre admitted, "but I did not want to embarrass you as we had never discussed your inability to write. I saw you working with Euphemia and anticipated the outcome. But, *chérie,* I did not marry you for your literary accomplishments. I married you because you are the most beautiful, understanding and loyal woman I have ever known."

"And because I waited for you," Juliette teased.

Suddenly Pierre gasped and hit his forehead with his palm.

"What is wrong?" Juliette was alarmed.

Pierre searched the pockets of his jacket until he found the envelope he sought. "Speaking of letters, a French gentleman who recently arrived in New York brought this to the shop today," Pierre said as he opened a letter from Mlle. Aurore Bérard.

Juliette saw the frown on Pierre's face. "Is she ill? What did she say?"

"She does not think it would be wise for us to move to France just to be near her."

"She must have said more than that," Juliette prodded.

"Jean Sorbieu called on her and they discussed my desire to come to France. She writes," and Pierre smiled before he proceeded to read:

> This gentleman appears to be much attached to you, which gives me great happiness. We talked together of your wish to come to France.
>
> If I consulted only my own desire to see you, I should say, come at once. But your happiness, my dear godson, is what I think of above all things, and since everyone from New York tells me that you are happy, highly esteemed and much beloved by most respectable persons there, would you be well off here?
>
> Those who know your resources better than I do may advise you with more confidence. If I were rich, it would be of little consequence. I would call you near to me, for I should be too happy to know a person to whom I could give all my confidence and of whose attachment I would feel certain....
>
> But my position is a sad one. I could not be useful to you, and I fear that you would not be as happy as you deserve.

Pierre let the letter drop to the floor. As Juliette picked it up he spoke. "I did not tell you that I heard from Mrs. Larue, and she said much the same thing. She and Mrs. Cruger had discussed the matter and decided it is best for us to remain in New York. It seems that the maids in France style the ladies' hair and a coiffeur is only used on special occasions. So these two hands could not make much of a living in France," Pierre laughed.

"It is for the best," Juliette smiled. "I had worried about how Euphemia would stand the long voyage."

"She is young and healthy. She would have enjoyed the sea."

"Euphemia is young, but she is only healthy because we feed and pamper her. She tires very easily."

"And who pampers her more than her Aunt Juliette?" Pierre laughed.

"Her dear uncle—who must be as tired as her Aunt Juliette."

"You go to bed," Pierre said as he took from another pocket several slips of paper and some money he had forgotten. "I must make these entries in the ledger. Sr. Cecelia is grateful for every penny."

"By all means take her the money," Juliette said, "or else I will have no excuse when Euphemia asks when she can bring all the orphans home to tea."

Not all of the freed blacks accepted the inferior role in the everyday life of New York to which they had been relegated. From time to time delegations would come to 105 Reade Street for the purpose of enlisting Pierre's aid in one cause or another. In most cases Juliette spoke for Pierre, who she knew was overburdened. But the group in favor of the Colonization Society's plan to send all those of African descent back to Africa persisted in trying to win Pierre's support. They thought his Haitian background would render him sympathetic to the Back-to-Africa Movement.

Pierre dismissed this delegation politely and suggested to them that since Haiti was now a black republic it might be easier for them to get there than to Africa. He was so courteous and pleasant that the men were outside Pierre's home before they realized he had refused all their requests.

Pierre had already encouraged Juliette and her mother

to contribute to the New York African Society for Mutual Relief when that society purchased a lot and erected a building at Orange Street (now Baxter) in 1820. Pierre approved of this group as they were dedicated to the purpose of caring for widows and orphans of deceased members.

That day in early 1820, when Pierre heard the *Elizabeth*—one of two ships outfitted to carry the Afro-Americans back to Africa—was to set sail, he avoided the blocks leading to the waterfront. He had heard that forty of the eighty-six blacks aboard were New Yorkers, but none of them were his friends. So he skirted the crowd and hurried to his appointments.

Neither Juliette nor Pierre were sure how Euphemia heard about the ship. Pierre was nonplussed that night when he came home and the little girl asked him to tell her about the ship going to Africa. Though she could barely pronounce the name, she insisted that he tell her where Africa was.

Pierre found an atlas that had belonged to the Bérards and pointed out the continent of Africa, which Euphemia had thought was a country. She asked so many questions that he told her about Tonette and Zenobie back at L'Artibonite. He pointed to Guinea and told her that had once been Tonette's home. Years later Pierre still remembered how he had prayed silently as he waited for Euphemia to ask him why Tonette and Zenobie had left Guinea and gone to St. Dominique.

Instead the child fell asleep in his arms.

As the years passed, Pierre knew he could not postpone the discussion he must have with Euphemia about slavery and how he, her mother and Juliette had obtained their freedom. Though Congress had passed a law in 1808 prohibiting the sale of slaves in the United States, the state of New York had taken no immediate steps to free those already enslaved. As far back as 1799 the New York Legislature had passed an act which stipulated that emancipation of slaves should take place in the state no later than 1827. Though

Pierre realized he could not avoid the discussion of slavery with Euphemia, he refrained from introducing the subject.

Cesarine Meetz, the musician, had grown even closer to the Toussaints since she offered to teach Euphemia. Their household was astir with excitement when they received an invitation to attend Miss Meetz' wedding. Then followed Euphemia's consternation when she learned that the young woman would be going to France to live after she married Charles Moulton. Juliette tried to cheer the little girl by telling her how she would enjoy receiving letters from her music teacher and how proud her uncle would be that she could answer these letters in French. The anticipation of the letters did not dispel the little girl's gloom. Then Pierre brought home a bolt of deep rose-colored chalis for Juliette to make dresses for the two of them to wear to the wedding. Euphemia's mood changed in the excitement of helping her Aunt Juliette select a suitable pattern.

The wedding must have been a pleasant experience for Euphemia since she wrote:

February 23, 1827

Dear Uncle:

O, how sorry I am that you were not there to see Miss Meetz married; she looked so sweet and beautiful; she looked like an angel; but what I think was so good in her, that she should come and kiss my aunt and me, before all the company. I believe nobody would do it but her. It will come quite difficult for me to call her Mrs. Moulton. I have made one mistake already.

Adieu dear uncle
Euphemia Toussaint

It would appear from this letter that Euphemia had understood her music teacher's relationship with them better than her uncle realized.

Euphemia was approaching her twelfth birthday when Pierre brought in a copy of the July 4, 1827 issue of the City

Gazette and read Governor Thompkin's message setting forth the act which called for state-wide emancipation of slaves.

That year the fourth of July had fallen on Sunday. So the big celebration and parade were to take place the next day. But Pierre heard that Rev. William Hamilton, said to be the illegitimate son of Alexander Hamilton, was scheduled to deliver an oration on emancipation that Sunday at the African Zion Church. He hoped the sermon would be more inspirational than exciting.

Pierre knew the streets would be filled with jubilant black men and women on July 5th. He also knew that Euphemia deserved an explanation of slavery and its consequences, in spite of his dread of having to be the one to tell her.

When the time came, Pierre explained to Euphemia that he could only tell her about his own family background and the slaves at L'Artibonite. He explained the so-called economic reasons behind the planters importing Africans who had been captured and taken away from their homes to become slaves in a strange land where they toiled from sunup to sundown without any rights or recompense. He felt compelled to admit that few slave owners were as kind as the elder Bérards. Once again he painted a word picture of L'Artibonite, even to describing the manor house and the huts where the slaves lived.

Juliette, who was listening nearby, wondered if Pierre would tell his niece about Maurice and Berto. Though he referred to men like Caradeux and Ducheine, who had brutalized their slaves, Pierre could not bring himself to burden Euphemia with the gory details.

He admitted that he knew little about slavery in the southern states but told Euphemia that Juliette's master had threatened to sell her to a southern planter before her mother raised the money to purchase her freedom. He had to explain his relationship with Madame Bérard as he told the little girl how the Frenchwoman had freed him on her deathbed.

Overwhelmed by all her uncle was telling her, Euphemia had remained silent. When Pierre was explaining how Madame Bérard-Nicolas had insisted that a lawyer come and draw up his papers of manumission, the little girl spoke up.

"It was about time!" she said.

Pierre and Juliette exchanged glances. It was almost as if Rosalie had spoken.

When Pierre had finished, he could tell that Euphemia was trying to reconcile all he had told her with her sheltered existence at 105 Reade Street.

"And what about my father?" she asked. "Was he a slave?"

"No, you were born of free parents. But it has been difficult for black men to find jobs. Your father, who like your Aunt Juliette, was a Noel, never seemed to be able to keep the type of employment that would enable him to provide for his family."

"You are black, but you always have work," Euphemia pointed out.

"Monsieur Bérard made sure that I had a profession. That is why I have tried to remind you that not all slave owners were evil men."

"If he was such a good man, why didn't he free you before he went back to St. Dominique?" Euphemia demanded.

Pierre was thoughtful. There was no way of evading Euphemia's question. He was paying the price for having delayed this moment of truth. Yet truth was on his side.

"As I look back over the years," he began, "I was never made to feel like a slave. There was only a few years' difference in my age and Jean Jacques Bérard's. His parents, his brothers and sisters all went to France. In St. Dominique he only had my family—and me—until he married. In matters pertaining to the habitation he depended on me, knowing my family would support whatever he did. In New York, we became even closer. We—we were almost like brothers, only he was white and I was black."

"Then why didn't he free you?"

"I honestly think he had forgotten I was a slave," Pierre found the memory of his relationship with Jean Jacques Bérard pleasant. "Just," he continued, "as some of my patrons appear to forget that I am black."

Juliette placed a tray with a pot of chocolate and cups on a table near Pierre's chair in time to hear Euphemia's next question.

"Did my father ever see me before he went away?"

"Your Aunt Juliette and her mother were with Dr. Berger when you were born. She told me that your father was very proud when they told him he had a daughter." Pierre wondered what would come next.

Euphemia sighed. "Well, if he had not gone away," she sat at Pierre's feet and rested her head on his lap, "my dear uncle would not have adopted me, and just think of all I would have missed. God was in the plan. And do you know what?"

"No," Pierre was spent from the interrogation.

"I think I am the luckiest girl in New York—black or white!"

"You are God's blessing upon the marriage of your Aunt Juliette and your Uncle Pierre," he said, and the three Toussaints embraced.

The next day when the emancipation celebrations took place in the neighborhoods where most of the citizens of New York of African descent lived, Euphemia insisted that her uncle should come home early and take her for a walk. That morning at Mass, Pierre prayed that the festivities would be peaceful. That afternoon as the two of them started out for the walk, he prayed that the child would not pull him into some of the sidestreets where he knew many of his people lived in squalor. But Euphemia loved to walk down Broadway and sit in City Hall Park. She enjoyed the warm greetings of friends who recognized her uncle and complimented him on his lovely daughter. Sometimes one of his many patrons would pass in a carriage and wave to her uncle. Pierre would bow gracefully but Euphemia returned a wave with a wave.

Pierre's fears disappeared that July 5th as they sat in City Hall Park. Several black men and women he knew came over and commented on the significance of the occasion. They were all sober, hardworking people who were pleased with the turn of events. In a little while Euphemia announced that it was time for a visit to St. Peter's since she had to get home to help her aunt and prepare her lessons for the next day.

"Maybe one day, if it is God's will, I can teach other black boys and girls to read and write and play the piano," she said soberly as she pulled Pierre along toward the church.

Pierre felt that his relationship with Euphemia had been even more rewarding after their discussion of slavery. Her teachers all said she was applying herself more consistently than ever before. Her letters continued, but more and more religious references were included. Juliette was puzzled when Pierre showed her one of the letters and Euphemia had written "if it is God's will that I live another year." To Pierre it was merely a pious phrase. From time to time she wrote of her determination to support her aunt and uncle when they grew old so as to show her appreciation for all they had done for her.

Juliette and Euphemia made a point of standing in the doorway of 105 Reade Street each morning when Pierre set out for his appointments or the shop. A few yards from the corner he would look back at the two of them, and they would wave him on his way.

Pierre's last stop of the day was usually at the home of Mary Anne Schuyler, who looked forward to these late afternoon chats with Pierre. When he left Mrs. Schuyler's, he would stop at a confectioner's or a flower shop to carry some token of his love to the two loved ones he knew would be watching and waiting for him. The leavetaking and home-coming continued to be a ritual for Pierre, who still walked to all of his appointments.

Some of the trams now carried signs which said "colored" were allowed to ride. When Pierre's friends suggested that his work would be much easier if he rode the trams, he replied: "I am still black," and continued to walk.

Throughout each day Pierre would chuckle over some-thing Euphemia had written in one of her letters or some endearing remark she had made. Juliette saved the child's wittiest sayings for their late night talks when there was no danger of Euphemia overhearing them.

From time to time Pierre shared Euphemia's letters with a few of his patrons. Mrs. Schuyler was much impressed with Pierre's reports of Euphemia's progress, and Mrs. Cruger, who spent much time in France, saw the notes Euphemia wrote Mrs. Larue, who regularly sent Pierre her contribution for the orphans.

As each year began Euphemia wrote her uncle a letter of greeting. On January 1, 1829, she wrote:

Dear Uncle

Will you be pleased to accept my most respectful compliments on the close of the old and the commence-ment of the new year. Give me leave, dear uncle, to tell you as well as my poor mind can express itself how truly sensible I am of all your favors. I will try by my conduct to merit the continuance of them.

As it has pleased God to give you good health during the course of the last year, I beseech him to grant you the same to the end of the present and many more, my prayers are morning and night offered up to heaven for your preservation. Nor are you ever in the day absent from my thoughts.

I remain your dutiful niece,
Euphemia Toussaint.

Pierre was touched by the tone of the entire letter but most of all by the passage saying he was never in the day absent from her thoughts. From Euphemia's infancy he could not think of a day when she had not been in his thoughts and prayers.

Juliette, who continued to make all of Euphemia's clothes, noticed one day as she fitted a dress that the child's collar bone was excessively protruding. Then she noted that Euphemia's arms looked thinner than she had recalled.

Juliette redoubled her efforts to coax the child to eat, but she could not fail to admit that Euphemia was becoming more listless. Then one afternoon she found the girl with her head on the piano. She was fast asleep. That evening Euphemia begged to take a little nap until it was time for "dear uncle" to come home.

Pierre was apprehensive when he saw Juliette waiting for him alone. "Where is Euphemie?" he asked.

"In bed. She is not well. I felt her forehead and she is feverish," Juliette was obviously worried.

"It is probably another cold," Pierre tried to appear casual. "Just the same, I'll send one of the boys for Dr. Berger. He will have her back on her feet in no time."

"I—I hope so," Juliette said as the tears she was fighting rolled down her cheeks. "My mother is in the kitchen, and we are both worried."

"Women, women, women," Pierre chided. "You are always worrying. Euphemia will have a good dinner, and Dr. Berger will come and prescribe medicine for the child. In a few days she will be filling this house with music and chatter."

Juliette and her mother watched Pierre as he climbed the steps to Euphemia's room. They had fought to keep this child alive for almost fifteen years, and now they were fearful that the disease which claimed Rosalie's life would take Euphemia away from them.

Dr. Berger, who seldom made house calls at night any-more, came before the Toussaints had finished their evening meal. Juliette let him in.

"Don't tell me that Pierre Toussaint has finally caught a cold," the old doctor teased.

"It's Euphemia," Juliette explained, as she took Dr. Berger's coat.

"Euphemia?" the doctor stroked his chin. "The last time I saw her she was leading her uncle down Broadway at a pace that made me fearful for Pierre. How long has she been complaining?"

"She is not really complaining, Doctor," Juliette explained as Pierre joined them. "She—she's just listless, drowsy and feverish."

"Thank you for coming out on such a cold night," Pierre shook hands with the doctor. "I will take you to your little patient."

Juliette went back to the kitchen. She made no effort to hide her fears from Claudine.

"You had better go to your husband," the old woman told her daughter. "I've a feeling he'll need you."

Juliette was grateful for her mother's advice when Dr. Berger took the two of them aside after he examined Euphemia.

"It is much harder for me to tell you this now," the doctor began, "than it was when she was born."

"Are you saying it is not an ordinary cold?" Pierre asked.

"Far from it. I am afraid Euphemia has advanced tuber-culosis."

As hard as Pierre tried to control himself, Juliette felt him trembling when she reached for his hand.

"There must be something I can do. I'll take her to the finest health spa. Surely the baths at Baden-Baden will help."

"I have to make one or two more tests, but I'm almost sure there is nothing we can do," the doctor said solemnly. "The child is wasting away."

"You don't mean," Pierre was incredulous, "you don't mean Euphemia—no, not my little Euphemia! Doctor Berger, just tell me what to do. I won't stand by and see her die—Tell me what to do!"

"Pierre, I'm afraid there is nothing you can do now. You once told me Euphemia was your miracle. You've had her for a number of years now, and we will have to accept the inevitable," the doctor motioned to Juliette to bring him a basin so he could wash his hands.

"You are right," Pierre could not even force his usual smile. "God gave Euphemia to me, and if it pleases him to take her back I must accept his will. But this will be the heaviest cross I have ever borne."

Dr. Berger became a constant visitor at the Toussaint home. After a number of tests he knew there was nothing he could do for Euphemia but make sure she was comfortable. The old doctor worried about Pierre and Juliette. Juliette and her mother gave Euphemia every attention. From time to time Mrs. Ruckel came and looked over whatever lessons Euphemia felt like completing. Pierre's knees were often stiff from kneeling so long before the crucifix at St. Peter's. On days when he was most despondent, he would kneel in prayer until he could make himself repeat with conviction: "I will take it as God sends it."

In the beginning, Euphemia sometimes felt good enough to get up. When she talked about going to Mrs. Ruckel's classes, Juliette reminded her that Mrs. Ruckel would be coming to her room as everybody wanted her to rest until she was strong again. After a while the girl made no attempt to leave her bed. And if she felt any pain she never complained.

"She's just wasting away," Claudine Gaston reminded Juliette, "like her mother."

"But she doesn't have that hacking cough like Rosalie," Juliette found herself building hopes she knew to be false.

"That—and the hemorrhages—will come later."

"Poor Pierre! I fear he will never be the same. Euphemia means so much to him."

"And what about Juliette?" her mother asked.

"From the moment she came into this world—when her mother was more dead than alive, she has been like my own child. I'll never forget how I felt after you bathed her and put her in my arms. Dr. Berger was calling for you. He told you to forget about the baby, since she would never live, and help with Rosalie, who was barely breathing. It was as if that baby was my flesh and blood, and I was ready to fight anybody or anything that tried to take her away from me.

"Her father preened himself when I told him he had a daughter, but he never offered to take her, and Rosalie was too weak to hold her. I put her in your arms when I came home to tell Pierre. When we brought her, here Pierre nursed her night and day. When he had to go to work I took her. All Rosalie could do was look at her baby and smile her thanks to me. She was never strong enough to hold the child in her arms. Rosalie wanted me to have Euphemia. She's mine! And now God wants to take her from me," she moaned.

Claudine had listened as her daughter talked. She knew how Juliette had struggled to improve her speech and her manners after Pierre came into her life. Now her defenses were down and Claudine heard accents and intonations she had not heard for years. Then the uncontrolled sobbing began.

"I'm not sure even Pierre can accept this," Juliette said between sobs. "Euphemia means everything to him!"

"If you keep carrying on like this, Euphemia will hear you," Claudine warned. "As much as Pierre prays, God will comfort him. They say the kneeler in pew #25 at St. Peter's has been smoothed down by Pierre's knees."

"I know," Juliette tried to smile, "but Euphemia was the

first person he felt was all his own. He said God gave her to him."

"What about you?"

"That's different. She was so little and helpless, but Pierre would not give up, even when Dr. Berger said there was no hope. He not only nursed her, but he also planned for her future. That worried him."

"He worried about you, too, when we thought you might be sold to that southern planter," Claudine reminded.

"Did he really?" Juliette wiped her eyes. "Was he that much in love with me? I used to think he thought Rosalie and I were the two silliest girls in the whole world."

"I think Pierre loved you from the day he saw you. That's why I had to turn to him for help when I thought you were going to be sold."

"Are you telling me that Pierre paid for my freedom?"

"Where else would I have gotten that much money?"

"That was money he was saving to buy Rosalie's papers," Juliette reminded her.

"I knew he wanted Rosalie to be free before she married Jean, and I never felt that would work out because I knew Jean so well. So I figured Pierre would have time to save more money for Rosalie—after he helped me save you," the older woman was afraid of her daughter's disapproval.

"Why didn't you tell me before?" Juliette asked.

"Pierre made me promise I would not tell you."

"I always suspected—from different things you said. But Pierre acted as if my freedom was a big surprise to him, and after a while I stopped thinking about it. Now I must try to help him face the loss of—of the only daughter we ever had."

Claudine was troubled about breaking her promise to Pierre. But when he came home the next day he barely spoke to his mother-in-law after he kissed his wife in his hurry to get back to Euphemia's room. The two women saw the packages he had brought, but that had become a daily occurrence. Pierre's patrons had learned of Euphemia's illness, and they sent candies, toys and flowers of every description to the girl they had come to know through her uncle.

Madame Larue, who had entrusted the care of the orphans to Pierre, also sent candy from France, and Pierre's godmother assured him of her prayers for Euphemia's recovery. Fr. Powers came often. The priest marveled at how Euphemia demonstrated the Christian upbringing she had received and wondered how he would console the Toussaints when she died.

On the rare occasions when Pierre felt Euphemia's brow and Juliette confirmed the fact that the child had not been running a temperature that day, Pierre decided his prayers were being answered. If he came home the next day and Euphemia was in a feverish stupor, he would alternate between applying wet cloths to her forehead, praying or sending one of the boys from the basement to get Dr. Berger. The doctor never refused Pierre's requests and near the end refrained from telling him his services were useless, as he knew Pierre no longer heard what he was saying.

As the trees began to bud, Pierre made sure the shutters were open so Euphemia could see the miracle of another spring. But the cough Juliette had anticipated began to wrack the tiny frame, and finally there were flecks of blood in the girl's sputum.

Pierre refused to see anything but the feeble flame of life in his beloved Euphemia. He would read to her, then take her in his arms and when she was able to talk she would tell him about things they might do one day and places they would visit. Sometimes Juliette, who was always nearby, saw how hard he was trying to control himself and suggested that he take a walk while she sat with Euphemia.

As Pierre went out to St. Peter's each morning, he was reminded of how Euphemia had enjoyed watching the new leaves on the trees. His patrons continued to send flowers, but watching the child waste away rendered him little more than a robot. Juliette and her mother bathed the feverish child and tied ribbons on her thick braids when she could stand for them to comb her hair. Fr. Powers, who had had much experience with such illnesses, had spent almost an hour with Euphemia the morning of the day she died. Her death was peaceful, more like a deep sleep.

It was May 11, 1829. Pierre forced himself to make the arrangements for the funeral. Euphemia Toussaint was buried in St. Patrick's Cemetery, where Pierre had buried her mother.

Juliette's grief was obvious, but Pierre did not weep. Neither did he talk. His shop was closed and his patrons began to worry about him. The strong Pierre they had known had become an enigma.

CHAPTER 17

Pierre's Long Night Begins

When Pierre reopened his shop after Euphemia's death, his patrons made sure there were numerous demands for his services awaiting him. Yet when Pierre kept these appointments, his closest friends were perplexed by the change in the man. He was punctual, polite and as skillful as ever. But the amiability of the old Pierre who would go out of his way to give advice or assistance to any who asked seemed to have disappeared.

Not even Juliette was aware of the fight Pierre was waging to make himself submissive to God's will. His kneeling figure was a familiar sight at St. Peter's. Juliette went with him daily to early Mass, but she knew he stopped in whenever he passed the church. Juliette's brother Joseph, a drifter much like Euphemia's father, told his sister he had followed Pierre into the church one day but that his brother-in-law had prayed so long he left, then came back and found him still on his knees praying.

"You probably went back because you wanted to borrow some money," Juliette said, and she soon knew she had not misjudged her brother.

"Doesn't matter," Joseph defended himself. "Your husband is *fou*—crazy!"

"Pierre is not crazy! He is heartbroken! Euphemia meant

so much to him. Before she came I never realized how much he loved children," Juliette admitted.

"No need to go crazy over one child. I'll give him one of mine," Joseph laughed.

"Get out!" Juliette picked up a broom, and her brother ran out the door laughing as his sister ran after him. "I feel sorry for the poor children who have you for a father," she called, her anger drying the tears she might have shed.

Night after night Pierre read Euphemia's letters. He never saw a black child in the street without thinking of the little girl he had lost. Pierre began to realize that few if any children of Euphemia's age and race had enjoyed the advantages he had given her. Looking at children who were obviously in need made him wonder what he could do to help them.

Many letters of condolence came to the Toussaints from Pierre's patrons and friends. Mlle. Bérard and Madame Larue wrote from France, as did Mrs. Cruger, who had been visiting in that country and was informed of Euphemia's death by Madame Larue. Men and women Pierre had helped came to the house and stopped him in the street to offer their sympathy.

Juliette had been especially touched by the concern shown by former slaves from their island home. They brought cakes and other native dishes, and each had a story to tell of how Pierre had helped them.

"I'm still learning what kind of man I married," Juliette told her mother one day when an old woman came with a coconut she must have picked up on the wharf and tried, in broken English, to tell what Pierre had done for her.

Claudine recognized the woman as a slave from St. Dominique, and she spoke to her in Creole.

The old woman then told them about her son. Her master had beaten the boy repeatedly because of his laziness. She begged her son to do his work. Instead he ran away and the master was so glad to get rid of him he refused to help her find him. Months had passed and the mother had not seen the boy until one day she was passing 105 Reade Street and he came out of the basement. The woman said she had not recognized her son at first but was attracted to him when he saw her and began running. She succeeded in following him to Pierre's shop, then waited a few moments before she went in and met Pierre, as the boy was hiding in the rear. Pierre told her the boy had been living in his home, the clothes he was wearing were not stolen as she had suggested, and that he was taking her son that day to the home of a family he hoped would employ him.

Though expressions of sympathy continued to arrive at the Toussaint residence, requests for aid seemed to multiply. A widow needed wood. An impoverished French refugee begged financial assistance so he could bring his family back to America from France. And there were always the poor priests who appealed to Pierre for funds to study or carry on their mission work. If these priests were visiting New York, they were sure of a meal with the Toussaints and if need be there was always an extra bed. From time to time Juliette, who had learned to read with Euphemia, saw letters of appreciation from young seminarians studying in Rome. Always they assured Pierre of their prayers.

Pierre and Juliette observed that Old Cabress, whose senility fluctuated like an ebbing tide, always seemed to come out of her shell when the young priests were visiting. She would tell these clergymen long rambling stories that they seldom understood. What they did understand was that she was well into her nineties, alone in a strange land and waiting to join her loved ones who were in heaven. Some days nobody saw the old woman, but Juliette knew her well enough to know she had stored up enough food to exist on before she went into these days of seclusion. She never neglected to tell Juliette she was praying for Pierre.

Juliette knew Pierre was wracked by grief, and she struggled to push aside her own sorrow in order to console

him. Her mother reminded her that Pierre had not brought
a stray boy home since Euphemia's funeral and that he was
taking more interest in efforts being made to help runaway
slaves from the South. Juliette remembered he had told her
that two of New York's leading merchants, Arthur and Lewis
Tappan, were secretly leading a movement to aid the fugitives. From the manner in which Pierre spoke, she knew he
would find a way to help, though she also knew he would
elect to remain anonymous.

Juliette was surprised one day to open her door to Mrs.
Mary Anne Schuyler. The gentlewoman said she came because all of Pierre's patrons and friends were worried about
him and wondered if there was anything they could do.

"My sons, who have known and loved Pierre all their
lives, keep asking me how they can cheer him up. They
wondered if a trip would help," she said.

"Madame, there is nothing anyone can do. It is all in
God's hands. But," Juliette added, "I do appreciate your
interest."

As her carriage drove away, Mary Anne Schuyler looked
back at Juliette standing in the doorway. "Poor woman," she
thought. "Pierre always told me what a delight it was to come
home at the end of a day and find Juliette and Euphemia
waiting at the door. Now Juliette is alone."

Then the break Juliette had been praying for came. It
was as unexpected as a deafening bolt of lightning zigzag-
ging across a clear blue sky. Pierre was smiling when he
came home that evening. She could not remember seeing a
smile on her husband's face since Euphemia's death.
Juliette was glad she had prepared an appetizing meal in
spite of the fact that Pierre had been pushing his plate aside
with half the food uneaten, and though he always apologized, Juliette worried because she knew he had begun to
keep a grueling schedule again.

Pierre's wife watched him as he ate heartily and then

asked for a second cup of chocolate after pastries. Juliette poured herself another cup and returned to the table.

"Stupid, stupid Pierre!" he began.

"I won't listen to such talk," Juliette put her hands over both ears.

"I keep thinking God took Euphemia. He did not take her—he gave her to me and let her live for almost fifteen years. He let me hold her like a beautiful gift to me."

"God gave her to *us*," Juliette reminded him.

"Forgive me," Pierre begged. "I have been so wrapped in my own grief, I lost sight of your sorrow. And you had her from the day she was born. This morning at church it was as if a voice was whispering—*the Lord giveth and the Lord taketh away*. Then I remembered how you said Dr. Berger insisted she would never live. He even told me that. But God heard my prayers and let her live. Do you realize those were the happiest years of my life?"

"And mine," Juliette added.

"We were blessed to have had her," Pierre repeated, but Juliette, seeing him emerge from his sorrow, vented her own grief.

"My dear wife," Pierre embraced the weeping woman, "God will sustain us. And we must take it as God sends it."

Juliette smiled through her tears. "Rosalie and Euphemia would expect you to say that."

The next day after Pierre left the house, Juliette draped one of her most colorful scarves about her head, threw a bright shawl about her shoulders and hurried to the Schuyler residence on Canal Street to tell Pierre's friend that their prayers had been answered. They agreed that nobody was to comment on the change in Pierre, and Mrs. Schuyler said she would share the good news with the Stevens, Crugers, Hamiltons and all the others who had been so worried.

That night Pierre busied himself with the ledger in

which he kept an account of the funds he turned over to Sr. Cecelia on the first Monday of each month. Other than the officers of the Roman Catholic Benevolent Society and the Ladies' Auxiliary, the sisters had no one to look to for their support but Pierre. He said Sr. Cecelia and her companions in religion, Sr. Rose and Sr. Elizabeth, always made him wish he could have collected twice as much. The orphans, too, made him feel they appreciated his visits. The sisters had cautioned the children not to ask questions about Euphemia, who had turned each September 16th, her birthday, into a gala for the orphans.

As grateful as the sisters were for the funds Pierre collected, sometimes they had to ask him to help them place some orphan who had come of age in a home where he or she might earn a living. Pierre never refused and kept a watchful eye on the boy or girl thereafter.

For a while it was as if circumstance had again agreed to smile on Pierre. His collection for the orphans showed a marked increase. He was negotiating with Abraham Bloodgood for the purchase of 105 Reade Street, and he had opened a larger shop at 141 Canal Street.

Now Pierre seldom spoke of Euphemia, but Juliette learned that he went across the street to the cemetery each first Monday after he turned his collection over to the sisters and put a bouquet of flowers on the grave. He still read Euphemia's letters, which he kept on his desk tied with a ribbon, but his prayer to be submissive to God's will had been answered.

Mary Anne Schuyler was delighted that Pierre had opened a shop on Canal Street. If an urgent problem came up, she would send a servant to fetch Pierre. In matters pertaining to the health of members of her family—and her husband was continually ailing—she asked Pierre for prayers. "Nobody," she said, "could have a better saint than my dear Pierre!" And her "dear Pierre" came daily to style her hair for the social function of the evening and accept her confidences.

When the Schuylers were at their country estate in Rhinebeck, New York, where Philip Jeremiah's health often improved, Pierre looked forward to the notes Mrs. Schuyler wrote almost daily. She reminded him to keep an eye on the Schuyler's Canal Street house, to be sure to pray for her husband's health and to remember to visit George Lee Schuyler at Laight Street, who was now married to Eliza Hamilton, daughter of James Hamilton. Having known George Lee and Eliza all their lives, Pierre was pleased to have an excuse to visit them.

Mrs. Schuyler's friend, Marie Stevens (Mrs. John C.), also relied on Pierre to insure that she was always beautifully coiffed. She, too, trusted Pierre's advice on matters pertaining to household help and often conversed with him about the new republic of Haiti. She mentioned to her friend, Mary Anne Schuyler, that even during the period immediately following Euphemia's death, she had never detected any traces of bitterness in anything Pierre said. True, there had been those weeks when communication was a one-sided affair and Pierre had gone about his work as though in a trance, but never once had he questioned God.

"You don't understand that saints don't question God," her friend chided her.

"If you're saying Pierre is a saint, I'm not an authority on saints. But I do know that if all I hear about him taking in homeless black boys and collecting money for the orphans is true...."

"I know Pierre has found household help for you," Mrs. Schuyler interrupted. "The young men he brought you were homeless boys he took in, clothed and fed, then trained. Sr. Cecelia over at the orphanage on Prince Street will tell you that Pierre's collections on their behalf keep their doors open. And everybody knows he supported Madame Bérard until she died—even while he was a slave. Now if he isn't a saint, I don't know what a saint is."

"Mary Anne, I love Pierre, too. It's just that I never knew anybody like him. He is a most unusual black man."

"He is an unusual man! And you'd be surprised if you knew how often I ask him to pray for me—especially for my husband's health—and things always seem to get better after Pierre has assured me of his prayers. You should hear Robert and George Lee Schuyler talk about Pierre. They go to him with all their problems. Sometimes I think their father is a little jealous—though he says he isn't. But Pierre is a saint!" Mary Anne Schuyler insisted.

Though these two women had been friends for years, the friendship had been cemented by their husbands' business association. John C. Stevens and Philip Jeremiah Schuyler were partners in a quarry business. Stevens and Schuyler had described to Pierre the many exciting experiments made by the elder Colonel Stevens, who had pioneered in steam navigation.

During the years when the plague came every August, Pierre had reason to remember that it was the elder Colonel Stevens who, after having served as treasurer of the Continental Army, had developed the system of wooden water mains for New York City which was now inadequate for the swelling population.

Pierre, who remembered the rivalry between Robert Fulton and Colonel Stevens, was relieved when the steamboat became a reality. There was much excitement when the Stevens family inaugurated a ferry service between New York and Hoboken, New Jersey. They had turned a part of their country estate at Hoboken into the Elysian Fields, an amusement park. Pierre heard his friends talking enthusiastically about a new game, baseball, which had been introduced at the Stevens' Elysian Fields.

Pierre had a retentive memory, and Juliette looked forward to their talks at the end of a day. He often told her how fortunate he was to have friends like the Schuylers and Stevens who had long ago taken time to brief him on matters of political importance.

Juliette said nothing but she often wondered if the Schuylers and Stevens had been aware that they were briefing Pierre, or if they had just been having heated political discussions while Pierre was in their company.

Pierre had been a much younger man when he first heard Philip Jeremiah Schuyler discuss the differing theories of government held by Alexander Hamilton, whose followers were known as Federalists. Those who subscribed to the views of Thomas Jefferson eventually became known as Republicans. As Secretary of the Treasury, Hamilton had favored central control while Jefferson, as Secretary of State, espoused the cause of a purely democratic government. Pierre recalled that he was still an apprentice, cutting the children's hair, when he had first overheard these discussions of the two men who were both members of George Washington's cabinet but held opposing views, sometimes placing the President astride a dilemma. Pierre eventually decided the Schuylers and Stevens favored Hamilton's Federalist point of view.

Then Jefferson had defeated John Adams for the presidency, and Alexander Hamilton had been killed. The Federalists had lost their champions.

In other homes Pierre had tried hard not to hear whispers about how Jefferson had been fascinated by the charm of Angelica Schuyler Church during the years when he represented his country in France and Angelica Church spent much of her time abroad. Pierre did not usually share rumors with Juliette, but the matters pertaining to government and the revolutionary theory of steam navigation were brought to her attention, since he tried to comprehend the effects of these developments on their lives. Juliette redoubled her efforts to converse intelligently with Pierre about such matters.

Pierre took no notice of the fact that his wife appeared less effervescent than in years past. Juliette was not sure why she had to make a determined effort to continue to entertain Pierre's friends from all over the world who now visited their home. She finally decided it was the aftermath of Euphemia's illness and the grief over the child's death which had sapped her energy.

Claudine had observed the change in Juliette. The woman made a quick decision when her former master informed her he was moving to Charleston, S.C., to live with a married daughter. The man wanted Claudine to accompany him in order that she might serve as a nursemaid for his grandchildren. Juliette's mother had no intention of leaving New York. She discussed the situation with Pierre, and in a matter of days they had found another freedwoman who was willing to go to Charleston. Claudine immediately moved into 105 Reade Street, hoping to be in a position to relieve her daughter of many household responsibilities. The one surprise was that she brought her son Joseph with her. Juliette was not on good terms with her brother, but Pierre was glad to have the family under one roof.

Pierre and Juliette were delighted with the letters Fanny Montpensier was writing from Baltimore. Four of Fanny's friends, working girls like herself, who had been assisting the Sulpicians in their efforts to educate and instruct the black children of Baltimore, had formed a religious order. They called themselves the Oblate Sisters of Providence, and Fr. Jacques Marie Joubert de la Muraille was their spiritual advisor. They had founded the first religious community of black women in the world. They devoted their services to teaching black children.

In October 1829 the Oblates formally announced their intentions and took their vows. Fanny Montpensier was glad to have another project to offer Juliette and Pierre, as Claudine had sent word of Juliette's protracted grief.

The Toussaints immediately sent a contribution to the newly founded order. But Fanny initiated an even more active role for Juliette.

It was common knowledge among her friends that Pierre's wife was a shrewd shopper and demonstrated excellent taste as far as apparel was concerned. Soon after the Oblates were founded, Fanny Montpensier was informing her cousin Juliette of the needs of the children the sisters had taken in. Fanny gave Juliette detailed descriptions of the materials she should purchase for the girls' dresses or the boys' pants and shirts. She knew of Pierre's connection with the orphanage on Prince Street and a priest, Fr. Deluol, from St. Mary's College at Baltimore, made periodic visits to the Sisters of Charity who conducted the orphanage in New York. Soon Juliette was packing boxes of apparel for Fr. Deluol to carry back to Baltimore for the children the Oblates were teaching. Fanny's requests were not confined to calico or other materials. She sometimes asked Juliette to shop for fish and other foodstuffs with explicit instructions that they be packed in ice and addressed to Fr. Deluol at St. Mary's.

Claudine was pleased that this new interest had come into her daughter's life and assured Juliette that Pierre would be well looked after if she decided to visit Baltimore and meet the Oblates. At first Juliette was reluctant, but as the months passed and Pierre became more involved in his own charitable projects, Juliette decided to go to Baltimore, visit her relatives the Noels, and meet the Oblates.

Pierre was busy helping a young priest prepare to go to Rome to study. He was also excited over the experimental cruises George Lee Schuyler was making now that the Erie Canal had been opened and the Hudson River was linked to the Great Lakes. Pierre absentmindedly agreed for Juliette to go to Baltimore and then was dumbfounded when he came home and learned she had already taken a boat.

Pierre had brought the young priest home for dinner with the promise that the good father would meet his wife.

"Who took Madame Toussaint to the boat?" he covered his embarrassment with a blustery manner.

"Her mother and her brother—because her husband was nowhere around," Claudine reminded. "Did you remember to stop by the Schuylers?"

"I forgot that, too," Pierre admitted. "But I did get a letter from George Lee Schuyler. He wrote while aboard the S.S. Magnolia on the Ohio River, and he actually wrote me in French. They were approaching Pittsburgh after sailing almost 2,000 miles. In a few days they will be in Niagara and then New York. He sent regards to Juliette, and his mother asked to be remembered. I must stop by tomorrow to make sure all is well at the Canal Street house. But tonight I must write my apologies to my dear wife for not escorting her to the boat."

"Pierre, you don't have to apologize to Juliette. She knew how many appointments you had today. And she heard you promise Fr. Powers to meet the young priest. I suspect you have already invited him to stay here until he sails for Rome."

"How did you know?" Pierre appeared startled.

"We did not meet yesterday," Claudine laughed. "So you can go to the parlor and tell your guest that dinner will be served shortly. I need his prayers for my children."

"Your children?" Pierre was curious.

"In many ways, my Joseph is like Jean—Euphemia's father. He can't keep a job."

"I will find work for him," Pierre offered.

"He must find work for himself," Claudine insisted. "Otherwise it will be the same old story; I will not have you embarrassed by Joe's laziness. Until he finds work I will make sure he looks after this house. You only have a couple of those boys downstairs now, but that basement needs a good cleaning."

"You said you needed prayers for your *children.*" Pierre was puzzled.

"Did it never occur to you that Juliette would have wanted a child of her own?"

"But I was so much older," Pierre began, "and then Euphemia came."

"And now Euphemia is gone and Juliette is lonely.

"Her life revolved around that child. You were out each day meeting all kinds of interesting people, but Juliette and Euphemia were never separated."

"What can I do?" Pierre asked. "Should I plan a voyage—maybe to France?"

"She is on a voyage now," Claudine reminded. "That is why I encouraged her to go to Baltimore. The Oblates will console her. She will hear a few good French sermons and, I hope, return in better spirits."

"I had not noticed that she was in poor spirits," Pierre insisted.

"Because she always shows her husband a smile. Now enough of this talk. You are leaving your guest alone too long, and I must prepare dinner."

Pierre kissed Claudine's hand. "No man ever had a more understanding mother-in-law," he said.

Claudine hurried to the kitchen where Joe sat at a table fast asleep.

"And no woman ever had a son-in-law to whom she owed more," she addressed the pots on the stove.

Despite Claudine's assurance, Pierre wrote Juliette and begged her forgiveness for being absent at her leavetaking. He wrote her each night and treasured the little scrawled notes she wrote in return. He was alarmed to learn she had been slightly ill and suggested that he would come to Baltimore to bring her home if she needed him. But in the same letter he was telling her about a visit from Fr. Herard, a priest stationed at Bottle Hill, New Jersey, who received much of his mail at the Toussaint house and was often an overnight guest.

The Schuylers had returned, and Pierre listened to his friend Mary Anne describe the voyage aboard the S.S. Magnolia each evening as he stopped in to style her hair or just for a friendly talk, as had become their custom.

Soon after Juliette returned from her visit to Baltimore, Pierre came home telling her about the excitement in the Stevens and Schuyler homes over the yacht John C. Stevens was having built. Then in 1832 the Stevens' yacht, the *Wave,* was launched, and George Lee Schuyler and John Stevens regaled Pierre with the beauty of the vessel. Pierre in turn shared the excitement with Juliette, who tried hard to be as enthusiastic about these developments as her husband.

On a sultry summer night in 1834, Juliette stood on the steps waiting for Pierre and wondered why he was walking so slowly when he came into view.

After their usual embrace Pierre led Juliette to the parlor and sat at the table on which she had placed the lighted lamp. Slowly he took a letter from his pocket.

"It is from Madame de Berty, Mlle. Aurore's sister," he explained.

"And Mlle. Aurore?"

"She is dead. Death came suddenly—and before she received my last letter, which was delivered after she died."

Juliette knelt at her husband's feet and laid her head on his knees as she had often seen Euphemia do, and wept quietly until she felt they had both regained their composure.

Pierre had not had any communication from his loved ones at L'Artibonite since the year Euphemia was born. Now and then a sailor would give him an account of what was happening on his island home, but he had no idea whether

Zenobie, his mother and father, or any of the others were still alive. Now his godmother Aurore was dead. Other slaves from L'Artibonite had made their way to New York years ago. They always managed to find Pierre, and as long as he lived Pierre contributed to their upkeep. But L'Artibonite was a part of his past, and the hope of ever seeing it again grew dim.

During the period when Pierre was saddened by the death of his godmother, a patron teased him about working so hard and asked him why he continued at such a steady pace, instead of retiring.

The lady reported to Pierre's friends that he smiled and said: "Then, Madame, I should not have enough for others!"

That night as Pierre made his way home, he kept remembering what the woman had asked him. "I would not know how to remain idle," Pierre mumbled and unconsciously rubbed a troublesome knee which had slowed his gait. "And in my life trouble has a way of coming in waves."

CHAPTER 18

Facing Reality

Pierre's negotiations with Abraham Bloodgood were at a standstill. Bloodgood was asking six thousand dollars for the house, and Pierre insisted that he could only pay five thousand. Juliette, who did not want to leave the house to which she had come as a bride, tried to persuade her husband to close the deal, but Pierre would not budge. Juliette's mother supported Pierre since she felt 105 Reade Street held too many memories of Euphemia. She felt Juliette would benefit from a change.

While Pierre was in the midst of house hunting, he was informed there was a real possibility that his beloved St. Peter's might be condemned. He had known the church needed repairs but never thought it might be torn down. Each morning Pierre had long talks with James Theil, the sexton, and they decided a few sturdy beams here and there with a generous amount of plaster and paint would save the structure.

Pierre must have had a premonition when he scoffed at the idea that he no longer needed to work. On the coldest night in mid-December 1835, the business district of New York City was almost completely destroyed by fire. The river was frozen over and there was little the hand engines could do. Fire fighters from as far away as New Jersey were helpless except to blow up buildings in order to keep the fire from spreading. The Merchants Exchange, a center of commerce built on Wall Street east of Broadway only eight years before, crashed before the eyes of horrified spectators. It was reported that seven hundred buildings were either destroyed by fire or blown up that night.

This fire spelled ruin and bankruptcy for many merchants, as banks and insurance companies were also destroyed. The building where Pierre had located his shop was among those burned.

News of persons whose property had been lost spread quickly. But the morning after the fire Pierre was out visiting those he knew who had suffered losses. When his patrons attempted to set up a fund for him, he diplomatically reminded them that his losses were as nothing compared to others.

"My needs are few. There are those with far greater responsibilities who are forced to mortgage whatever they can in an effort to protect hundreds of investors who have placed their life savings in their care. I would be embarrassed if it became known that I presumed my loss, as compared with theirs, to be significant," he insisted.

The wave that Pierre foretold was rolling. Soon after the fire St. Peter's was declared structurally unsound. Pierre, who was a member of the Society of St. Peter, the Society of the Blessed Sacrament, and active in all parish affairs, immediately began calling meetings for the purpose of raising funds to build a new church. He had hoped the old building would not be condemned, but once it had happened he assured Fr. Powers that he would devote his energies to the erection of a new structure.

Juliette accompanied Pierre to the last Mass at old St. Peter's on August 28, 1836. She knew Pierre was not only worried about the church. The first Catholic burial ground, adjacent to the church, would have to be used in laying the foundation for the new structure.

Arrangements had to be made for the transfer of the remains of all buried there to the cemetery uptown at the new cathedral.

The following years were crammed with activity. Fr. Powers depended on Pierre to appeal to those French refugees who had managed to salvage enough of their worldly goods to live comfortably in New York. Some of them had left St. Dominique even before the Bérards, and their investments had yielded handsome profits. Pierre lost no time in reminding them that now was the time for them to come to the aid of mother Church.

Amid the constant round of committee meetings and benefits, Juliette assumed the role of Pierre's social secretary, though most of the correspondence was from those who sought Pierre's help. Juliette was glad she had learned to read and write enough English to sort out the appeals which came to 105 Reade Street. Claudine carefully examined those written in French or Creole. When Pierre came home the women had two neat piles of letters on his desk waiting for him.

Sometimes Claudine marveled that her daughter did not protest her husband's charity.

"You never seem to be angered by the constant stream of requests," the older woman said. "Don't you ever resent your husband giving his money away?"

"It would do no good," Juliette laughed. "Pierre feels that God has made it possible for him to live in comfort, and he, therefore, has an obligation to share whatever blessings he has enjoyed. He says he gets the highest possible rate of interest on his money because the sisters and all of the young priests he helps have assured him of their prayers."

"Pierre is lucky to have a wife like you," Claudine commented.

"I am the lucky one," Juliette declared. "Among those we know, what other black woman lives as I do?"

Pierre was working harder than ever at seventy-one years

of age. He was collecting funds for the orphanage, assisting Fr. Powers in raising funds to rebuild St. Peter's, responding to any call for assistance from Bishop DuBois, training boys to assist him or work in the homes of his patrons, and making all of his visits on foot.

Pierre's gait became slower and slower due to the rheumatic knee which constantly pained him. Whenever a friend made so bold as to remind him again that there were trams which carried signs on both sides of the cars stating: "Colored People Allowed in This Car," Pierre's reply was always: "I'm still black!" and he would walk away making an almost superhuman effort to avoid limping.

Pierre knew that the blacks of New York bitterly resented this form of "branding," as they called what later became known as Jim Crow. They contended that it existed in saloons, theaters, churches and the union halls of New York City. In spite of the grumbling and complaints, it was not until 1853 that a Rev. W. C. Pennington, who had been thrown off one of the Sixth Avenue Railway cars, sued that company. After two hours of deliberation, the jury ruled against Rev. Pennington and in favor of the Sixth Avenue Railway Company. But in 1854 Elizabeth Jennings, a black woman who taught in one of the public schools for blacks, refused to leave her seat and was dragged away and thrown off the car. This determined woman went to court with Chester A. Arthur, later to become President of the United States, as her attorney. The court awarded Elizabeth Jennings monetary damages, but more importantly ruled that Jim Crow was unconstitutional.

Elizabeth Jennings' victory was too late to benefit Pierre. Though he was considered by all who knew him to be one of New York's outstanding citizens, he was never free to ride on any New York railway system without running the risk of being relegated to special cars—because of his color.

The new St. Peter's was blessed by Coadjutor Bishop Bernard Hughes on February 25, 1836. Juliette and

Claudine later commented that Pierre's limp, which worried them both, was hardly noticeable that day. As people came up after the service to congratulate him for his success in raising funds to build the new church, Pierre reminded them that they were still faced with an enormous debt.

In spite of the drain on his resources made by the fire, the building fund for St. Peter's, doles to the needy and the anonymous contributions he had encouraged Juliette and Claudine to make to organizations working to improve conditions among his own people, Pierre made the first one hundred dollar contribution toward the establishment of a French church in New York City. It was 1841, and Pierre had listened to an impassioned plea for such a church made by Bishop Charles August Count de Forbin-Janson from the altar at St. Peter's. The church of St. Vincent de Paul was built at Canal Street and Broadway, then later moved to West 23rd Street.

The wave continued to roll, and in May 1842 Pierre received a disturbing letter from one of his friends who had gone back to their island home. Haiti had suffered a devastating earthquake. Pierre awoke the next morning to find a crowd of weeping black women and men on his doorstep. They, too, feared that their loved ones were lost and came to Pierre for information and help. He took as many as would follow him to Mass. Then Pierre enlisted the aid of the priests at St. Peter's so he could tell the people what cities had been affected. A sailor had already brought him another letter from a friend who wrote that Cap Haitian, Santiago and Portau-Paix had been destroyed. At Gonnaive, which was close enough to L'Artibonite to give Pierre grave concern, it was said the earth had opened up and a stream of water had gushed out, followed by a fire that had raged for hours.

For weeks 105 Reade Street was a clearing house for information on this disaster which had ravaged Haiti. Fanny Montpensier wrote from Baltimore that one of Juliette's

dear friends had decided to go back to Haiti shortly before
the quake and was presumed dead. A number of the Oblates, Fanny said, had lost relatives. By August 1842, the
Oblates had a Mass said in their chapel at Baltimore for the
relatives they presumed had died in the May quake.

Even during the years when reports of Pierre's charitable
acts were common knowledge and his advice and assistance
were sought by many of the city's most distinguished families, he did not escape the humiliation many New Yorkers
reserved for people of his race.

The role Pierre played in raising funds to build the new
cathedral was a source of pride and admiration among his
many friends who had contributed. In the summer of 1842,
Pierre and Juliette decided to take Old Cabress with them to
a ceremony which was to take place in the cathedral. The
old woman had recently been slipping out of the house to
take long walks. This worried the Toussaints, and they decided to include her on this outing. No sooner had Pierre,
Juliette and Old Cabress entered the church than a young
usher barred their way and informed them there were no
pews set aside for black people.

Pierre was startled. The women were frightened, but as
Juliette glanced at Pierre's face she became fearful that he
would not succeed in controlling the temper which had
always been one of his hair shirts.

Then suddenly Pierre shook his head, crossed himself
and led Juliette and Old Cabress out of the church. As they
passed the cemetery where Euphemia was buried, Juliette
felt the pressure of Pierre's hand on her arm and stopped.

"Thank God," he said, "she will never know the humiliation to which we were just subjected."

By the time Louis F. Binsse, who was president of the
board of trustees, and other friends of Pierre discovered
what had happened, he was out of the reach of their voices.

The grief these men felt was expressed in the following
letter which Mr. Binsse wrote to Pierre.

It would be difficult for me to express to you the grief which has been caused me by the insult which you have received in the Lord's house. It has given me all the more pain, because, wishing to have order in the church, it was I who begged this gentleman to be one of the masters of ceremony. This young man is truly very repentant for it, and he has been reprimanded most severely by several of the trustees.

Everybody knows, my dear Toussaint, that if God by his will has created you as well your good wife with a black skin, by his grace he has made your hearts and souls as white as snow. While many others (and you know them well) to whom God has given a white skin, having repulsed this same grace, have made their souls, and hearts also, as black as coal.

You have been disgusted, my dear friend, by such an insult. I can well believe it. I should have been so, as much as you, and perhaps more than you, because you are human and I also. Our divine Master is the only one, who, insulted, beaten with rods and crucified, submitted himself with meekness to the will of his Father, when he could by the breath of his mouth have crushed his executioners.

What ought we to do, then, my dear Toussaint? Imitate him as much as our weakness and his grace will permit us to do. If by our weakness we resent insult, by his grace it should be forgotten. For my part, I should find myself more at ease seated in the house of the Lord between you and your wife and the good Cabress, than beside many other persons whose skin is as white as satin. In the house of the Lord there is no distinction. God looks at the heart, but never at the color of the skin. These are the sentiments of all the trustees, and of him who is most sincerely your friend.

Louis F. Binsse

The letter was dated August 24, 1842.

The story of Pierre being ejected from the cathedral

spread throughout the community. Protestants as well as Catholics were indignant. Pierre did not encourage those who sought to discuss the incident with him. Yet he would not completely hide his true feelings from his friend Mary Anne Schuyler.

"Juliette understands these things, but just think what it would have been like if my little Euphemia had been with us," he said to Mrs. Schuyler. "That is one pain God saved her. And yet such things happen to my people every day."

Mary Anne Schuyler was so surprised that Pierre showed no outward signs of indignation that she confided her reaction to her friend Maria Stevens.

"You said he was a saint," her friend reminded Mrs. Schuyler.

"I can't find anybody who was there to tell me what Pierre did when that man refused to let him in the cathedral," the woman admitted.

"If you must know, why don't you ask Juliette?" Mrs. Stevens suggested. "She was there."

A few afternoons later when these two women were out driving, their carriage stopped in front of 105 Reade Street just as Juliette was returning from the market. They had brought Pierre's wife a basket of fruit which she graciously accepted. Suspecting that they had heard about Pierre's encounter and wanted to make amends, she invited them in. Though both of the women had insisted they were hurrying to a tea, they followed Juliette into the house.

"I'm so upset over what happened at the cathedral," Mrs. Schuyler began as soon as they were in the tastefully arranged parlor.

"All New York is talking about it. We consider it an outrage! Madame Toussaint," Mrs. Stevens lowered her voice, "what did Pierre say to this—this nobody—whoever he was?"

Juliette recounted the happening, described how she had seen the anger on Pierre's countenance, then how he had crossed himself and had led her away. She described the scene and Pierre's remark as they passed the cemetery.

"Only a saint would thank God for an insult," Mrs. Stevens rose and handed Mary Anne Schuyler a handkerchief, since Pierre's dear friend was in tears.

"I wish I could get somebody to tell me that usher's name," Mrs. Schuyler said. "I would give him a piece of my mind!"

"I think the trustees have already reprimanded him," Juliette ventured as she opened the door for Pierre's two dear friends.

Juliette's mother was curious about the women's visit. Her daughter showed her the fruit and told her about the conversation. Claudine sucked her teeth and grunted. "You'd think Pierre was the only black man in New York who was ever insulted," she said.

"It was the first such experience for Pierre," Juliette explained. "He has made sure he never went places where he ran any risk of not being accepted. If you remember, he would never take Euphemia to the Cruger's or the Schuyler's until they insisted. He never expected this to happen at church."

"And a church he helped to build!" Claudine shook her head. "But I guess it is better late than never. Now he can understand how Joe is always getting into fights with the Irish."

"How can you compare Joe to Pierre?" Juliette asked.

"Joe is my son and your brother," Claudine reminded. "And every time he gets a job some hungry-looking Irish immigrant comes along and agrees to work cheaper."

"And Joe doesn't look too hard for another job because he is lazy," Juliette smiled. "I know he hasn't been here for a few days and you are worried about him. Make sure those children and his wife have enough food, though he acts as if they do not exist."

"I carried them food already," the older woman admitted. "Young Gaston still talks about Euphemia. He wants to come here to practice on the piano."

"The last time they played a duet we had to send for the piano tuner the next day," Juliette laughed. "But there is no reason he cannot practice after Mrs. Ruckel's classes are over."

Juliette thought it strange that they never heard the name of the usher and mentioned it to Pierre.

"It is easier to forgive an unnamed person than one whose name is known to you," Pierre smiled. "I only wish he had been faceless as well."

It was not too long after the cathedral affair that Pierre had cause for another worry. He learned that his beautiful young friend Catherine Cruger was seriously ill, though few of her friends were aware of her illness. He had known Catherine Church Cruger since she was a young girl when he cut and styled her hair before she went for dancing lessons. As a prominent young matron, she had been one of his best advertisements. Now he was begging God for her life.

Pierre paid the rent on 105 Reade Street but had no other transactions with Abraham Bloodgood. He knew Juliette did not want to leave the neighborhood, and he located another house nearby which was for sale. Again Pierre found the price of this house to be the same as the price Bloodgood was asking for 105 Reade Street. Again he refused to agree to the deal. His friend Sarah Anne Moore pointed out a house on Franklin Street, number 144, near her own home. The house was for sale, and the owner agreed to sell it to Pierre for $5,000.

One of the first things Pierre did after he bought the house was to look for quarters for Mrs. Ruckel, since there was not enough room in the new home for this woman who had taught his Euphemia to read and write English.

It was a sad day for Juliette when the drays drove off with the furniture, much of which had been inherited from Madame Bérard-Nicolas, and all of their other belongings. The two young men who helped Juliette and her mother pack, as the move took place during one of Joseph's disappearances, had once been among the homeless black boys Pierre brought to the house. They had grown up working for Pierre at the shop and assisting him whenever it was necessary.

"I can remember the first time I ever saw them," Claudine told Juliette. "They looked like two bundles of rags—and dirty ones at that."

"Pierre says they are both learning the trade. They have excellent manners, and he has been allowing them to cut all of the children's hair. They are a great help to him, and they have certainly helped us."

"They are the two who used to fight so much," Claudine laughed. "Many is the time I caught Euphemia standing at the bottom of the steps. She would put her finger to her lips so I wouldn't call you."

"Then that night she'd tell Pierre what you said about the boys being rowdy and him being too soft," Juliette recalled. "On the day I die I'll still miss Euphemia."

"Don't talk like that! It was God's will."

"I accept God's will. But something went out of our lives when she died. And—and leaving this house makes me feel like I'm leaving her behind," Juliette whispered to her mother as she heard Pierre coming to take her to her new home.

Pierre left the carriage he had engaged standing at the curb. As he entered the house he hurried upstairs, though he saw at a glance that Claudine and Juliette were ready and waiting. Old Cabress had not been out of her room recently, and he did not relish the prospect of having to bring her down the steps and deposit her in the carriage with all the neighbors watching. When he opened the door to the room the old woman occupied, he found her dressed and waiting. Pierre was so surprised he held the door and pointed her toward the steps.

As he walked toward the quarters he had shared with Juliette, Pierre thought back over the years. It was now 1845 and the Bérards had brought him to 105 Reade Street in 1787—fifty-eight years before. In the bedroom there was a large box which demanded his attention. He had packed these keepsakes in the box because they were too valuable to be hauled with the furniture.

There was the old, tattered copybook Zenobie had found in Jean Jacques' trunk so long ago. He looked at the ledger in which he entered the donations he collected for the orphanage and the rosary Sarah Anne Moore had sent him from Tabor, which she said she had laid on the Holy Sepulcher at Jerusalem. He patted a stack of scribbly notes from Mary Anne Schuyler, which he placed next to Euphemia's letters. Pierre chuckled when he read a note which fell to the floor that Mary Anne had written on one of the trips she had taken to Baden-Baden for her husband's health. A sprig of olives someone had sent him from Rome fell beside the note. Pierre took his crucifix from the wall, then tied the box with a piece of string so it would be easy for him to carry.

He was halfway down the steps when Pierre remembered the prie-dieu which his aunt, Marie Bouquement, had given him the day after they buried their young mistress.

Juliette and Claudine saw Pierre run back up the steps to their bedroom. Instinctively Juliette knew what he had forgotten and ran up to meet him.

Neighbors stood outside watching while the little family climbed into the rented carriage. As they drove away, Pierre tipped his hat to the ladies and ordered the driver to proceed to 144 Franklin Street.

Pierre held Juliette's hand all the way to their new home. Claudine chattered away in order to keep her daughter from weeping and called attention to the homes of people they knew as they reached Franklin Street.

The young men from Pierre's shop had unloaded the furniture and placed it around so that Juliette did not get the feeling of entering a strange place after Pierre unlocked the door and ushered them in.

"Welcome to your new home, Madame Toussaint." He showed them around the house, which Juliette decided was not as bad as it had seemed when she had first seen it.

Pierre went back to the carriage to get his precious box, which the driver offered to bring into the house, but Pierre would not hear of it. He did let the man bring in the prie-dieu as he led Juliette up the steps to their bedroom where he had already had new furniture delivered as a surprise for his wife. There was a little alcove just outside the bedroom where he sat the prie-dieu. In a second he untied the box, retrieved the crucifix and with the help of a nail and a little silver hammer hung it over the prie-dieu. Juliette took a pair of rosaries from her bag and they both knelt and asked God's protection on their new home.

In the days which followed their move, Claudine warned Juliette over and over that she was working too hard, that she was not eating enough and that she did not like the way she looked. But Pierre's wife was determined that her husband would be proud of his home, the first he had ever owned, when his friends came to call.

Pierre, too, thought a great deal about the joys and responsibilities of being a homeowner. He also thought about making a will. He had been greatly affected when his young friend Catherine Cruger died. Now he decided it was time for him to make some disposition of his worldly assets so that Juliette and Claudine would be properly taken care of when God called him home to heaven.

Euphemia's death had left the Toussaints without an heir. Claudine was already an old woman whom Pierre would care for until she died. Old Cabress, much like a member of the family, was so elderly she had long since lost track of her own age. They had recently learned that Joe's wife had disappeared with her children and there was no news of Claudine's only son.

Pierre postponed making a will, but the impact of the loss of his young friend Catherine Church Cruger finally made him act. Pierre remembered how Euphemia had thought that every picture of a beautiful lady was a picture of Mrs. Cruger. Then his mind went back to the days of this woman's childhood, and he found it difficult to believe that she was dead and he was still alive. Pierre knew he could not postpone this matter any longer.

As Pierre made his way to the offices of David C. Golden and George Wilkes on Laight Street, he kept calling to mind his association with the Schuyler family. He could even remember the old General Philip Schuyler of Saratoga fame, whose grandsons George Lee and Robert Lee, insisted their grandfather was extremely enthusiastic in his admiration of the young Pierre. Pierre had always marveled at the fact that General Schuyler, who was 71 when he died in 1804, always seemed more robust than Mary Anne's husband, Philip Jeremiah. General Schuyler had enjoyed talking to Pierre about the turmoil in Haiti and the military mistakes he thought the French had made. Yet Pierre never indicated to the older man how painful to him were these discussions of the St. Dominique he had known and loved.

Pierre sighed as he thought of how Mary Anne Schuyler had taken her husband all over the world seeking a cure. Pierre had recently become concerned about Mrs. Schuyler's health, and more than once he had been puzzled by the reference George Lee and his brother made about their grandfather's description of Pierre. Just as Pierre had never dared ask Mary Anne Schuyler the nature of her husband's illness, he had never asked the Schuyler sons what their grandfather had said about him. The Schuylers knew that Pierre would have been embarrassed if he had known that General Schuyler, in speaking of Pierre, had said: "I have known Christians who were not gentlemen, gentlemen who were not Christians. I know one man who is both, and that man is black."

In this frame of mind Pierre reached the offices of the lawyers where his will was to be drawn up. Pierre listened as the lawyers advised him on how this document should be legally phrased. Then he asked if they would, be kind enough to give him a pen and paper and a place to write where he would not be disturbed.

There was no doubt in Pierre's mind about who his heirs would be. He had no knowledge of any living blood relative. Not one of his friends who went back to their island home had found it possible to get to L'Artibonite. Letters no longer came even from the sister who had escaped to Cuba. News of internal affairs was especially distressing. That part of the island which had formerly been under the yoke of the Spanish had now declared itself independent as the Dominican Republic.

"Though I have long since given up hope of finding any living relative, I will make provisions for $100 to be set aside for any who may later make a valid claim," Pierre informed the lawyers before he began the document. Then slowly and thoughtfully, he began:

> It was the holy will of God to take from me my beloved and adopted daughter Euphemia, and I submitted to the blow with faith in the wisdom of my heavenly Father....
>
> But then especially did I appreciate the friendship and sympathy of my two friends, Catherine Cruger (who has finished her life of constant benevolence and disinterestedness) and Mary Anne Schuyler, now of the City of New York.
>
> Their friendship for many years has been more to me than that of any others, though there are many others whose regard I highly value and appreciate, and I determined after my Euphemia's death that when my estate should no longer be required by my beloved wife Juliette

or her mother, it should pass to the benefit of their children to whom I have been known from their infancies.

Pierre wrote on and on explaining his relationship to all
of the Schuyler children and grandchildren, for Catherine
Cruger had been the daughter of Angelica Schuyler Church,
and referring to the youngest Schuyler grandson, Philip,
whom Pierre was leaving the greater share of his estate. A
bequest was included for St. Peter's and the new pastor. A
sum was also specified for Masses to be said for the repose of
the soul of Pierre Toussaint whenever it became appropriate. George Lee and Robert Lee Schuyler were named as
executors of the will. It was duly witnessed and signed.

In the days following the writing of the will, Pierre was
almost like a young man in love for the first time. He felt at
peace with the world and worked harder than ever to express his gratefulness for so much good fortune by sharing
with all who sought his help. He contributed generously to a
benevolent society made up of French men of color. Juliette
and Claudine questioned him as to why he did not insist on
being anonymous when he made donations to this *Frères
réunis pour se secourir en cas de Maladie et Mortalité.*

"I do not have to explain myself to them. They know I
am the product of the conditions under which I grew up—
no better and I hope no worse than any of them. With the
blacks here in New York, my accent and my profession mark
me as 'Frenchy,' who loves to work and associate with whites.
How can I explain that everything I have, even to what I give
them, comes from whites? And to those fugitives who I hear
are escaping from slavery in the South, they would never
understand for they have been maimed by the cruelty of
white men. There is a young man I would have liked to
know—under different circumstances—a David Ruggles
who has a bookstore on Lispenard. I have reasons to suspect
he is assisting the fugitives. I would suggest you ladies find

some reason to patronize his store." Pierre handed Juliette a small purse of coins. "I hear you can purchase old copies of *Freedom's Journal* there. I would like to read them."

Each night when Pierre came home to the Franklin Street house, he looked around in amazement. There was hardly a day that Juliette did not add some touch of her homemaking skill which attracted his attention. The exquisite pieces of French furniture he had helped Jean Jacques crate to bring to America were shown off to an advantage in the parlor. In the dining room sat the silver tea service and the hand-painted chocolate pot, with the dainty cups on a miniature rack. In the hallway on the marble top below a tall mirror, sat a silver tray to receive the cards of callers. The curtains at the parlor windows were lace, and the furniture shone with a gloss from frequent polishings.

At the end of his long nights, after he finished entering the monies he had collected for the orphanage or setting aside sums to be paid out—as Pierre forbade Juliette and her mother to buy anything they could not pay for on purchase—he would kneel down on the prie-dieu outside the bedroom and thank God for his mercy and kindness.

Pierre made it a habit to surprise his wife each night with a posey, pastries or a box of chocolates. Recently he had added ice cream for which she had developed a fondness. Juliette always tried to meet him at the door, and he would hide the gift in a hand behind his back as he made a sweeping bow and then presented his surprise, much as he had seen the elder Monsieur Bérard present gifts to his wife.

Pierre had found a bunch of fresh violets out of which the florist had fashioned a lace-trimmed posey the night he had to use his key to let himself in. He peered in the dark parlor where Juliette always kept a lamp lighted as soon as dusk fell. Smelling food, he hurried to the kitchen and found his mother-in-law.

"Where is Juliette?" he demanded.

"Upstairs—in bed," Claudine answered, without turning from the stove where she was stirring a soup.

"Why is she in bed?" Pierre asked. "I don't understand."

"Your wife is sick—very sick!" the old woman whispered and when she faced Pierre he saw her eyes were puffed from crying.

"Juliette cannot be sick—she—she is too young! This must be just some slight indisposition," Pierre told the old woman and went up the steps to the bedroom muttering, "She is too young! Much too young!"

CHAPTER 19

The Shadows Lengthen

And why is Madame Toussaint in bed so early?" Pierre forced himself to smile at his wife.

"Madame Toussaint is not feeling well," Juliette replied softly.

Pierre sat beside the bed and looked at his wife. Juliette was often asleep when he retired, and he had insisted that she blow out the light when he was outside writing at the desk which sat in the alcove. He suddenly realized that the outline of her body beneath the covers looked smaller than when last he had noticed.

"We will get a doctor." Pierre was still trying to treat the matter lightly. "Too bad Dr. Berger is no longer practicing."

"I have been to the doctor," Juliette said quietly.

"Without telling your husband?" Pierre playfully waved a finger at his wife.

"I didn't want to worry you."

"And what did the doctor say?"

"He was not sure." Juliette was vague.

"Never mind. We will get a doctor who is sure." Pierre began pacing the floor. "I will speak to Mrs. Schuyler. She has an excellent physician. My Juliette will be well in no time."

"Thank you, Pierre," Juliette murmured and closed her eyes.

Pierre closed the door softly, leaning against it for support. "Nothing can happen to Juliette—she is too young. O God," Pierre prayed, "please protect my Juliette."

Pierre engaged a succession of doctors to examine Juliette. They all told him the same thing; his wife had cancer and had evidently had it for a long time. At first Pierre was so stunned he could barely function. He would sit at the table as Claudine prepared a tray for Juliette, whispering: "She is too young! She is too young to die!"

"And all Juliette says is, 'Poor Pierre. He will feel so alone when I go.' You are only making it harder for Juliette—and for me," Claudine chided.

"Forgive me," Pierre begged. "But you must know I would gladly give my life in return for Juliette's. She is so much younger. If only I had known earlier, I might have saved her."

"I tried to warn you," Claudine reminded. "But from the first time you noticed Juliette in the kitchen with Rosalie, you only saw beauty in Juliette—nothing else. Her tray is ready."

Pierre attempted to tell Claudine his many reasons, other than her beauty, for being attracted to Juliette, but she stopped him.

"Take the soup to Juliette while it is still hot."

As Pierre started out of the kitchen with the tray, Claudine spoke again. "Who was that man who always said we have to take it as God sends it?" she asked.

"Thank you for reminding me. From now on I will leave it in God's hands," he promised.

Pierre kept his promise. The boys at the shop were instructed to inform his patrons that Mr. Toussaint had illness in his family and was not available. When Pierre was not attending to Juliette's needs, he was either exploring the markets and stores for delicacies that he hoped might delight his ailing wife or kneeling before the crucifix at St. Peter's. At night after he was sure she was comfortable, he would kneel at the prie-dieu in the alcove outside their bedroom and beg for God's help.

Pierre's patrons soon learned of Juliette's illness and offered any service they might render. Mary Anne Schuyler, who was not enjoying the good health she had formerly boasted, sent her sons to visit the Toussaints and express the concern of the entire family. Pierre's friend and neighbor, Sarah Anne Moore, visited often.

Though Juliette was resigned to death and must have suffered greatly in silence, she begged all her visitors to try to comfort Pierre who would soon be alone.

Some nights when the dying woman could not sleep, she would weep at the sight of Pierre kneeling before the crucifix outside her room. The flickering flame from the lamp sometimes made a noise as it burned out and reminded Pierre that he had been kneeling for hours. He would tiptoe into the room where Juliette lay and kiss her forehead lightly. Once he made sure the shutters were secure so as to keep out the light, he would go to a nearby bedroom and try to sleep.

Sometimes Juliette was already asleep when Pierre kissed her goodnight. Other times she pretended sleep so as to be left to suffer her pain alone. Always, though, her prayers were for Pierre.

Claudine's face masked her feelings as she catered to the needs of her dying child. She had stopped worrying about Joseph, who had been missing for months, but from time to time there was compassion in the glance Claudine gave Pierre when he placed a flower on a tray she had prepared for Juliette and insisted on feeding his wife.

Some days Juliette was moderately comfortable. Then Pierre would tell her about the Schuyler grandchildren or the school "for colored children in the church basement" of the church of St. Vincent de Paul. Juliette knew Pierre was pleased about this school, and she remembered he had been the first contributor to the establishment of this French church. She found herself wondering how Pierre would react if one day an usher stopped him from entering St. Vincent de Paul Church because he was black.

Pierre took great pride in showing his wife the record of the money he was still collecting for the orphanage, and he told her the Sisters of Charity were all praying for her.

With the wisdom that God sometimes bestows on those about to approach the portals of heaven, Juliette began to discern a degree of resignation to God's will in her husband. He had stopped talking about the trips they would take when she recovered or the colorful material he saw in some shop that would make a beautiful dress for her. He had asked Fr. Quinn, now the pastor at St. Peter's, to administer the last sacraments. More and more he sat by her bed and prayed. He was with her the day her breathing became labored to the point she was gasping. Claudine was in the room, and he asked the old woman to open the shutters and pull back the curtains. Then he held Juliette's hand until she gave one last deep breath. When Claudine saw him bow his head, she knew her child was dead.

The old woman pulled to her face the white apron she was wearing. She looked back at the still figure on the bed and the grieving man who sat holding the lifeless hand of his wife. She wiped her eyes with the apron and closed the door. She had brought Juliette into the world a slave but Pierre had made her a free woman and the object of his affections. Claudine left Pierre alone with the wife whose body would soon grow cold.

Juliette died on May 14, 1851. She was buried beside Euphemia, though Fanny Montpensier and the Baltimore Noels had wanted Pierre to bring his wife's remains to that city.

Just as he had finally reacted after Euphemia's death, Pierre began a round of visits to the ill and infirm. He brought homeless boys to the Franklin Street house to live until he could find jobs for them, and he redoubled his efforts to solicit funds for the work of the Sisters of Charity. Claudine smothered her distaste for the ragged boys he brought home and instructed them in matters pertaining to cleanliness and how to keep house and serve a meal. With the taller boys she gave them clothes her son Joe had left behind.

Pierre was pleased at the manner in which Claudine assisted him, since he knew she was not inclined to favor these unfortunate boys from the streets.

Pierre's friends, however, began to notice a physical change in him soon after Juliette's death. Nobody would have guessed that New York's most renowned coiffeur was in his mid-eighties. His smooth skin was still like sable. Though the bad knee caused a limp, he was otherwise erect and stately. His closely cropped hair was receding and sideburns were gray, but still nobody thought of him as an old man who had been twenty years the senior of the wife he had just buried.

Pierre's friends remembered how Juliette had begged them to look after her husband. The Schuyler sons came with more stories of the grandchildren of Mary Anne and their escapades at Nevis. It was the home on the banks of the Hudson near Tarrytown where James Hamilton, father of Eliza Hamilton Schuyler, had built a mansion and named it for the West Indian island on which his father, Alexander Hamilton, had been born.

The Sisters of Charity praised Pierre for his efforts on their behalf and involved him in placing orphans who were old enough to find jobs.

In spite of the efforts of his friends, they eventually had to admit that the stalwart Pierre suddenly became a crippled old man. His body was beginning to refuse to respond to his efforts to carry on the many charitable causes he served.

Pierre was not aware of his friends' great concern for his

welfare because he was becoming increasingly worried about
Claudine. True, he had not seen her cry since the day
Juliette had died, but she seldom spoke other than to greet
him. The house was clean, his meals were prepared and the
old woman was unusually kind to the boys he brought home.
But Pierre missed her pithy and sometimes humorous remarks. He thought about the zombies he had heard about as
a child in St. Dominique. Claudine was like a dead woman
who walked, talked and once in a while made a grimace
which she passed off as a smile. Old Cabress was more like a
ghost; now you saw her and then she disappeared.

Unlike Pierre, Claudine was almost wholly confined to
the house as she now had no outside interests other than an
occasional visit to St. Peter's. She understood what was happening to Pierre and to herself. They had both lost the
desire to live.

Pierre had gone to deliver his collection to the sisters at
the orphanage the day the Schuylers' coachman came to the
Franklin Street house. Mary Anne Schuyler had been taken
dangerously ill and was asking for Pierre. Claudine told the
man that Pierre was not at home, but she would deliver the
message.

"My mistress is asking for him," the man insisted. "What
shall I say?"

"Just say Pierre will be there as soon as possible,"
Claudine suggested.

Once the carriage was out of sight, she threw one of
Juliette's shawls about her shoulders and hurried over to
Broadway. She had gone as far as Canal Street when she saw
Pierre slowly walking home.

"Claudine, why are you here?" he asked.

"Mrs. Schuyler is very sick. She wants you." The old
woman turned away to avoid seeing the startled look on
Pierre's face.

Mary Anne Schuyler was asleep when Pierre reached the
Schuyler residence. Pierre saw from the faces of the mem-

bers of the family who had gathered that there was cause for grave concern. The doctor, who had also attended Juliette, was leaving.

"She wants you to pray for her," Pierre was informed.

"I will pray for her each and every day," Pierre told his friends. "I will visit tomorrow as soon as it is convenient for her to receive guests and assure her that I will storm heaven for my dear and loyal friend."

During the weeks of Mary Anne Schuyler's illness, there was not a day that Pierre did not come bringing a bouquet for the sickroom. He would sit beside his ailing friend and pray for her.

Mrs. Schuyler's sister Hannah Lee, who became Pierre's first biographer, noted how Pierre had aged after Juliette's death and wrote of seeing him sitting beside her sister's bed, his head covered with "blossoms of the grave."

During this period Pierre quoted often from the Sermon on the Mount and the Beatitudes. When his loyal friend died he sat by her bier, tears streaming down his face until Mary Anne's son sent him home in the family carriage.

Pierre no longer had any interest in his work. With Catherine Cruger and Mary Anne Schuyler gone, he instructed the boys at his shop as to the likes and dislikes of his regular patrons. When he made a call, it was more social than professional, or maybe to introduce one of his apprentices.

One morning not long after Mrs. Schuyler's death, Pierre returned from the six o'clock Mass at St. Peter's and found the house ominously quiet. He went to the kitchen which was cold and dark. He called his mother-in-law's name, but there was no answer. Pierre knocked on the door of Claudine's bedroom, but there was still no answer. As he turned away he heard a sound, much like a grunt or a moan, that attracted his attention. He put his ear to the door and listened. Again he heard the sound. Pierre flung open the door. There on the floor was Claudine. Her face was twisted

and she could not move. He knew she had suffered a stroke
as it was obvious that she was paralyzed. As Pierre struggled
to get her on her bed, the old woman regained consciousness. She tried vainly to speak but Pierre assured her that
she would soon be all right, though his hopes were dim. As
soon as Claudine was comfortable, Pierre ran to Sarah Anne
Moore's and asked one of the servants to go for a doctor.

No patient ever had more tender care than that Pierre
lavished on the ailing mother of the wife he had so loved.
Pierre reckoned that Claudine was well into her nineties,
according to events he had heard her recall. Black men and
women, who like Pierre had once been slaves in St. Dominique, heard of Claudine's illness and came to help Pierre in
any way they could. Miraculously, they found Joseph,
Claudine's wayward son, and he held his mother's hand
before she lost consciousness.

Once more Fr. Quinn came to the house and adminis-
tered the last sacraments. And once more Pierre had to
follow one he loved to the cemetery.

Now Pierre was glad to know when the first Monday of
each month arrived. He would deliver the money he had
collected to Sr. Cecelia, then go across the street to the
cemetery and place flowers on the graves of those he had
loved in life. Each visit reminded Pierre that he had to
change his will.

When Pierre went to the lawyers' office on December 3,
1852, he had already informed them that he had to add a
codicil to the will he had made earlier. The lawyers also
knew there was no need for them to advise Pierre, since he
had carefully weighed the matter of the codicil and decided
on what should be included.

> In the name of God, Amen. I, Pierre Toussaint of the City
> of New York, do publish and declare the following to be a
> codicil to my last will and testament made and published
> on the fifteenth day of September in the year of Our

Lord one thousand eight hundred and forty-two, the day of the date thereof.

I do declare that it is my intention hereby to ratify and confirm my said will, except so far as I may expressly modify and alter the same by provisions of this codicil, and though the pleasure of my heavenly Father has taken from me my beloved wife Juliette, and her mother Claudine Gaston, and thus all the provisions of my said will have become inoperative as to them, yet it is most congenial to my feelings to have the assurances of my deep interest and affection in those now departed ones, as I made them when they were the objects of my daily concern and care....

Pierre left the bulk of his estate to young Philip Schuyler, much as he had done in the first will. But he also made provisions for numbers of "memorials" of remembrance for many of his friends. He added a bequest for young Elizabeth Meyer, the daughter of his friend Francis Meyer, who looked in on him every day to be sure he was well cared for.

Pierre then hired a woman to keep house for him as he continued his calls on the sick or those in need. He was pleased when Fanny Montpensier wrote from Baltimore that the Oblates had a Mass said for Juliette on the anniversary of her death. She assured him that these sisters never forgot Juliette's charity and that they also prayed for his continued good health.

The winter of 1853 was one of the most severe Pierre could remember. Every morning as he walked to St. Peter's he had the feeling that each step put him farther than closer to the church. One morning he could only limp the distance between his bedroom and the alcove. He fell against the prie-dieu and cried: "My Lord and my God, help this miserable creature!"

Pierre was still half-kneeling, half-leaning against the prayer stool when the woman he had hired found him. He instructed her to bring him a cup of black coffee and then gave her the address of the doctor who had taken over Dr. Berger's practice. The physician came and after examining Pierre, was surprised to discover that this well-known patient was 87 years old. The doctor also insisted on sending a nurse to care for Pierre.

The nurse had only been looking after Pierre a few days when the housekeeper found Old Cabress in her room dead.

"Her body died," Pierre told the woman. "The good Cabress left us a long time ago." Pierre sent for the priest and asked him to make the necessary arrangements, for which Pierre paid.

For a short while Pierre rallied, and it was only when Fr. Quinn and Pierre's friends no longer saw him at the early Mass that they realized something was definitely wrong. When the report spread that Pierre was bedridden, friends and those he had helped came to Pierre's home. The nurse was courteous, but she insisted that her patient was quite ill and could not be disturbed. The Schuylers appealed to the doctor, who explained the close relationship between Pierre, the Schuylers and all their relatives and friends. Exceptions were made so they could visit Pierre. The nurse also agreed that the visits of young Elizabeth Meyer always seemed to cheer Pierre. Fr. Quinn was a constant visitor, and the nurse complained to the priest and the doctor that Pierre had started speaking French most of the time and this made it difficult for her to care for his needs.

The woman did not realize that Pierre was beginning to relive his early days at L'Artibonite. Though he had long since accepted all he had endured as the will of God, Pierre had never admitted to himself that he had really suffered. He had never had time to devote exclusively to conjuring up old memories. So now his memory discriminated in favor of the happy days of his childhood. He relished the memories of his withered great-grandmother Tonette who talked about "Guinee." He smiled as he recalled the dominance of Zenobie and the pleasant days with his mother and father, as his brother and sisters sat outside their hut. Once again he was the little Pierre whose mimicry delighted and entertained the Bérards on their lush habitation. He tried to move his stiff fingers when he thought of Zenobie teaching him to scrawl his name and once again he was with the elder Monsieur Bérard, who was helping him to learn to read the books he stacked on the shelves of the library at L'Artibonite.

Then there was De Pointe, his little godmother. The name Aurore only confused him. How they enjoyed their childish play with his sister Rosalie, whom he would send to gather flowers so he could fashion a garland for De Pointe. Pierre remembered how miserable he had been when his mother told him De Pointe was going to Paris to be educated in the manner of a young lady of wealth. It was the first time he was to suffer the pain of separation. The first time....

Pierre also had memories of the harvest feast in St. Dominique, which had become Haiti. Hadn't Zenobie told him that the natives, who disappeared after the white man came, had once called their home Hyati?

But the harvest was something to remember. Pierre would close his eyes and see vast fields of cane and waves of slaves moving through the fields in long lines swinging machetes until the cane was cut down to stubble. He could see the sweat pouring from the backs of the slaves as they made tonal sounds—more groans than the music he later heard white men say they made.

Pierre frowned as he remembered the grumblings of other slaves when he was old enough to work in the fields but instead was kept on in the "colon's" house, as they called the Bérard residence.

This made Pierre remember the contrast of the lifestyle of the slaves who worked all day in the sun and then after sundown went to huts which they called home, whereas the

Bérards or their neighbors, the Bossards, the Dessources or Roundanes, all lived in the comfort of ornate manor houses built with riches amassed from the labors of the slaves.

Pierre knew his childhood had been happy because he had been unaware of the nature of his station in life or the plight of black slaves on other habitations throughout the island.

Few people—then or now—knew how Pierre had to struggle to overcome a violent temper. Maybe Zenobie and perhaps Juliette had observed his attempts to master his anger. It was almost a secret between Pierre and his God.

In childhood his temper had flared between Pierre and Zenobie and Ursule. Then had come that night at L'Artibonite when the beat of the drums hidden high in the hills above his home had made sleep impossible. He had stolen away to hide in the bushes and the shadows to listen as the slaves and their leaders plotted the death and destruction of the white planters who had torn them from their African homes and condemned them to lives of drudgery and degradation.

Once again Pierre was listening to the conversations in the Bérard drawing room where he served tall cooling drinks and dainty sandwiches and pastries when other planters came calling. The planters thought that the *gens de couleur* posed the greatest threat to their way of life. By the time he was of age, Pierre knew that the slaves, who had never enjoyed the education and small luxuries which many of the planters had given their biracial children, far outnumbered the *gens de couleur*. The undiluted blood of the African slaves would not allow them to be satisfied until they had avenged their captivity and the cruelty they had suffered in this strange land.

Pierre could remember hearing the slaves whisper about the other Toussaint, the coachman at Breda, Count de Noe's estate, who was to give the signal for the uprising. He had heard the other slave leaders exhort their brethren to spill the blood of the French planters until they were no more. He had been fascinated when for the first time he saw his people revert to their tribal customs and engage in African dances and rituals.

The old, ailing Pierre shuddered when he remembered the young Pierre who had momentarily considered how easy it would be for him to destroy all the Bérards and their friends. Zenobie and her mother Tonette, as well as his aunt, Marie Bouquement, who nursed all the Bossard children, were known for their ability to mix strong potions from herbs. These potions could cure and they could also kill. Pierre's African heritage had made him aware of the various ways his people could be avenged.

As an old man, Pierre felt a sense of remembered guilt. Yet he had at one time had such murderous thoughts when he realized the plight of his people and how his mother and grandmother had isolated him from the other slaves. Then Pierre had finally realized that it would be impossible for him to raise a hand against the Bérards. Yet he knew that neither he nor his family could save them once the revolt came. He also knew the slave revolt would come. Poor Jean Jacques had thought it would be the *gens de couleur* they would have to reckon with.

Then there had been Maurice and Berto. Pierre still shook his head at the manner in which his dilemma had been resolved. Young Monsieur Bérard had asked him to go to New York.

Those first days in New York Pierre recalled as bewildering, but he had to fend for Rosalie and his Aunt Marie. He recalled his apprenticeship with Mr. Merchant and how the young master had gone back to St. Dominique and left him in charge of the family. Pierre remembered the struggle to keep the house going and save money for Rosalie's freedom, and then for that of the lovely Juliette Noel.

Madame Bérard and Rosalie had slipped away, but Euphemia—lovely, delicate, little Euphemia—came and the Reade Street house was like unto a heaven on earth to which he returned each evening to find Juliette and Euphemia, dressed in look-alike outfits, waiting for him.

There were all his friends, the Schuylers, the Church family, the Crugers, the Stevens, the Hamiltons, the LaFarges, the Lees, the Binsse family, the Bancels and many more.

The joyful memories of the years with Juliette and Euphemia acted as an opiate for the pain which Pierre suffered. He accepted it as God's will that he would soon join them, and he looked forward to the reunion.

Eliza Hamilton Schuyler went to see Pierre almost every day. Hannah Lee, Mary Anne Schuyler's sister, was also a constant visitor. In Mrs. Lee's book she wrote:

> When I last saw Toussaint, I perceived that his days were numbered, that he stood on the borders of the infinite. He was feeble, but sitting in an arm-chair, clad in his dressing-gown, and supported by pillows. A more perfect representation of a gentleman I have seldom seen. His head was strewn with the "blossoms of the grave."
>
> When he saw me he was overcome by affecting remembrances, for we had last met at the funeral obsequies of the friend so dear to him [Mary Anne Schuyler]. He trembled with emotion, and floods of tears fell from his eyes.
>
> "It is all so changed! so changed!" said he. "So lonely." He was too weak to converse, but his mind was filled with images of the past....
>
> The next day I saw him again and took leave of him to see him no more in this world. It was with deep feeling that I quitted his house—that house where I had seen the beings he dearly loved collected.
>
> It was a bright summer morning, the last of May; the

windows were open and looked out into the little garden with its few scattered flowers. There was nobody there I had ever seen there, but himself—the aged, solitary man....

Spring had brought back many more memories for Pierre. Once again he was in City Hall Park with Euphemia, who loved to imitate the sounds of the birds. That was why he had laughed when Cesarine Meetz said the child had a voice that required cultivating. How Euphemia had loved walking down Broadway in the spring. Then she would come home and imitate the vendors they had passed who were hawking their wares. His Aunt Marie would remember the little Pierre whose mimicry had delighted the Bérards and the Bossards. Now it was spring, but where were they all? Pierre sometimes wondered and expected them to appear momentarily. At other times he knew they were waiting for him and begged God to take him—but only when it was his will.

One day when Eliza Hamilton Schuyler went to see Pierre, she wrote of her visit:

> Toussaint was in bed today; he says it is now the most comfortable place for him, or as he expressed it in French, *"Il ne peut pas entre mieux."*
>
> He was drowsy and indistinct, but calm, cheerful and placid—the expression of his countenance truly religious. He told me he had received his last Communion, for which he had been earnest, and mentioned that two Sisters of Charity had been to see him and prayed with him.
>
> He speaks of the excellent care he receives—of his kind nurse (she is a white woman)—and said "All is well." He sent me away when he was tired, by thanking me.

The young Mrs. Schuyler, who had known Pierre all her life, visited her friend again on June 26, 1853. She wrote:

> I saw him on Sunday; he was very low and neither spoke

nor noticed me.... On Monday when I entered, he had
revived a little, and looking up, said,
   "Dieu avec moi"—God is with me.
   When I asked him if he wanted anything, he replied
with a smile, *"Rien sur la terre"*—Nothing on earth.

Four days later on June 30, 1853, at twelve o'clock on a
Thursday, Pierre Toussaint died. He was with God and his
loved ones gone before him.

As word of Pierre's death spread, men and women who
had benefited by his charity gathered in front of his house
on Franklin Street. Fr. William Quinn, who had been with
Pierre at the end, immediately notified Robert Lee and
George Lee Schuyler, executors of Pierre's will. The house
at Franklin Street was crowded with members of the French
Benevolent Society and boys who had grown up in the basement at 105 Reade Street and obtained jobs in the homes of
the patrons Pierre served for so many years. Parish societies
from St. Peter's and the French Church of St. Vincent de
Paul sent expressions of condolence. Though Pierre had no
living relative to mourn his passing, the entire community
was aware of a great loss.

The church, Pierre's beloved St. Peter's, was crowded
the day of his funeral. There were members of the great
families of New York, grown men and women who had been
at the orphanage when Pierre and Euphemia came each
September 16 with gifts, widows from whom Pierre had supplied fuel and food during the long winters, and household
help who had been placed in their jobs by Pierre in the
homes of New York's prominent citizens. Those who had
once been homeless black boys wept for the man who had
been the only father image they had known. The Sisters of
Charity were there, as were many of the priests Pierre had
helped.

The remaining members of the Schuyler family, the
Stevens, LaFarges, Binsses and the Hamiltons watched as the

casket of the man they had known all their lives was lowered into a resting place at Old St. Patrick's Cemetery on Saturday, July 2, 1853, beside his loved ones.

Fr. William Quinn, the pastor at St. Peter's, had closed the eulogy by saying:

"There are few left among the clergy superior in devotion and zeal for the Church and for the glory of God; among laymen, none."

Eliza Schuyler, who had once been Pierre's "little Eliza Hamilton," was among those who attended Pierre's funeral and later wrote:

> I went to town on Saturday to attend Toussaint's funeral. High Mass, incense, candles, rich robes and solemn music were there. The Church gave all it could give, to prince or noble. The priest, his friend Fr. Quinn, made a most interesting address. He did not allude to his color and scarcely to his station; it seemed as if his virtues as a man and a Christian had absorbed all other thoughts. A stranger would not have suspected that a black man of his humble calling lay in the midst of us. He said though no relative is left to mourn for him, yet many present would feel that they had lost one who always had wise counsel for the rich, words of encouragement for the poor, and all would be grateful for having known him.
>
> The aid he [Pierre] had given to the late Bishop Fenwick of Boston, to Fr. Powers of our city, to all Catholic institutions, was dwelt upon at large. How much I have learned of his charitable deeds which I had never known before.

The Schuyler brothers, George Lee and Robert Lee, the appointed executors of Pierre's will, went to his Franklin Street house to decide the distribution of his belongings. On his desk they found Euphemia's letters, which Pierre had read over and over until he could no longer read. There was the ledger in which he had entered every donation he had collected for the orphanage. Beside the ledger was a purse containing the exact amount of the last entry. Pierre missed keeping his date with Sr. Cecelia on the first Monday in July 1853, but he knew the Schuyler brothers would make sure the orphans received the money he had collected for them. Pierre also knew that the Sisters of Charity, the spiritual daughters of Mother Elizabeth Seton, would remember him in their prayers because Pierre's efforts on their behalf was a part of that order's early history in New York. Pierre insisted that prayer yielded the highest rate of interest.

Many who attended Pierre's funeral could have told Eliza Hamilton Schuyler even more about Pierre's charity. But generations of Schuylers to come would remember that their ancestor of the Battle of Saratoga fame had said of Pierre: "I have known Christians who were not gentlemen, gentlemen who were not Christians. I know one man who is both, and that man is black."

Epilogue

The death and funeral of Pierre Toussaint, considered by many to be New York's outstanding black citizen, did not go unnoticed. The city which never made it possible for Pierre to ride on any public conveyance mourned and lamented the demise of the black man whose charity transcended the artificial barriers of race.

In her *Memoirs of Pierre Toussaint,* published soon after his death, Hannah Lee Sawyer included the following accounts which appeared in the newspapers of the day.

Pierre Toussaint, whose funeral will take place this morning at ten o'clock from St. Peter's Church, Barclay Street, was born in the servitude of St. Domingo, and in devoted attendance upon Madame Bérard in her flight from that island, arrived in this city in 1787. Here the former dependent became the support of the unfortunate lady, and her most disinterested friend until her death.

The occupation of ladies' hairdresser gave him admission to the houses of the influential families of that day, and his good manners, unusual discrimination of character and high sense of propriety insured him the countenance, courtesy and esteem of all to whom he was admitted, and the confidence and friendship of many to whom the excellence of his life and character were more intimately known. All knew his general worth, but few

347

knew the generous qualities of his heart, and with those
principles of disinterested daily conduct.

His charity was of the efficient character which did
not content itself with a present relief of pecuniary aid,
but which required time and thought by day and night,
and long watchfulness and kind attentions at the bedside
of the sick and departing. Thus goodness springing from
refined and elevated principles and from a sense of religious duty, which never permitted him to omit a most
scrupulous compliance with all the requirements of his
faith, formed the prominent feature of his character and
made his life a constant round of acts of kindness and
sympathy.

By such a life, governed by such principles of integ-
rity, charity and religion, Toussaint secured to himself
the respect, esteem, and friendship of many of our first
citizens, and though death has made the circle small in
which he had moved, there are yet remaining many who
remembered his excellence and with the kindest appreciation.

Though this tribute, which appeared in two papers on
July 2, 1853, was only signed with the letter "S," there is
reason to believe that it might have been written by one of
the Schuylers.

Mrs. Lee also included an extract from a longer tribute
to Pierre written by Henry T. Tuckerman, an outstanding
writer of that period. This article appeared in the *Home
Journal* a few days after Pierre's death.

Died on Thursday, June 30th, at his residence in this city,
Pierre Toussaint, in the eighty-seventh year of his age.

We cannot allow this brief announcement to form
the sole record of one whose example is a higher vindica-
tion of his race, or rather a nobler testimony to the
beauty and force of character, than all the works of fic-
tion that studious invention ever conceived.

Pierre Toussaint for more than sixty years had been
the most beloved Negro in New York. He came here in

1787 with his mistress.... He soon began to exercise his rare talent as a hairdresser, and became indispensable to the ladies of New York, and their children. A very few of the brides, whose tresses he so daintily arrayed, yet survive, and as long as any of them lived, Pierre paid them regular visits and was always certain of a kind reception. He supported his beloved mistress not only in comfort but in luxury when her means failed, until the day of her death.

Meantime, he had associated himself with all the best families. The wives and daughters loved to listen to his tropical reminiscences, or his cheerful comments on the news of the day as he adorned their heads for the evening party, and the children delighted to put themselves under his kindly hands when the time came for a hair-cutting. Pierre was thus busy from morning to night....

After the death of his mistress, he married and was enabled to purchase a very good home in Franklin Street. He retired from business with an adequate fortune and thenceforth devoted himself to social and benevolent duty. His relations in the former respect were threefold; first, to his cherished lady friends and their families, whom he had attended in youth, and toward whom he exhibited a disinterested and loyal attachment, which seemed to belong to a past age or a different country so unique and touching was its manifestation; second, to the French population of New York, to whom he was attached by early association and native language; and thirdly to his own race....

By these so widely different classes, Pierre was both respected and beloved. He moved among them in a way peculiarly his own. He possessed a sense of the appropriate, a self-respect and a uniformity of demeanor which amounted to genius. No familiarity ever made him forget what was due to his superiors, and prosperity and reputation never hardened his heart toward the less favored of his own class.

For sixty years he attended Mass at six in the morning, as punctual as a clock, until prostrated by illness. His days and nights were given to visits, ministrations to the sick, attendance upon the bereaved and attempts to reform the erring and console the afflicted.... Often strangers paused to look with curiosity and surprise upon the singular tableau presented in Broadway of the venerable Negro, with both his hands clasped in greeting by a lady high in the circles of fashion or birth, and to watch the vivid interest of both as they exchanged inquiries for each other's welfare.

The last time I saw Pierre, he was seated among a group of mourners beside the coffin of a lady venerated for years in the highest social sphere of the city. She was almost the last tie that bound him to the past. He had visited her daily for the past thirty years and brought his offering of flowers, and there he sat with his white head bowed in grief and every line of his honest sable face wet with tears. It was a beautiful homage to worth—a beautiful instance of what may be the disinterested relation between the exalted and the humble—when the genius of character and the sentiment of religion bring them thus together.

Pierre was buried in the cathedral churchyard beside his wife and adopted child, and his funeral was attended by gentlemen and menials; his death-bed soothed by the fairest as well as venerated by the most humble representatives of the wide circle included in his sympathies and attracted by his worth.

Peace to the ashes of good, noble, loyal Pierre Toussaint!

As late as 1893, Emma Carey, who had known Pierre when she was a child, wrote an article which appeared in *Ave Maria* magazine. In setting forth her childhood memories of Pierre, Emma Carey wrote:

When I was young I used to hear Protestants speak with

reverence of two Catholics—the great [Bishop] Fenelon and the humble Pierre Toussaint.

I believe Pierre Toussaint to have been a man who dwelt above the region of human passions and personal interests. He had a strong sense of dignity of being a creature of God, and no outward circumstances of birth, of station or even of bondage could lessen his interior contentment.... I believe he never gauged his own merits by any measure of man's making, but said, like St. Francis of Assisi: "What I am in thy sight, O God! that I am, and no more."

Emma Carey, who had grown up in a Protestant home before she converted to Catholicism, wrote of Pierre's ability to explain the teachings of the Church with intelligent simplicity. She credited him with explaining the devotion to the Mother of God with the utmost clarity and quoting from the great spiritual writers in a manner which accounted for the faith he espoused and so eloquently defended. There is little doubt that Pierre sowed seeds of faith in Emma Carey's heart and soul. The debt this writer owes Emma Carey is set forth elsewhere in this book.

Illuminating stories about Pierre were handed down to the children of the families with which he had been associated. The Rev. John LaFarge, S.J., who founded the Catholic Interracial Council, remembered and often spoke of his parents' accounts of Pierre's charities. Fr. LaFarge lived to witness a revival of interest in the life of the black man about whom his family had always spoken in such glowing terms. Much of this revived interest in Pierre's life was due to the untiring efforts of Fr. LaFarge's cousin, Schuyler Warren, and Schuyler Warren's sister, Hope Warren Wilberforce.

Pierre's humble efforts to aid suffering humanity had a profound effect on all the Schuyler children and grandchildren. George Lee Schuyler preserved a trunk full of Pierre's letters and papers, which Schuyler's daughter Georgina do-

nated to the New York Public Library in 1903. Louisa Lee
Schuyler, another daughter, was among the first group of
women who gathered at Cooper Union in April 1861, and
organized for the purpose of nursing the sick and wounded
in the Civil War. Louisa Lee Schuyler was elected as first
president of the women's Central Relief Association, as this
organization was called. This grandchild of Pierre's friend
Mary Anne Schuyler, who was also a great-grandchild of
Alexander Hamilton, later founded the first School of Nursing at Bellevue Hospital. Louisa Lee Schuyler no doubt
remembered the stories she had heard her parents tell
about Pierre jumping over barricades to nurse victims of
the plague which hit New York each August. She was also
one of the founders of the American Red Cross and the
National Society for the Prevention of Blindness. She advo-
cated the removal of children and the insane from all poor
houses and was one of a group who spearheaded the anti-
tuberculosis campaign. Tuberculosis had claimed the lives
of Pierre's sister Rosalie and his beloved Euphemia.

Over the years, Old St. Patrick's became a parish church
as the new St. Patrick's Cathedral was located on Fifth Avenue at 50th Street. The neighborhood around Old St. Pat's
has undergone a drastic change, and the cemetery is now
surrounded by aging and nondescript tenements. Though
the cemetery is like an oasis in the midst of this rundown
neighborhood, with age-old trees spreading their branches
high above the stone wall surrounding the burying ground,
few New Yorkers are aware that the remains of more than
thirty thousand early Catholic inhabitants of this city are
buried there.

A young seminarian, Charles H. McTeague, became interested in the life of Pierre Toussaint through the writings
of Fr. LaFarge and George Hunton, executive secretary of
the Catholic Interracial Council and editor of *The Interracial
Review,* and subsequently began a search for Pierre's grave.
Time and weather had obliterated names and dates from

many of the tombstones. From scant records made available
to him, Charles McTeague, now the Rev. McTeague of the
Apostolate of the Sea, in the Archdiocese of Newark, New
Jersey, located the row of graves where he thought Pierre
might have been buried. He took pictures of the stones on
two graves he suspected to be those of Pierre and Euphemia.
The markings were so faint he enlisted the aid of his
mother. She went to the cemetery with him and at high
noon held a mirror so he could see if the correct shadows
were falling on the stones before he took the pictures. When
the film was developed the young seminarian was still unable
to decipher the faint markings. He showed the photographs
to George Hunton at the Catholic Interracial Council. Mr.
Hunton took the negatives to a bright window, held them up
to the light and called McTeague. Together they read
"...saint" on one stone and "...emia" on the next one. The
"saint" was the last part of Pierre Toussaint's name and the
"emia" was for Euphemia. After more examining they deci-
phered the date of Euphemia's death—1829. Charles
McTeague then knew he had found Pierre Toussaint's
grave. What he did not know then was that he, as a priest,
would spend the remaining years of his life working and
praying for Pierre's cause.

In 1951 the late Francis Cardinal Spellman, then Archbishop of New York, visited Pierre's grave for the purpose of
blessing a plaque on the tombstone which had been placed
there by the John Boyle O'Reilly Society for Interracial
Justice.

On June 29, 1953, a pontifical Mass was celebrated in
Pierre's memory at his beloved St. Peter's on Barclay Street.
A bronze tablet commemorating Pierre's years of service was
affixed to the right outer wall of the church and blessed by
Bishop Joseph Donahue, as clergymen, city officials and resi-
dents from all walks of life read the following inscription:

Pierre Toussaint
1766—1853

Catholic Negro Layman, Member of Old St. Peter's Parish. For 66 Years Revered for his Exemplary Life and Many Works of Charity.

This Tablet Affixed June 29, 1953, by the John Boyle O'Reilly Committee for Interracial Justice.

Just above the plaque in memory of Pierre is another one in memory of Elizabeth Ann Bayley Seton—August 28, 1774—January 4, 1821.

It was a great day in 1968 when His Eminence Terence Cardinal Cooke presented documents in preparation for the cause of Pierre Toussaint's canonization to the Congregation for Sacred Causes at Rome. The faithful few surviving members of the Pierre Toussaint Guild, under the direction of the Rev. Benjamin J. Horton, S.S.J., found it difficult to believe that their many years of work had finally begun to bear fruit. Once Pierre's cause was introduced, the guild members began re-examining the miracles attributed to Pierre's intercession.

In St. Marc, Haiti, a parish priest related a story which fascinated this writer. According to Fr. Joseph Saget, one Gesner Lamothe, a young Haitian athlete, was taken ill. When his condition did not improve, he was accepted for treatment at the Albert Schweitzer Hospital near his home, where his illness was diagnosed as cancer. The priest encouraged Lamothe to beg Pierre's intercession, since the ailing man had been born near Pierre's birthplace. When hope for the young man's life was almost abandoned, he was accepted for treatment at the Center for the Treatment of Cancer in Port-au-Prince, where the doctors agreed that Gesner Lamothe was dying.

Following is Fr. Saget's story. Though this good priest spoke and wrote in French, I am indebted to my friend Joyce James for this English translation.

In 1966, I was responsible for a small church in Liancourt, a small village located in the Artibonite Department. I received a visit of a sympathetic young man, 25 years of age, named Gesner Lamothe, who was just appointed as the manager of a football [soccer] team in that locality.

After this first contact with him, I was glad to see how he was devoted to his work. He had to quit his job because the office which appointed him was not able to pay him because of a lack of funds.

A few weeks later Gesner Lamothe decided to open a primary school. He did not have a place to open that school, so I shared my place with him. I helped him by allowing him to use the church during the week. I was very glad to be helpful to him and to my parishioners.

The school became so popular that he was not able to stay in the church, which was too small, so an unoccupied house in the neighborhood became the new school. One day we received the visit of a few people who said that the house belonged to them, and they took the property away from us. They were from the Bahai region.

Gesner was disappointed but had to surrender the place. With the help of the inhabitants of Liancourt and Marie, we built a hall where the children could come for their education. At that time there were 300 pupils.

A few months later, I noticed that the devoted director was losing weight. I suggested that he see a doctor. We went to Albert Schweitzer Hospital which is at Deschapelles, not too far from Liancourt.

The checkup showed a tumor in his abdomen, and he was operated on. They found two cancers, one in the abdomen, the other in his lung. After spending eight days at the hospital, the doctors suggested to him to join his parents and relatives because he could only expect to live about three more months. The night the doctors told him this he became so upset that he wanted to kill himself.

Later, having calmed down, he accepted the will of the Lord. Because he needed some moral support, he asked for me. I went right away, finding him in low spirits.

Gesner was transferred to the Centre de Treatment du Cancer [Center for the Treatment of Cancer] located at Port-au Prince. There the doctors did not have any hope for him and agreed with the former ones.

Facing this tragedy, this young man, devoted, enthusiastic for the work he was doing and wishing to help the young of this place, prayed to the soul of someone who died a century ago. He did it on my suggestion, as I did it, too.

I prayed to the soul of Pierre Toussaint, who was an apostle in life and an example of kindness to the people of his time. This will be for him, the teacher, a way to recognize the power of God through this soul.

After his therapy, he was discharged. A few months later, he noticed that he was again losing weight. He went back to the clinic for another cure. There he learned from Dr. Chevaleir that he was completely cured. All the X-rays did not show any trace of his illness.

Happy, he came to tell me the news. He told me that he had prayed with confidence to the soul of Pierre Toussaint and had asked him to cure him not for himself but for his pupils.

I can certify that this recovery is the work of Pierre Toussaint, a blessed soul.

Now Mr. Gesner Lamothe is living in that locality [Liancourt]; he is the principal of a school with 600 pupils.

Director of St. Marc Parish
Haiti, West Indies

On December 11, 1964, Lorraine Ferranolo, age 12, of Cliffside Park, New Jersey, was taking her sister Maria, age 4, and her brother Andrew, 6, to a nearby store to buy Christmas presents. The three children were struck by an automobile and taken to Englewood Hospital. All three of the children were unconscious when admitted, and according to the hospital records there appeared to be slight hope for their recovery. Little Maria, who was listed as having a gross deformity of the left thigh in the upper one-third femoral region, had to undergo a "tracheostomy, duodenotomy and litigation of bleeding artery." She was by far the most seriously injured, though all three of the children had suffered concussions.

The mother of the children, Mrs. Joseph (Mary Lou) Ferranolo, who was praying for the recovery of all three of her children, writes: "...Fr. McTeague visited us in the hospital to bless the children and console us. He told us about a saintly Negro, Pierre Toussaint, and suggested we seek from God the children's recovery. As a sign of the heroic sanctity of Pierre Toussaint, our prayers were answered and all three children recovered.... We have to attribute this to God through Pierre Toussaint's intercession."

Another man, John S. McBride, writes that he had first learned about Pierre Toussaint only two days before he was mysteriously awakened at 3:30 a.m. and for no apparent reason decided he should go to the next bedroom and look at his son Joseph, who had not been feeling well the night before. Mr. McBride claims he found his son unconscious, that the boy had already turned a "blueish shade" and he could hear what the father described as the "death rattle." Mr. McBride called the police, and Joseph was rushed to the Englewood Hospital where the admitting doctor is reported to have said: "This boy is dead—clinically speaking."

Joseph was placed in intensive care, but eventually recovered and was released.

Mr. McBride writes: "I am convinced that it was the prayers and interest of Pierre Toussaint that woke me and saved my boy's life."

It would appear that Pierre Toussaint is still nursing the sick and begging God's help for the afflicted.

A friend I have never met wrote of Pierre Toussaint as follows:

> He was a fellow human being and the bearer of the image of God; this image being in him so bright that all who came in contact had to see it. It obliterated all forms of social, legal and racial distinction, not because he [Pierre] ceased to be a slave or a black but because he was who he was, and his humility, being a real Christian virtue, was not such as to feed the pride of his owners and the local whites, but rather such as to humble them and make them realize how empty were the racial and social feelings that made such a man a slave and them his masters.

As hard as I have tried to paint a word picture of Pierre Toussaint, this black man summarized and set down all I had come to believe about Pierre. I am grateful to Jaime Vidal for adding his masculine insight to my female interpretation of a post-Revolutionary black who displayed the virtues and characteristics of a saint.

Appendix

The Cause of Pierre Toussaint

On December 5, 1989 with John Cardinal O'Connor presiding, the first session of the diocesan inquiry relating to the life and sanctity of Pierre Toussaint was held at the Catholic Center, 1011 First Avenue in the Archdiocese of New York, thereby formally opening the cause for sainthood of this Servant of God.

Cardinal O'Connor, upon taking an oath, established the Archdiocese of New York as the promoter of the cause of canonization of a former Haitian slave who is known to have performed many outstanding acts of charity in old New York during the early years of the 19th century.

As early as 1968 the late Terence Cardinal Cooke had alerted Rome to the sanctity and good works of Pierre Toussaint and initiated preparations for opening a formal process. However, the cause appeared to have been dormant until December 5, 1989.

In 1987 Cardinal O'Connor had instructed Msgr. Michael J. Wrenn, pastor of the Church of St. John the Evangelist in New York, to begin preparations for this formal opening of the Pierre Toussaint cause. Cardinal O'Connor had also ascertained from the Congregation of Sacred Causes that there was no objection to this cause. The prefect

of the congregation, Angelo Cardinal Felici, had replied to
the inquiry by granting the *nihil obstat.*

Cardinal O'Connor, actor in the cause, appointed the
Rev. P. Carlos Lizarraga, C.P. (Rome), as postulator of the
cause. On December 1, 1989, the Rev. Lizarraga appointed
Msgr. Robert M. O'Connell, pastor of St. Peter's Church on
Barclay Street, where Pierre Toussaint had worshipped for
sixty years, as vice-postulator for the cause.

Cardinal O'Connor appointed Msgr. Michael J. Wrenn,
president of the historical commission, in view of the exten-
sive research Msgr. Wrenn had already done on Pierre
Toussaint. Bishop Norbert M. Dorsey, C.P., whose doctoral
dissertation on Pierre Toussaint was well known, and Rev.
Thomas J. Shelley, professor of history at St. Joseph's Semi-
nary, Dunwoodie, comprised the historical commission.

Cardinal O'Connor then appointed Bishop Patrick J.
Sheridan as episcopal delegate, Msgr. Desmond J. Vella as
promoter of justice and Rev. Lawrence M. Connaughton as
notary actuary.

Msgr. Wrenn later commissioned Rev. Cyprian Davis,
O.S.B. to prepare a background study on Haiti, Pierre's
birthplace. This study, when completed, was included in the
findings of the commission.

On May 15, 1990 a second session of the diocesan in-
quiry was held at the Catholic Center in the Archdiocese of
New York. The following persons testified regarding their
knowledge of the sanctity and good works of Pierre
Toussaint: Mr. Herbert A. Johnson, executive secretary of
the Archdiocesan Office of Black Ministry; the Rev. Charles
H. McTeague, who had located Pierre Toussaint's grave so
many years before; Rev. John F. X. Smith, historian; Rev.
Joseph I. Dirvin, C.M., secretary, St. John's University; and
Ms. Ellen Tarry, author. Testimony was subsequently taken
from Bishop Norbert M. Dorsey, C.P., *ex officio,* in the diocese of Orlando, Florida.

A third session of the diocesan inquiry was held on October 30, 1990. Those who gave formal testimony were Bishop Emerson J. Moore, auxiliary bishop of the Archdiocese of New York; Msgr. Michael J. Wrenn, *ex officio;* Msgr. Florence D. Cohalan and Rev. Thomas J. Shelley, *ex officio.*

The historical commission members under Msgr. Wrenn were aware of the formidable task confronting them. They knew that it would be difficult and time consuming to gather all of the necessary and proper legal instructions for the cause of canonization of the Servant of God, Pierre Toussaint.

Msgr. Wrenn had to instruct the members of the commission that they had to carefully examine all and any documentary sources, letters or writings left behind, inasmuch as this is an ancient cause in which there are no living eye witnesses of the life and heroic virtues of Pierre Toussaint. The proof of his heroically virtuous life must be evident in documentary sources and any letters or writings which may have been left behind.

The historical commission had the responsibility to collect all or any proof as stated above. (Much of this had been done by Bishop Dorsey who had treated Pierre's life and works in his doctoral dissertation.) The three members of the historical commission would have to prepare a report known as the *Relatio.* The *Relatio* would have to be submitted to the canonically erected tribunal. The three members of the commission would have to answer any questions which the episcopal delegate might ask.

The reputation of sanctity would have to be proved. Eye witnesses to this must be called by a canonically erected tribunal consisting of a episcopal delegate, a promoter of justice and a notary. The Cardinal is to preside at the first and last sessions, and the delegate presides at other sessions.

Though there were other stipulations which would have to be followed, the historical commission was duly in-

structed, and work began on collecting the documents necessary to presenting the cause for the canonization of the
Servant of God, Pierre Toussaint.

It is fortunate that through the years there had been a
little band of Pierre's loyal admirers who had passed on their
knowledge of his saintly life and works. The Rev. John
LaFarge, S.J., whose parents had known Pierre, was joined
by his relatives, Schuyler Warren and Hope Warren
Wilberforce (who had married the son of the great English
abolitionist William Wilberforce), and they made sure
Pierre's life and works were not forgotten during their lifetime.

After years of missionary work in Maryland, Fr. LaFarge
was transferred to New York where he became editor of
America, a national Catholic weekly, and the founder of the
Catholic Interracial Council. Through the latter organization's organ, *The Interracial Review,* Fr. LaFarge and a
group of followers kept the story of the life and works of
Pierre alive.

The story of how St. Peter's Church was crowded with
friends and mourners at Pierre's funeral even though he
died without leaving any relatives behind is known by all who
have read books on Pierre's life. Yet Catholics are not proud
of the fact that Pierre's grave in Old St. Patrick's cemetery
had been overlooked for so many years.

However, once the grave was located, a steady stream of
Pierre's admirers began visiting his grave in Old St. Patrick's
cemetery.

In an article by John C. Armstrong and Paul F. Bryant,
which recently came to my attention, they describe a visit to
Pierre Toussaint's grave as follows:

> On the sunny afternoon of June 29, 1941, the usually
> deserted graveyard around Old St. Patrick's Cathedral
> was alive with the shuffling of feet, singing of choirs and
> the rhetoric of distinguished speakers. The ceremony
> there that day moved Fr. John LaFarge, S.J., a prominent

leader in the Catholic interracial movement, to be reminded that America has....

A religious history, a vast thrilling history that began
in adventure and romance. Saints, martyrs, confessors
and virgins have walked these streets.... Prayers of real
contemplatives have risen from within New York's walls,
as pure and as fervent as any that rose to heaven from the
Theban Desert.

On June 10, 1965, the Pierre Toussaint Guild was
founded with ecclesiastical permission. Cardinal Spellman
appointed the Rev. Benjamin M. Horton, S.S.J., who also
headed the Catholic Negro-American Mission Board, as director of the guild.

In addition to distributing leaflets on the life of Pierre
Toussaint, in the years after its organization the Pierre
Toussaint Guild became the source of information for men
and women throughout the country who had heard the
story of Pierre Toussaint's charity and good works.

Fr. Horton was fortunate to have the cooperation and
counsel of Fr. McTeague, who had located the Pierre
Toussaint grave site, and Arthur Sheehan, who with his wife
Elizabeth had written a biography of Pierre Toussaint which
was published by P.J. Kennedy & Sons in 1955.

For many years before publishing the book on Pierre,
Arthur Sheehan had carried on a correspondence with Sr.
Mary Timothy, SBS, who became interested in Pierre after
reading the magazine article in *Ave Maria* by Emma Carey in
1893. In a letter to this writer from Arthur Sheehan dated
June 4, 1974, Arthur says of Sr. Timothy: "She had been
propagandizing for Pierre Toussaint's cause forty years....
She told me that Mother Drexel's sister had brought a set of
old copies of the *Ave Maria* magazine to the convent. I am
sending you a photocopy of the article in this magazine
which drew her attention to Pierre Toussaint..."

The memory of Sr. Timothy's devotion to the Pierre
Toussaint cause impressed all who knew her. Sr. Timothy

corresponded with Fr. Horton and the guild during the remaining years of her life. Blessed Katharine Drexel knew and approved of Sr. Timothy's devotion to the Pierre Toussaint cause.

The Pierre Toussaint Guild also fostered the practice of placing a wreath on the grave of Pierre Toussaint at Old St. Patrick's cemetery for the anniversary of his death (June 30) and on All Saints Day. Scholars from all over the world wrote the Pierre Toussaint Guild for information, prayer cards and articles on the life of Pierre Toussaint.

It was only in 1971 after Cardinal Cooke had asked me to do a book about Pierre Toussaint that I became a member of the Pierre Toussaint Guild. The many meetings with Fr. Horton, Fr. McTeague and Arthur Sheehan during years of research were an enriching experience.

Members of the Pierre Toussaint Guild were saddened when the Rev. Benjamin M. Horton, S.S.J., was transferred on July 1, 1980 to Pascagoula, Mississippi, to serve as pastor of the Church of St. Peter the Apostle. Later Fr. Horton was assigned to a mission outside Mobile, Alabama, where he died in 1988.

The Rev. Benjamin M. Horton's memory lives on each year when the Archdiocese of New York's Office of Black Ministry sponsors a Pierre Toussaint Mass at the Cathedral of St. Patrick. The medal which Fr. Horton commissioned and Fr. Thomas McGlynn executed is bestowed on a member of the community deemed to exemplify the virtuous charity for which Pierre Toussaint is widely known.

The zeal and enthusiasm of the remaining members of the Pierre Toussaint Guild was a rich source of enthusiastic dedication which was tapped when Msgr. Robert M. O'Connell, vice-postulator of the cause, appointed Waldemar A. Roebuck as director of the Pierre Toussaint Guild in 1989.

Waldemar Roebuck was one of the early commissioners of the office of black ministry and had served almost a half century as a Secular Franciscan. He held the office of national chairman of the North American Federation of the Third Order of St. Francis.

The reactivated Pierre Toussaint Guild immediately began publishing a Pierre Toussaint Guild Newsletter informing its readers of developments in the cause for canonization of this Servant of God. Msgr. O'Connell as vice-postulator and Msgr. Wrenn as head of the historical commission were pleased to observe the enthusiasm for and about the cause, which was evident in the meetings of the reactivated Pierre Toussaint Guild.

Cardinal O'Connor requested a rescript from the Congregation of Sacred Causes on August 17, 1990 for permission to exhume the remains of Pierre Toussaint from the cemetery of Old St. Patrick's for the purpose of examination and re-interment in a crypt beneath the main altar of St. Patrick's Cathedral on New York's Fifth Avenue. This request was made in order to provide a more convenient location for veneration by the faithful.

Justice Phyllis Gangel-Jacob of the Supreme Court of New York gave the required civil permission on August 28, 1990. Though the Archdiocese of New York had moved cautiously in this matter so as to avoid widespread media coverage, several newspapers, radio and television stations managed to have representatives follow the proceedings.

While being interviewed by a young reporter from CNN on November 1, 1990, I casually mentioned the significance of the proceeding. In a few moments the reporter as well as the photographers and all their equipment had vanished from the living room where I was giving the interview and they hurriedly made their way downtown to Old St. Patrick's cemetery.

Newspaper articles, pictures and commentary followed in the wake of the exhumation proceedings, which took place on All Saints Day in the presence of Cardinal O'Connor and others involved in the cause. Excavation continued until

November 15, 1990. The Metropolitan Forensic Anthropology Team of the department of anthropology of Lehman College, City University of New York, conducted exhaustive studies of the skeletal remains. A computerized superimposition of an image of a skull on the only known photograph of Pierre Toussaint, which was taken by Nathaniel Fish Moore, president of Columbia College about 1851, was entered as evidence. The team finally concluded that the remains were those of the Servant of God, Pierre Toussaint. The team also found an arthritic condition in the right knee bone, corresponding to the fact that Pierre walked with a limp in his declining years.

On December 4, 1990, the remains of Pierre Toussaint, in a metal container encased in a solid hardwood mahogany-stained casket, were brought to St. Patrick's Cathedral. The Cardinal bestowed his blessing on the casket, then led a procession to the main altar and from the main altar to the crypt.

Pierre's coffin was placed in a niche in a bottom row of three directly under the tomb of Coadjutor Archbishop John H. Maguire. Other niches in the crypt contain the remains of all previous heads of the archdiocese, two former rectors of the cathedral and Archbishop Fulton J. Sheen.

The marble slab which encloses the Toussaint niche reads: "Pierre Toussaint, Servant of God, 1766-1853."

At the top of the steps leading down to the crypt opposite Our Lady Chapel, an inscribed prie-dieu has been installed for the convenience of those who come to pay reverence to Pierre or beg his intercession.

In June, 1991 Rev. Paul Molinari, S.J. was appointed Roman postulator for the Pierre Toussaint cause. The Rev. Peter Gumpel, S.J. was named relator for the cause later in that year. Rev. William S. Elder, who had been acting as theological censor, was appointed to assist the Rev. Gumpel.

On June 18, 1991, the final session of the diocesan inquiry was held with Cardinal O'Connor officiating. The *Acta* (all papers and documents relating to the cause) were gathered and placed in sealed boxes for safe shipment to the congregation in Rome. The following week Msgr. Robert M. O'Connell delivered them to the congregation. On July 9, 1991 Cardinal Felici granted permission for the sealed boxes containing the *Acta* of the diocesan inquiry to be opened. Cardinal O'Connor issued the decree of *non cultus* on November 12, 1991. The Congregation of Sacred Causes issued a decree declaring the re-validity of the diocesan inquiry on November 16, 1991.

It was then the duty of Rev. Peter Gumpel, S.J. and Fr. William S. Elder to prepare the *Positio* from the *Acta* and all relevant actions or papers.

Though the relator faced a formidable task, the fact that many of Pierre's papers plus his will had been kept safely by his friends the Schuylers and donated to the New York Public Library upon his death was a blessing.

A news release dated August 13, 1991 distributed by the New York Public Library referred to the papers as follows:

> The New York Public Library's holdings of the papers and correspondence of Pierre Toussaint (1790-1853) recently served as vital testimony in Toussaint's candidacy for sainthood in the Roman Catholic Church. If the petition for beatification for the Haitian-born slave meets approval by the Vatican, Toussaint would become the first African-American saint.
>
> As part of the beatification, a process stemming from medieval times, the Vatican requires proof that the candidate lived a life of "heroic virtue" and that a miracle was performed either by him or through a prayer for his intercession. Cardinal Cooke of the Archdiocese of New York used as central evidence the library's collection of Toussaint's papers in the petition for beatification made in Rome....
>
> The collection of Toussaint's papers, part of the library's rare books and manuscripts division, includes over 300 letters between Toussaint and friends and rela-

tives in the United States, the Caribbean and France. Among other notable items in the collection are many appeals made to Toussaint for charity, as well as the letters and poems of Toussaint's niece and ward Euphemie.

As a whole the collection illustrates the extent of Toussaint's involvement in all levels of New York society. Manumission papers in the collection, for example, document Toussaint's efforts to gain freedom for many slaves, while correspondence with the Schuyler, Hamilton and Moore families chronicles his intimate connections with prominent New York families. A letter in the library's collection from Sarah Anne Moore provided the means for identifying a photo of Toussaint taken by Moore's brother, Nathaniel Fish....

In the January 1993 issue of the Pierre Toussaint Guild Newsletter, Fr. Elder gave a report from the Vatican which follows:

One of the amazing aspects of the recent progress of the cause for canonization of Pierre Toussaint is the speed with which it has moved since Cardinal O'Connor formally opened the cause in December 1989. In short order the entire diocesan process (that part of the investigation which took place here in the Archdiocese of New York) was completed. In June 1991 Msgr. Robert O'Connell, the vice-postulator for the cause, personally delivered to the Sacred Congregation for Causes of Saints the several cartons of documents which were the fruit of that inquiry. One would have reasonably expected that the congregation, which with a limited staff has to process hundreds of cases from around the world, would not have been able to move very quickly on this new case. But in fact the cause was greeted with great enthusiasm, and much to my surprise Bishop Patrick Sheridan asked me to begin my full time work on the cause as soon as possible. In order to do that, I had to take a leave of absence from my job as a judge on the marriage tribunal, which has left them a bit short-handed. But Msgr. Desmond Vella, who heads the tribunal, has been most enthusiastic in his support of the cause, and himself played a major role in the diocesan process.

My task at this time is to function as the full-time collaborator to the relator of the cause, who is Fr. Peter Gumpel, S.J. The relator is the Vatican official who makes the formal presentation of the cause to the Sacred Congregation for the Causes of Saints. In order to do that, he must work with a collaborator who writes the *Positio*, a rather large book containing all the information and documentation which the members of the congregation need in order to conduct their investigation. So most of my time now is spent preparing the *Positio*....

Fr. Gumpel has been most friendly and helpful to me, and he is quite enthusiastic about the cause of Pierre Toussaint. Before my arrival the staff of the congregation had sorted through all the documentation we had sent and had arranged them in two sets of seventeen bound volumes. (All of the documentation had been sent in duplicate.) My first task was to make an initial assessment of the contents of those volumes, called the *Acta*, or acts of the cause. Fr. Gumpel requested that I examine everything carefully and thoughtfully with one question in particular always uppermost in my mind: Did I think that Pierre Toussaint was a saint? That was the burning question I faced during the hot Roman summer: Is Pierre Toussaint really a saint, not just a saint with a small "s," but the real thing, a saint with a capital "S," a man of extraordinary holiness worthy to take his place with the heroes of our faith, with St. Peter and St. Augustine and St. Francis of Assisi and all the rest?

Living in the shadow of St. Peter's, I realized why it was important for me to re-examine that question. It is quite easy back in New York to get excited about the prospect of canonizing one of our own, a genuine New Yorker who is so much a part of the history of this great city. But in Rome one looks at the question from a different angle: Is Pierre Toussaint something more than a local hero? Are his life and his sanctity so extraordinary that they can rightly be held up as examples for the universal Church, so that he can be venerated not just by New Yorkers, not just by Americans, but by Europeans and Asians and Africans as well?

With all those weighty considerations in mind, one day last summer I sat down in a room of the North American College with several volumes of the *Acta* on a table in front of me. The room had a spectacular view of the dome of St. Peter's Basilica. I picked up the first volume and started reading about Pierre Toussaint with a new perspective. I read the story of a slave from a very poor country who came to New York. I read the story of a man of tremendous passion and dignity and, above all, charity. I read the story of a man whose warmth and love and active concern for others made him beloved of all who knew him. I read the story of a man in love with God and his Church. I read the story of a man whom I myself would have loved to have known. I also read about people whose lives he had touched, people who even in his own lifetime revered him as a saint. I read about how his memory had been carefully preserved and handed down, and how many people had expressed the hope that one day he would be canonized a saint.

And as I was sitting in that room far from home, reading about the history of my city and someone whose personality is an indelible part of that history, I was suddenly startled to hear the bells of St. Peter's ringing out loudly and joyfully. Perhaps now, I thought, this treasure of old New York is about to add to the richness of the universal Catholic Church.

Yes, Fr. Gumpel, I believe Pierre Toussaint is a saint!

As the Pierre Toussaint Guild has been kept informed of the stages through which the cause of Pierre Toussaint is moving, the guild has made a special effort to inform and encourage those congregations or organizations that have shown continued interest in the cause.

One of the first parishes outside the Archdiocese of New York to invite members of the guild to attend a Mass honoring Pierre Toussaint was St. Vincent Ferrer in Brooklyn, where many of Pierre's fellow Haitians reside. The Vice-Postulator, Msgr. Robert M. O'Connell, was the celebrant at this Mass in September 1993.

The following April, guild members were invited to attend a Mass in honor of Pierre Toussaint at St. Jerome, also in Brooklyn. The pastor at St. Jerome is the Rev. Guy Sansaricq, a native of Haiti and a former recipient of the Pierre Toussaint Medal. This Mass was conducted in Creole and English as the congregation is almost entirely Haitian. Msgr. O'Connell and the Rev. Sansaricq officiated, and a Haitian band provided appropriate and stirring music. The Haitian custom of young maidens processing with gifts during offertory was picturesque and uplifting.

The Pierre Toussaint Guild later sponsored a concert at one of New York's oldest mid-town churches, the Church of St. Paul the Apostle. Choirs from Harlem churches along with the choir and band from Brooklyn's St. Jerome offered musical praise in memory of Pierre Toussaint.

One of the highlights of the St. Paul the Apostle concert was the presentation by Msgr. O'Connell of a document and medal from the Holy Father to the Director of the Guild Waldemar A. Roebuck, making him a Knight of the Order of St. Gregory.

Masses in memory of Pierre are said every first Saturday at Mt. Carmel Church in Harlem, and periodically at St. Ann's Church in Nyack, New York, where Haitians comprise a large percentage of the membership.

In meetings of the Pierre Toussaint Guild, the members often express their desire to know more about the cause. In February 1994 Fr. William S. Elder, in the guild's newsletter, assured them that the cause is moving forward inasmuch as the *Positio*, a volume containing the *Acta* and all information which has been submitted to the Congregation of Sacred Causes, is completed.

In the February issue of the Pierre Toussaint Guild Newsletter, Fr. Elder wrote:

> Some 140 years after the death of Pierre Toussaint, the most important part of the preparation of his cause for canonization has been completed. The process began immediately after his death, when the Schuyler family and others began carefully preserving his papers and his story. Such was the devotion of those who had know him—Mary Anne Schuyler affectionately called him "Saint Pierre"—that his first biography by Hannah Sawyer Lee was published only a few weeks after his death. For well over a century, stories continued to be told; books and articles continued to be written, and groups continued to meet, until it became clear that the time had arrived to begin the formal process leading toward sainthood. Cardinal Spellman and Cardinal Cooke oversaw important preparatory work, and the cause itself was finally opened by Cardinal O'Connor.
>
> Every cause for canonization must pass through two major stages. The first is an investigation by the local bishop, usually in the diocese where the Servant of God died. When that investigation is completed, all the material that has been gathered is sent to the Sacred Congregation for the Causes of Saints in Rome, and the second stage begins. The cause of Pierre Toussaint is now well into the second stage.
>
> The heart of the process at the congregation is the preparation and evaluation of the *Positio*. The *Positio* is essentially a scholarly examination of all the material that has been gathered on the life of the Servant of God. It must be as detailed and as accurate as possible in order to enable the members of the congregation to reach a well-informed decision.

The *Positio* for Pierre Toussaint, which was completed just before Thanksgiving, is divided into four sections. The first, called the *informatio,* is a brief study showing how all the major virtues were exemplified in his life. The second, called the *vita documentata,* is the heart of the work. It contains a critical biography and a great deal of supplementary information. Since most of those involved with the cause at the congregation will not be from the western hemisphere, it is necessary to include brief histories of Haiti, the United States, New York City and the Catholic Church in New York. The final two sections contain the testimony of witnesses and the report of the historical commission, which was presided over by Msgr. Michael J. Wrenn. Altogether the *Positio* comprises two volumes with a total of approximately seven hundred pages.

At the congregation the *Positio* will be evaluated by three separate committees. The first is an historical commission which examines the historical completeness and accuracy of the work. The second is the theological commission which thoroughly debates the central question of heroic virtue in the life of Pierre Toussaint. Next the cardinals and bishops who are members of the congregation meet to vote on the cause. Finally the recommendation of the congregation is sent to the Holy Father. If he decides—and *only* he decides—the Servant of God is then declared heroically virtuous and is given the title Venerable.

In order to proceed further in the canonization process, there must be a formal investigation of a miracle. If the miracle is accepted, the candidate is beatified and given the title Blessed. After beatification a second miracle is required in order to complete the process of canonization and bestow the title of Saint. Someday, we pray, the title given by Mary Anne Schuyler will prove prophetic: "Saint Pierre!"

Since Fr. Elder wrote this, the cause of Pierre has advanced even more. On December 17, 1996, Pope John Paul

II bestowed the title "Venerable" on Pierre Toussaint, thus bringing him even closer to canonization.

In spite of the many outpourings of love and devotion to Pierre, some are critical of this Servant of God. As one priest said in commenting on those who have criticized Pierre for not having been more militant in the fight against slavery: "Pierre did not appear to have been politically correct" during the period of slave insurrections in Haiti and in the following years.

As regards more recent criticism of Pierre, few readers of most of what has been written about Pierre and his relationship with the family of his owners have realized that Pierre and his family had over the years developed a close relationship with the Bérards that transcended the cruelties of master to slave or vice versa.

Though the young Pierre Toussaint left Haiti before the slave insurrections began, his papers and other records indicate that he shared all he had with escaped slaves who sought his help, even to the extent of helping some of them to purchase their freedom. Pierre Toussaint fought injustice with prayers and good works instead of using the sword against his fellow men.

During my 1977 visit to Pierre's beloved Haiti, I noted with interest that few Haitians knew anything about Pierre Toussaint. Yet when highlights of Pierre's life were shared with group after group, the men and women addressed were proud that one of their countrymen had become an outstanding citizen of old New York. They understood the limitations of Pierre's youth and thrilled to the stories of how he frequented the New York waterfront seeking news or information from seaman about loved ones he had left behind.

Helene Morpeau, one of Haiti's most respected poets, was also an exception among Haitians who knew nothing of Pierre Toussaint's charity and good deeds. Miss Morpeau presented us with a poem (in French) which she had dedicated to Pierre. She also informed us that her brother Pierre

Moraviah Morpeau, who had migrated to Argentina, wrote a book in Spanish about Pierre Toussaint. Unfortunately we were never able to get a copy of it.

Soon after I visited the birthplace of Pierre Toussaint and sometime before drastic changes took place in the Haitian government, a Senator Dietel Toussaint visited my home. Dietel Toussaint, whose father was Horace, told us his grandfather's name was Zoe, which he said was the male form of Zenobie, Pierre's grandmother's name. Senator Toussaint was inclined to believe that his grandfather was an older brother of Pierre's who had been given the name of Zoe out of respect for the grandmother. This assumption had been strengthened by the fact that an elderly aunt had always and repeatedly told them that they had a relative in New York who was prosperous and highly respected. Another member of this family also wrote. It is almost certain that distant relatives of Pierre Toussaint still live in Haiti.

At the time of the 1994 crisis in Haiti, when the possibility of the invasion of U.S. troops appeared imminent, a Mass was celebrated by a Haitian bishop at the Church of St. Gregory the Great on New York's upper West Side. The predominantly Haitian congregation prayed, sang and responded in Creole, outwardly hopeful that their loved ones in Haiti would be safe from all harm. Though there was every indication that an invasion was inevitable, hope persisted and was expressed in supplications.

Late that evening and the next morning when news bulletins informed the public that a peace keeping force of American troops had landed on Haiti without bloodshed, there were many who felt Pierre had heard their prayers and in heaven pled the cause of his beloved homeland.

A friend of Pierre's from London, England wrote as follows:

Dear Sir/Madam:

I am writing because last night I prayed to God asking

Pierre Toussaint to intercede that a miracle be granted and that it be used toward his canonization. On the news that night America was about to invade Haiti. I prayed and asked for Pierre Toussaint's intercession so that neither one drop of blood nor one life be lost and that God's will be done in this matter.

Before going to bed (between 10:00-11:45 p.m. London time), I picked up the picture of Pierre Toussaint and noticed that he was a Haitian. That inspired me to pray.

Today (about 10:10 a.m. London time), I read in the paper that "an eleventh hour peace mission" was sent. The invasion has not taken place. My plea through Pierre Toussaint has reached God, our Father. I believe my prayer has been answered.

Thank you, God. Praise you, God. Thank you for answering my prayer through Pierre Toussaint.

Thank you, God, so much. Please let peace reign in Haiti. Please use this miracle towards making your son, Pierre Toussaint, a saint.

God bless you.

Kindest regards, in Jesus & Mary.

L.C.D.

London, England

Members of the Pierre Toussaint Guild have been encouraged by reports from localities all over the world of devotion to the cause of Pierre Toussaint. We had known for some time of the work of Fr. George Smulski, O.F.M. of Forest Gate, London, England, who works with many of the people from the Caribbean who have migrated to England. Along with a request for prayer cards and leaflets recently came beautiful photographs of ceremonies in which Pierre Toussaint is honored.

In Nassau, the capitol of the Bahamas, Fr. Patrick Pinder, rector of St. Francis Xavier Cathedral, is writing an article for the Catholic diocesan paper which will be shared with guild members.

The Pierre Toussaint Guild was especially interested to learn of the establishment of the Pierre Toussaint Foundation, New Orleans, Inc. which had been founded by the Rev. Joseph M. Doyle, S.S.J. to encourage and help African-American youths to advance from Catholic elementary schools to Catholic high schools with advice and assistance being supplied by mentors and sponsors.

In 1989 the Rev. James Goode, O.F.M., pastor of St. Paul of the Shipwreck in San Francisco, California, founded the Annual Day of Prayer for African-American Families. Fr. Goode, who also gives revivals all over the country, recently announced that Pierre Toussaint had been selected as a role model for the seventh annual observance of this day of prayer. Leaflets and prayer cards along with a brief sketch of Pierre's life have been made available to this group by the guild through the Josephite Pastoral Center, Washington, D.C.

While members of the Pierre Toussaint Guild are aware that the Pierre Toussaint cause is under favorable consideration by the Congregation for Sacred Causes, they continue to pray for reliable information regarding miracles attributed to Pierre Toussaint's intercession. Prayers are said daily for the one miracle which will contribute to the documentation that may help to elevate this Servant of God, Pierre Toussaint, to the altars of the Church.

Bibliography

Alexis, Stephen. *Black Liberator: The Life of Toussaint L'Ouverture.* Translated by William Stirling. New York: Macmillan Co., 1949.

Anthonian, "The Quiet Man." Paterson, NJ: St. Anthony's Guild.

Armstrong, Margaret. *Five Generations, Life and Letters of an American Family, 1750-1900.* New York: Harper and Bros., 1930.

Carey, Emma. "Pierre Toussaint." *Ave Maria* (1893).

The Catholic World, October 1950.

Cole, Hubert. *Christophe, King of Haiti.* New York: Viking Press, Inc., 1967.

Commonweal, July 4-18, 1941.

Dannett, Sylvia G. L. *Noble Women of the North.* New York-London: Thomas Yoseloff, 1959.

Dirvin, Joseph I., C. M. *Mrs. Seton, Foundress of the American Sisters of Charity.* New York: Farrar, Straus and Giroux, 1962-1975.

Durbin, Louise. *Inaugural Cavalcade.* New York: Dodd, Mead & Co., 1971.

Carruth, Gorton and Associates, eds. *The Encyclopedia of American Facts and Dates.* A Crowell Reference Book, 1956.

Hanley, Boniface., O.F.M. *Catholic Digest,* June 1980. Condensed from *Ten Christians.* Paterson, NJ: St. Anthony's Guild.

Interracial Review, 1935-1953.

La Farge, John, S.J. *The Manner Is Ordinary.* New York: Harcourt, Brace & Co., 1954.

Lee, Hannah Farnham Sawyer. *Memoir of Pierre Toussaint, Born a Slave in St. Domingo.* Boston: Crosby, Nichold & Co., 1854.

Meehan, Thomas F. "Pierre Toussaint: Catholic Negro." *America,* June 28, 1941.

Our Colored Missions, 1935.

Ottley, Roi and William J. Weatherby, eds. *The Negro in New York.* Dobbs Ferry, NY: Oceana Publications, Inc., and the New York Public Library, 1967.

Roberts, Kenneth. *Lydia Bailey.* New York: Doubleday and Co., 1947.

Schuyler, George W. *Colonial New York.* New York: Charles Scribner's Sons, 1885.

Schuyler, Georgina. *The Schuyler Mansion at Albany.* New York: The Devine Press, 1911.

Sheehan, Arthur and Elizabeth Odell. *Pierre Toussaint: A Biography.* New York: P. J. Kenedy & Sons, 1955.

Vandercook. John W. *Black Majesty.* New York: Harper Bros., 1928.

Wilson, Ruth Danenhower. *Here Is Haiti.* New York: Philosophical Society, 1957.

Copy of Pierre's will from Surrogate Court Valentine's Manuals, New York, the Pierre Toussaint papers in the New York Public Library, Manuscript Division, and the many volumes in the library of the New York Historical Society on the Old New York that Pierre Toussaint knew and loved.

About the Author

Ellen Tarry, Catholic author/lecturer, is well known for her work in civil rights circles throughout the United States. Miss Tarry has won recognition as an author of children's books and was acclaimed for her autobiography, *The Third Door,* first published on the anniversary of the 1954 Supreme Court Decision. Miss Tarry worked throughout the New England States with the Department of Housing and Urban Development as a Relocation Advisor for a number of years. Later she served as a Director of Equal Opportunity with HUD and worked in New York, New Jersey, Puerto Rico and the Virgin Islands.

Prior to joining HUD, Ellen Tarry was Director of the Community Center of Public School 68, New York City; Director of Community Relations, St. Charles School Fund; Director of Women's Activities in USO-NCCS Clubs throughout the country and Co-Director of Friendship House, a Catholic Interracial Center on the South Side of Chicago.

In addition to *The Third Door,* other titles published by Ellen Tarry are as follows:

Children:

    Janie Belle, Garden City Press, 1940
    Hezekiah Horton, Viking Press, 1942
    My Dog Rinty, Viking Press, 1946
    The Runaway Elephant, Viking Press, 1950

Teenage:

Katharine Drexel—Friend of the Neglected, Farrar Straus and Cudahy, Inc., 1960

Martin de Porres—Saint of the New World, Farrar Straus and Cudahy, Inc., 1963

Young Jim—The Early Years of James Weldon Johnson, Dodd, Mead and Co., 1967

Adult:

The Third Door, David McKay Co., Inc., 1955

The Third Door, an autobiography, may be of special interest to those who have followed recent incidents in the South. A paperback edition of *The Third Door* was published by All Saints Press in 1966.

The Other Toussaint: A Modern Biography of a Post-Revolutionary Black, Pauline Books & Media, 1981, 1998

BOOKS & MEDIA

The Daughters of St. Paul operate book and media centers at the following addresses. Visit, call or write the one nearest you today, or find us on the World Wide Web, www.pauline.org.

CALIFORNIA
3908 Sepulveda Blvd., Culver City, CA 90230; 310-397-8676
5945 Balboa Ave., San Diego, CA 92111; 619-565-9181
46 Geary Street, San Francisco, CA 94108; 415-781-5180

FLORIDA
145 S.W. 107th Ave., Miami, FL 33174; 305-559-6715

HAWAII
1143 Bishop Street, Honolulu, HI 96813; 808-521-2731

ILLINOIS
172 North Michigan Ave., Chicago, IL 60601; 312-346-4228

LOUISIANA
4403 Veterans Memorial Blvd., Metairie, LA 70006; 504-887-7631

MASSACHUSETTS
Rte. 1, 885 Providence Hwy., Dedham, MA 02026; 781-326-5385

MISSOURI
9804 Watson Rd., St. Louis, MO 63126; 314-965-3512

NEW JERSEY
561 U.S. Route 1, Wick Plaza, Edison, NJ 08817; 732-572-1200

NEW YORK
150 East 52nd Street, New York, NY 10022; 212-754-1110
78 Fort Place, Staten Island, NY 10301; 718-447-5071

OHIO
2105 Ontario Street, Cleveland, OH 44115; 216-621-9427

PENNSYLVANIA
9171-A Roosevelt Blvd., Philadelphia, PA 19114; 215-676-9494

SOUTH CAROLINA
243 King Street, Charleston, SC 29401; 803-577-0175

TENNESSEE
4811 Poplar Ave., Memphis, TN 38117; 901-761-2987

TEXAS
114 Main Plaza, San Antonio, TX 78205; 210-224-8101

VIRGINIA
1025 King Street, Alexandria, VA 22314; 703-549-3806

CANADA
3022 Dufferin Street, Toronto, Ontario, Canada M6B 3T5; 416-781-9131
1155 Yonge Street, Toronto, Ontario, Canada M4T 1W2; 416-934-3440

¡Libros en español!